Unwarranted Influence

Bombing of Nagasaki, Japan   August 9th 1945

"Nuclear destruction is the total and complete annihilation of a society, its culture, its language, its cities and its collective history and artefacts. As well as all these things, it robs humankind of the dignity of death or dying of a loved one, a family member or a friend. It is even more heinous than genocide."

Father and daughter in death, Kobane, Syria 2014   Ayn al Arab   AP

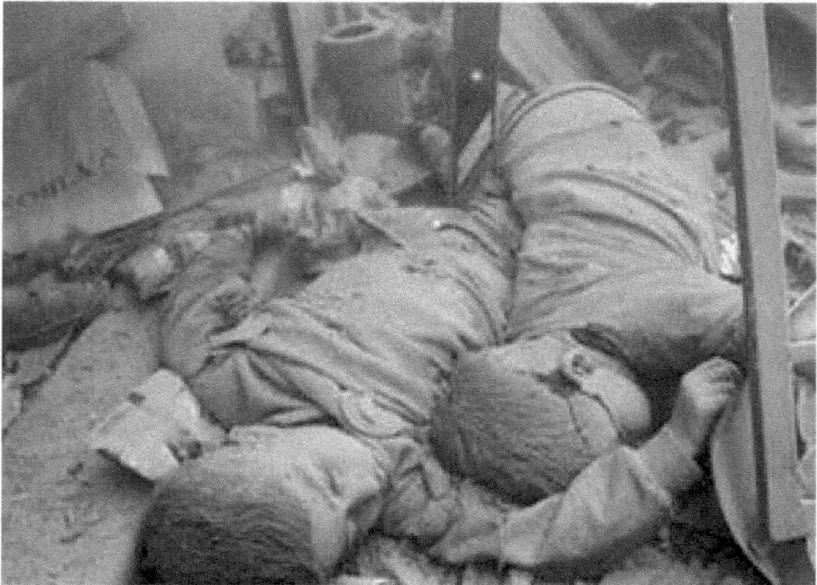

Brothers in death, Kobane, Syria 2014   AP

Unwarranted Influence

.. a cry and a plea for an end to global madness

"Think not that I am come to send peace on earth: I came not to send peace, but a sword."

Copyright © 2018 Tom Law

for Ita

and in memory of Razan al Najjar

ISBN 9780987629814

This 3rd Edition Published in Australia by:
Longership Publishing Australia
Swifts Creek Victoria 3896 AUSTRALIA
ABN 73446736413
email: longership@email.com
First published in Australia October 2018
as: What Have We Done, now re-titled.
Copyright © Tom Law Jan 2019
Cover design: Tom Law (see below)
The right of Tom Law to be identified as the Author of the Work has been asserted in accordance with the Copyright, Designs and Patents Act 1988.

Law, Tom
Unwarranted Influence
ISBN 9780987629814
p 464

Sales of this Edition will contribute to these organisations:

Save the Children

UNICEF

International Red Cross & Red Crescent

The Smith Family (Australia)

Cover: Hercule terrassant l'hydre de Lerne, Guido Reni (1617), Musée du Louvre, Paris.

Unwarranted Influence

Unwarranted

Influence

tom law

Longership Publishing Australia

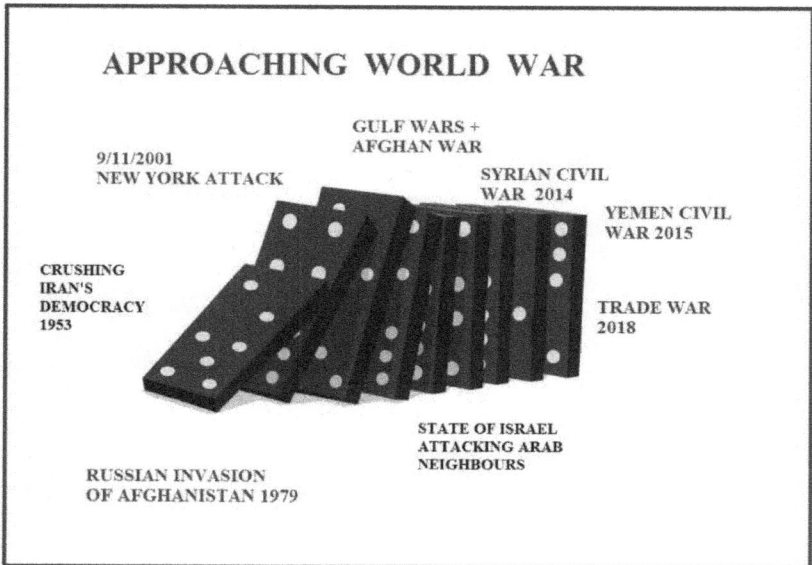

APPROACHING WORLD WAR

GULF WARS +
AFGHAN WAR

9/11/2001
NEW YORK ATTACK

SYRIAN CIVIL
WAR 2014

YEMEN CIVIL
WAR 2015

CRUSHING
IRAN'S
DEMOCRACY
1953

TRADE WAR
2018

STATE OF ISRAEL
ATTACKING ARAB
NEIGHBOURS

RUSSIAN INVASION
OF AFGHANISTAN 1979

"There is almost inevitability in certain outcomes!"

Cain said to Abel "Let us go over into the field"
And whilst in the field, it was there that Cain murdered
his younger brother Abel.
The Lord enquired of Cain "Where is your brother
Abel?"
"I do not know. Am I my brother's keeper?"
The Lord then said unto Cain "What have you done?
Listen, your brother's blood cries out to me from the
soil!"

Genesis 4, vs 8-10.

"In the councils of government, we must guard against
the acquisition of unwarranted influence, whether
sought or unsought, by the military-industrial
complex."

President Dwight Eisenhower, Jan 1961.

"In the modern world, every war is a war crime!"

Tom Law 2018.

Unwarranted Influence

Contents

Glasgow 1943

Gaza 2014   **AP**

Foreword

What this book is about: Predominantly it is about the foolishness and waste of human life as well as energy and resources pumped into wars between nations. Further, it addresses the current standoff between the super powers with their immoral and anti-humanitarian arsenals of nuclear weapons and their delivery systems. The book encourages ordinary men, women and even high school students to appraise this diabolical situation and take steps towards complete denuclearisation of the world. It demands all nations to use their power in the forum of the United Nations i.e the General Assembly to reach this objective before the end of 2025 by the instruments of international humanitarian law. It demands reform of how the UN works, particularly the Security Council which is currently a fundamental blockage to progress of the objective.

As well as this prime motive for the writing, the same organisation must bring about stricter rules dealing with the manufacture, storage and trading in traditional arms and military hardware so that human life and the dignity of nations and their societies are paramount over the evil of profit. One had hopes that the twenty first century would bring about a golden age of creativity, social improvement and a gross reduction in poverty and the death toll of children across the globe. However, the war mongering arms manufacturers and dealers stand in the way of such ideals and wanting progress. They must be swept aside and in many cases suffer consequences such as prison terms.

This book proffers the statistics of past major conflicts rather than any detail of their history. It is highly critical of politicians in governments of many nations that are there to serve the people but instead are serving their own pecuniary short term interests. The new age requires a new awakening to the lies and deceits of those holding power.

Tom Law   Mount Beauty, August 2018.

Feed the Birds

'The Tuppence Administration is hardly worth a Halfpenny' was my personal appraisal on the Trump-Pence power trip in the Whitehouse of the USA! But then I was trying to place an Australian bent on US politics and trying to comprehend how the American public think. This of course cannot be reached to any great depth; Americans think, behave and react very differently from us and the bottom line is generally we just have to accept the fact! This of course does not mean that we must not try to persuade them to change or adopt at least partially our ways and perhaps idiosyncratic dialectic! After all, they are sort of cousins and shared dialogue can sometimes result in good outcomes rather than political pits of despair. Whether we regard them as sometimes crass, big footed and big mouthed, we must never forget that they were there when we needed them most! For this we must demonstrate gratitude. However it would be self effacing and intellectually insulting if we did not raise our voice where we are justified to disagree! There are always many alternative roads and choices of action to solve the world's problems; it is better to hold to a perceived 'better solution' than go timidly and silently along the more disastrous route. A better man than this author once said:

> **"It is better that I offend you with my stance than to avoid pointing at the truth or worse still negating a truth to save that offense! Regardless of our friendship,   out of respect the truth must always out no matter the risk!"**

So I must take risks but at the same time state that no matter our differences, we will always remain as cousins and, as such, each deserves everlasting mutual respect!

To cite an example I was dismayed at the decision that an embassy be built in Jerusalem and recognising that city be the capital of Israel. It cannot solve the current dilemma of hatred and animosity between Palestinian Muslims and Israeli Jews and can only promulgate and exasperate the impasse forever into the future. Muslims around the world were shocked and horrified at the decision and immediately identified America as having chosen a side instead of remaining aloof and seeking a better solution. This author has always maintained a 'three state solution' where Jerusalem becomes a separate entity from Israel and Palestine and governed by a triumvirate of the three religions that have a vested interest. It would require a heavy UN presence of course to make a 'New Jerusalem' work efficiently and shine. As the 'centre of the world' perhaps it would be better to seat the United Nations in that city rather than New York! Sheer force and aggression will never work.

The other thing that gripes is the idea of America taking its military into space! I remember seeing the movie "Eye in the Sky" where satellite imagery was being used to assist a drone strike on a terrorist cell somewhere in North Africa. There was a delay in the strike as a child was on the street close by selling loaves of bread that her mother had made. After much hesitation and deliberation, the General decided that the child would be just unfortunate collateral damage. So in some respects, space is already being used as a military theatre. But arming satellites and creating military bases and military space vehicles is beyond the pale and against current treaties brokered by the United Nations. Any country taking military hardware and/or military personnel into space needs to be vehemently opposed by the international community. Otherwise we will see China, Russia, India and other nations following suit. We have not yet solved all the problems on this planet; we do not need to expand war into space! So regardless of the intentions of the US on this matter, the UN must be firm with economic consequences brought to bear!

The regular media has been problematic in that it tends to feed the public with information and stories framed in a propaganda way to support those decisions made in the halls of power.. usually the very rich and in the interests of global capital entities such as banks and corporations. Unfortunately armaments production and sales is now impacting in an evil way upon the lives of millions of innocents that have no knowledge of why their lives are being destroyed. And I am not being the disgruntled socialist or communist here when I point this out.. not at all. Both East and West are involved in this dirty conspiratorial weapons manufacture and distribution at unprecedented levels. The eyes of politicians, share holders and the moguls of the armaments industries shine bright as the dollars pour in to the destruction and devastation of whole segments of human civilisation at unfathomable cost! One can only weep for the mangled bodies of women and children like so much refuse cast aside to be charred and burned by horrific weapons. Where is God? How many will make it to His House? Certainly not the perpetrators! Only eternal nothingness awaits them but they realise this not and continue in their wickedness; both politicians and the industrialists. Many of us go to work each day and in some way are guilty and knowingly involved in this evil. But few look seriously at the consequences of their handiwork and ask of themselves: "What Have We Done?"

The Western forces that have played a role in Afghanistan, Iraq and Syria have, for the most part, now returned home. The daily news moves on to focus on other things particularly domestic events. But how many of us have an insight to the scope of damage and destruction to these countries? How many of us have taken in the cost to so many cities and smaller towns across these two countries? Have we viewed the desolation? Have we realised the death toll? Many cities resemble the aftermath of Dresden, Hiroshima and Nagasaki in 1945. To combat Islamic State the West pounded cities relentlessly for three and a half years day in and day out leaving the ground fighting to the Kurds and Iraqi troops. Millions of people have been dispossessed of their homes, hundreds of thousands killed by an onslaught of satanic proportion. The Coalition of Western air power has without any doubt and upon precise and inescapable evidence committed war crimes of a heinous nature. I recall the words of James Snowdon describing his brief entry to the American Forces:

> "I wanted to make a contribution to do some good in the world
> only to find that most of my fellow soldiers and their superiors
> had a single mind-set i.e to kill Muslims."

Just when everyone involved has packed their kit bags and returned home one can only surmise that this is not the end to some great battle. No sir-ree! As with the intent of the Japanese when they struck Pearl Harbor in 1941, the current wars in Iraq and Syria are but just the spark to a world conflagration not yet realised. We have NOT kept our nations

17

safe! On the contrary we are yet to feel a tsunami of hatred and reaction that has barely begun and will compound itself into destruction on a scale that the world has yet to experience. Woe to humanity!

It will quickly be noticed that I have made scant reference to those wars and conflicts in Africa, Central and South America other than a few well recorded and most significant. This tome is not meant to be encyclopaedic and I provide more than sufficient examples of horror and the appalling behaviour of contemporary man on this our beautiful blue planet set in an infinite sea and cosmos beyond our comprehending.

Don't Talk to Me about Religion:

Like all of us, I was greatly moved by the heinous beheadings supposedly perpetrated by Jihadi Jo and blazed sickeningly on the internet. I watched the sad memorial service in Manchester in November 2014 with the family of murdered Alan Henning. I felt deeply for his family left behind and wondered how anyone can stoop to such a depth

of depravity for a cause.

But then I recall the tragic death of Queen Jane Grey, beheaded at age nineteen to make way for Queen Mary, eldest daughter of Henry VIII. Known for her Protestant piety and learning, it was this religious devotion which persuaded Edward to alter the succession. Edward himself was a devout Protestant and did not want Roman Catholicism restored in England. With a superior army and defection of most members of the Privy Council, Mary Tudor claimed the throne with great popular support and Jane was imprisoned in the Tower of London. Her

18

subsequent execution in 1554 was a political necessity for Mary Tudor. Despite her youth, Jane met her end with great dignity and courage.

Mary brought England back to Roman obedience and many people were pleased. However it has never been easy to summon up much affection for Mary's Catholic revivalism, particularly if one reflects on the victims perishing in the flames. Religious strategy unfolding between 1553 and 1558 seemed dynamic but sometimes brutal. The protestant hydra was being decapitated at least for a while, but strongly resurrected with the coming of the reign of Elizabeth I. Both Britain and Europe have seen many a bloody war based on religious differences over the

Beheading of deposed Queen Jane Grey 1554
Oil painting by Paul Delaroche 1833   **National Gallery   London.**

centuries.

And so we have two remaining members of IS known to have committed bloody murderous crimes that perhaps should be extradited

Tears from a Persian Rose

Tom Law

longership

to America, executed in order to exorcise the evils of religious extremism? It is a question is it not? Would a greater punishment be for them to languish in prison for the rest of their lives rather than provide them with martyrdom? Had St Alban not been vilely executed, how would Christianity have fared in England? America has warned Iran not to make threats otherwise suffer (as so many other countries have suffered)... under the big Mother Of All Bombs! "My dad can beat up your dad any day!" As we will see later, the 'Leader of the Free World' also known as the 'Satan of the World' and 'Biggest Bully Boy of the World' doesn't take any nonsense from smaller countries! The 'last Trump' has tried to make friends with Russia and will not allow any new comer to the 'Nuclear Club'. This hypocritical nonsense remains a stumbling block to the complete elimination of these weapons of mass destruction. In the next chapter the author aims to get across the concept of a stronger UN General Assembly where it might be possible to accomplish the dream of a world without nuclear weapons. But we have already experienced the US exiting from the Human Rights Committee. It is to be hoped that this is only a temporary glitch. Hopefully governments the world over will lend an ear to the demands of people! Their voices are soon to reach a crescendo!

Police in America have gotten away with shooting people on the street since the time of the Founding Fathers. But having recently shot dead an

20

innocent Australian lady whose family are seeking extraordinary compensation, perhaps a final shake down will occur on that front. 'Moms Demand' and 'Black Lives Matter' form part of a movement to question negative attitudes and behaviours that need to be relegated to the trash bin of yesteryear. 'Making America Great Again' is not about money and power but about equality of opportunity and a free, happy and safe society where guns are seen only at gun club shoots, not in the supermarket or school yard! A sobering hard-look and self analysis is necessary in order to transform to something better.

The contemporary world with its expertise in industry, agriculture and art persuaded by the giant leaps in scientific and technological understanding all make for an exciting future with undreamed of possibilities. At the same time, if turned to 'the dark side', we may alternatively face a world which is a frightening nightmare for all. We must make the best choices for the sake of future generations. Nations can no longer go to war. They can no longer afford to waste their resources. Every nation is like a portion of a very large garden. Each must nurture its own plot and reap the benefits for all members of its society. The strong and rich have a duty to lift up the weaker and poorer. The vast monopolies of international armaments manufacturers are not serving the interests of the planet. They have become a 'law unto themselves' and need to be castrated and sterilised. National armed forces must be replaced by regional UN forces. Unilateral intervention in disputes between nations is not the way to go. The war mongers and those that seed hatred must be called out and shamed. The creative spirit in all of us must be fed and watered; our destructive nature tempered to logic and sensibility for better outcomes. It is up to all the nation states of the world collectively to entertain peace and harmony. Education of our children in these precepts is essential for a safe, happy and prosperous world. Let us not stumble!

American Nuclear Posture Review:

But that is NOT the way of America! Trump within his first two months of office called for a review of America's Nuclear Defense Capabilities and the American Nuclear Posture Review was the outcome, a document planning for the future of nuclear defence in protecting America and its close allies.

> "This review affirms the modernization programs initiated during the previous Administration to replace our nuclear ballistic missile submarines, strategic bombers, nuclear air-launched cruise missiles, ICBMs, and associated nuclear command and control. Modernizing our dual-capable fighter bombers with next-generation F-35 fighter aircraft will maintain the strength of NATO's deterrence posture and maintain our ability to forward deploy nuclear weapons, should the security situation demand it. Recapitalizing the nuclear weapons complex of laboratories and plants is also long past due; it is vital we ensure the capability to design, produce, assess, and maintain these weapons for as long as they are required. Due to consistent underfunding, significant and sustained investments will be required over the coming decade to ensure that National Nuclear Security Administration will be able to deliver the nuclear weapons at the needed rate **to support the nuclear deterrent into the 2030s and beyond.**"

And further, we read the hypocritical 'opt-out' clause:

> "While we will be relentless in ensuring our nuclear capabilities are effective, the United States is not turning away from its long-held arms control, non-proliferation, and nuclear security

objectives. Our commitment to the goals of the Treaty on the Non-Proliferation of Nuclear Weapons (NPT) remains strong.

[... interpret this as NOT wanting any new comers to the nuclear club!]

Yet we must recognize that the current environment makes further progress toward nuclear arms reductions in the near term extremely challenging. Ensuring our nuclear deterrent remains strong will provide the best opportunity for convincing other nuclear powers to engage in meaningful arms control initiatives. This review rests on a bedrock truth: **nuclear weapons have and will continue to play a critical role in deterring nuclear attack** and in preventing large-scale conventional warfare between nuclear-armed states for the foreseeable future. US nuclear weapons not only defend our allies against conventional and nuclear threats, they also help them avoid the need to develop their own nuclear arsenals. This, in turn, furthers global security."

[... that is until there is an accident or misidentification of a situation!]

So the bottom line is that we are forced to retain nuclear weapons because (i) its cheaper than fighting a conventional war; (ii) no other super power is about to give up theirs... in fact Russia and China are developing more sophisticated systems as well as carrying out research; and (iii) our allies do not need to develop their own (ignoring here Britain, France, India and of course Israel which ALL have their own!)

In fact, all of these allies have recently commited billions of dollars to update and replace the necessary military components supporting their individual nuclear deterent (in the case of Britain close to 100 billion pounds to 2025 with Israel not too far behind). The US will spend a trillion dollars and possibly more on its nuclear defence before 2030!

As repeated throughout this writing, it will take people and the smaller nations to achieve total disarmament by the application of international humanitarian law at the United Nations. The governments of the superpowers will NEVER give up their nuclear weapons if left to their own devices!

To the Prime Minister of Great Britain and Northern Ireland:

21st August 2018

Dear Prime Minister, I wonder if you would determine whether the human rights activist Esraa al-Ghamgam, a female citizen of Saudi Arabia was executed by beheading by the current regime of that country in the last few days. If so, I do hope that your government will make a protest in the strongest terms to the government of Saudi Arabia and consider some retaliatory action to invoke reform and end such barbarous behaviour.

Sincerely, Tom Law.

Esraa al-Ghamgam

Held in detention since December 2015 with her husband Musa al-Hashem, her crime was her defence of political detainees, her demands for civil rights, her participation in peaceful demonstrations and her expression of views on social media platforms. Al-Ghamgam is from Dammam city in Qateef, Saudi Arabia.

Q: Does the Koran state explicitly and emphatically that an apostate should be executed? (apostate: someone who leaves the religion)

A: No! The Koran does not say anywhere that apostates should be killed. It condemns apostates but punishment is left up to Allah.

The death penalty for apostasy is an example of Islam exceeding the mandate of the Koran in some applications of Sharia law.

In Islam, the Koran is supreme because it is the literal Word of God. When there exists a difference between the Koran and a hadith, the Koran is supposed to prevail. Yet Sharia law takes license from a hadith instead of the Koran where apostasy is concerned and has, traditionally, demanded the death penalty. A hadith is notoriously unreliable and was culled from a vast collection of sayings and accounts of Muhammad that had, over a long period of time, picked up many interpolations, interpretations and apocryphal details.

Speaking of interpolations and apocryphal details, another interesting example is the death penalty for adultery as proscribed in Sharia law. The Koran prescribes 100 lashes for adulterers but in the following sahih hadith, stoning for adultery is spoken of as something Muhammad *may* have done but not something he actually did. It's an assumption, not a claim of fact!

Actually, stoning was a favored punishment in traditional Arab culture and law *long before* Muhammad appeared. Beheading by the sword lies in the same category!

The claim that the death penalty is ordained as a *must* in the Koran in the name of an 'eye for an eye' is simply not true!

5:28 "If thou dost stretch thy hand against me, to slay me, it is not for me to stretch my hand against thee to slay thee: for I do fear Allah, the cherisher of the worlds."

Trinity was the code name of the first detonation of a nuclear weapon. It was conducted by the United States Army on July 16, 1945 as part of the Manhattan Project.   **US DoD**

Yield: 20 kilotons of TNT (84 TJ)   Device: Plutonium implosion fission

The United Nations and a Need for Reform

On reading 'Mullahs Without Mercy' by Geoffrey Robertson- a perspective on Iran and its struggle to attain nuclear weapons- it was a considerable time later before I picked up the book again to read the last few chapters. It was suddenly brought home to me that his essays on human rights and nuclear weapons were the most striking parts of the book and I kicked myself for not having read these important chapters earlier as they were pertinent and to the heart of what I myself wanted to discuss here in this current book i.e the role of the UN in putting a final end to 'Weapons of Mass Destruction' and curbing the unchecked flow of weapons and war materials across borders generally! The clear message from Robertson (a Queen's Councillor incidentally) is that real change can only come about by incremental steps in International Law.

The Snowden revelations began in June 2013, when *The Washington Post* and *The Guardian* revealed surveillance programmes which had allowed the NSA access to the personal data of millions of American and European citizens. The first legal ruling came when a federal Judge ruled that bulk collection of American telephone metadata was significantly likely to violate the Fourth Amendment.
In February 2014, an independent US body 'The Privacy and Civil Liberties Oversight Board' issued two extensive reports. The first concluded that the bulk metadata programme was illegal and must be stopped. On 2nd June 2015, by 67 votes to 32, the Senate passed the '*USA Freedom Act*' which prohibited bulk collection of US citizen' phone records.
Although it is true that the European Union has more detailed rules concerning the processing of ordinary data than the US, in respect to

intercepting and procuring data on national security grounds it offers very little protection, and these protections are likely to reduce even further, particularly in France and the UK.

The PCLOB report questioned the value of PRISM; it concluded: "The programme has proven valuable in the government's effort to combat terrorism; monitoring terrorist networks has enabled the government to learn how they operate and to

Geoffrey Robertson QC

understand their priorities, strategies and tactics. Further, to identify previously unknown individuals who are involved in international terrorism; it has played a key role in discovering and disrupting specific terrorist plots aimed at the US and other countries".

The significance of the whistle blowing by Snowden lies in the gut reaction of the populous and its anger against government infringements on liberty and accepted freedoms. We must fall back on the intentions of the law (and, in the case of the US, its constitution) to clearly define a line of what is acceptable for national security and what is not!

Let us now consider the ultimate theatre embodying democracy and freedom for the whole of humanity on the planet: 'The General Assembly of the United Nations'. With its various committees and institutions, the UN governs the behaviour of governments of nations, whether they are members or no. It aims to better the lives of people in its aid programs and emergency relief programs in times of great upheaval such as natural events (earthquakes, floods etc.) as well as the result of wars (refugees, famine and disease). The first Geneva protocol on the use of chemical weapons, 1925, banned their use permanently. However the first protocol did not prevent countries from stock piling these substances or carrying out research into them!

The Chemical Weapons Convention (CWC) is a multilateral treaty that bans chemical weapons and requires their destruction within a specified period of time. The treaty is of unlimited duration and is far more comprehensive than the 1925 Geneva Protocol, which outlaws the use but not the possession of chemical weapons.

CWC negotiations started in 1980 in the UN Conference on Disarmament. The convention opened for signature on January 13, 1993, and entered into force on April 29, 1997.

The CWC is implemented by the Organization for the Prohibition of Chemical Weapons (OPCW), which is headquartered in The Hague with about 500 employees. The OPCW receives state declarations detailing chemical weapons related activities or materials and relevant industrial activities. After receiving declarations, the OPCW inspects and monitors state facilities and activities that are relevant to the convention, to ensure compliance.

The CWC is open to all nations and currently has 192 signatories. Israel has signed but has yet to ratify the convention (as of April 2018). Three states have neither signed nor ratified the convention (Egypt, North Korea and South Sudan).

Destruction Implementation:

Stockpile   Agents   Remaining

Russia	40 000 metric tons	Lewisite, Mustard, Phosgene, Sarin, Soman, VX	None	Completed destruction on September 27, 2017.
South Korea	605 metric tons	Unknown	None	Completed destruction on July 10, 2008.
Syria	1308 metric tons	Sulfur Mustard	Declared stockpile has been eliminated but undeclared chemicals still exist	No projected timeline for destruction of undeclared chemicals.
United States	27 771 metric tons	Binary nerve agents, Lewisite, Mustard, Sarin, Soman, VX	2770 metric tons as of December 2015.	Will not meet deadline; US estimates: 2023.

In April 2009, President Obama assured the world that America would take steps to bring about 'a world without nuclear weapons', a most noble gesture and certainly an objective of the highest order. There was a treaty to reduce warheads and stockpiles but as 2020 approaches, still no complete elimination of these abominable weapons.

In theory, any non-nuclear state that acquires materials and technology with the intention of constructing a nuclear bomb can be prosecuted at the International Criminal Court for a 'crime against humanity'. But we have not seen such a prosecution of states such as Israel, Iran or North Korea. In the case of Iraq, we saw the US go to war along with many other nations to remove Saddam Hussein and any facility that might have been used to make a bomb. In the case of North Korea we saw economic sanctions applied with much posturing that might yet still lead to another war on the Korean peninsula! India and Pakistan joined the club without any ramifications by the international community.

[Note: Each of Iran, Libya, Syria and Iraq has had nuclear facilities destroyed by Israeli bombing at various times over the past decade or more.]

The IAEA has maintained the task over the past seventy years of inspecting nuclear facilities and checking inventories of nuclear materials held by nuclear states. By definition, a country is designated a 'nuclear state' once it builds a nuclear facility such as a research plant or nuclear power plant. Thus this agency is a 'Nuclear Inspectorate' that keeps a constant eye on all of the world's nuclear facilities and quantities of potential bomb material.

A step forward was made in Rome, 1998, with the signing of the Statute of the International Criminal Court defining 'crimes against humanity'. In particular, section 8(2)(b)(iv) reads:

> **It is an international offence to intentionally launch an attack in the knowledge that such attack will cause incidental loss of life or injury to civilians or damage to the natural environment which would be clearly excessive in relation to the concrete and direct overall military advantage anticipated.**

Clearly this now makes any use of a nuclear bomb illegal. There has been a rapid expansion of human rights law introduced across many continents in recent years and specifically demanding protection of citizens' rights to life, enabling them to live free of inhuman treatment. It is not much of a logical step to now assume that:

> **The production, testing, possession, deployment and use of nuclear weapons is each in itself a crime against humanity and infringes upon the health, freedom and human rights of all peoples of the Earth.**

As will be repeated on occasion in this text, there remains an inherent

[It is noted here that the United States, under President Donald Trump, withdrew from the UN Council of Human Rights in June 2018 on the pretext that the Council was prejudiced against the state of Israel.]

and high wall problem regarding the current structure and implementation of proceedings within the United Nations Security Council. Not long ago this body constituted the BIG FIVE i.e the five permanent members China, France, Russia, UK and the USA; all nuclear weapons states. More recently the council has been augmented to include an additional twelve states selected from General Assembly members on a rotational basis. The 'high wall' mentioned of course is 'the power of veto' permitted for any of the five permanent members.

This state of affairs eternally leads to an almost childish fall back where the motion at hand 'does not suit the interests of a permanent member state!' Because of this, on many occasions **the world has suffered!** It is the author's view that the only way forward is either:

(i)   Remove both the permanent member status AND the power of veto of any state or

(ii)   Scrap the Security Council permanently and let the General Assembly (and its various committees, organisations etc) deal with all business.

This author sees merit in the second of these two options!

Thus many obstacles preventing complete disarmament of both nuclear and chemo-bio weapons might be swept away sooner. If a super-power leaves the organisation and moves to an isolation policy, so be it. The General Assembly now has teeth to pull it into line by international law. Even a super-power would find it both disdainful and uncomfortable to be shunned by the international community and have severe economic pressures brought to bear! NO INDIVIDUAL NATION HAS THE RIGHT TO EMPIRE STATUS ACCOMPANIED BY BULLY BOY ACTIONS ON SMALLER NATIONS TO GET THEM TO BEND TO ITS WILL. Surely the days of empire and colonialism are past? Of course, we are still often beholden and at the mercy of international corporations that behave themselves like dominions or states, having fiscal collateral greater than some small nation states. But that scenario relies on and is in the realm of other rules of international law, some of which are yet to be written and acted upon!

Despite the proliferation of terror groups such as al-Qaeda and Islamic State, their impact upon the world, though nasty, has been greatly exaggerated and causal damage mere pin pricks when compared to the two former world wars or any major war between two belligerent nations. Neither ever possessed submarines, jet fighters, aircraft carriers or intercontinental missiles! That any rogue terror group could get hold of a nuclear bomb is a spurious notion and extremely unlikely. An attack by a sovereign nation on say Israel with a nuclear device is not impossible but given the present situation of it being a nuclear state (illegally, one might add) again is highly unlikely. Conventional armaments are more likely. This brings one to another question, discussed in more detail in a later chapter, on the rules and protocols of armaments trade between nations. This trade across the whole world has also reached an outrageous and immoral dimension causing the inhuman destruction of millions of lives with grossly insufficient action by the international community to curb its vile existence!

Israel/Palestine

> **Jerusalem Post: Haley warns US 'taking names' of UN opponents of Trump's Jerusalem move**
> **Monday's veto at the Security Council marked the first time the US has used its veto power since 2011.**
> **December 20, 2017**

…and again:

> **The Guardian: Donald Trump has threatened to withhold billions of dollars of US aid from countries which vote in favour of a United Nations resolution rejecting the US president's recognition of Jerusalem as the capital of Israel.**

His comments came after the US ambassador to the UN, Nikki Haley, wrote to about 180 of 193 member states warning that she will be "taking names" of countries that vote for a General Assembly resolution on Thursday critical of the announcement which overturned decades of US foreign policy.
December 21, 2017

... and lastly:

The Times of Israel: US vetoes Arab-backed resolution on Gaza at UN Security Council
The United States vetoed Friday an Arab-backed UN draft resolution calling for protective measures for the Palestinians that won backing from 10 countries at the Security Council. A US resolution condemning Hamas also failed.
China, France and Russia were among the countries that voted in favour of the draft put forward by Kuwait on behalf of Arab countries. Four countries, Ethiopia, the UK, the Netherlands and Poland abstained.
1 June 2018

Well, Ms Haley can certainly write down this author's name if she so wishes!

Ambassador Nikki Haley, UNSC

More on this in a later chapter. BUT we can see clearly that the UN Security Council under its present constitution is NOT a democratic organisation! We have to look back to its formation after WWII where the 'Big Five' as winners of that horrific war ensured that their say would over-rule that of all others and further, through money and the seat of the UN being in New York, USA, America will forever impose its will on the whole world! The problem we now face is that America, under Mr Trump, is starting to fly in the face of even its closest allies on many policies!

To summarise, we need reform in the United Nations that it can perform one of its vital tasks: to remove weapons of mass destruction from the world as well as bring about sensible rules that will lead to fewer wars between nations or at least restrict the availability of sophisticated weapons and weapons technology. It can only accomplish this by stepwise application of international law regarding 'crimes against humanity'. All nations must be engaged. Once accomplished it also needs to focus on the international arms manufacturers and dealers that profit from conflict and the misery inflicted on citizens of this, our global community. Punitive powers are essential to reach these goals. Any alternative to these evolutionary controls means 'more of the same and worse', inconceivable, untenable and cannot be imagined.

America is NOT an exemplary nation in this regard as it ever seeks more sophisticated weaponry and associated systems which go far beyond the requirements of self protection. It has problems enough with its domestic social structure where gun deaths are far too high for a civilised nation (though far less than those of Central and South American countries!) ALL the superpowers contribute to wars around the world, are involved heavily in the trading of armaments and retain their power of veto on the Security Council. The United Nations itself would be better placed on more neutral ground! In earlier writings I suggested a UN Jerusalem Free State. A small island in the middle of either of the Atlantic, the Indian or the Pacific oceans or perhaps ALL THREE on a rotational basis might be considered.

But the essential outcome is to build a United Nations that is democratic and addresses the pressing problem of Weapons of Mass Destruction soon if we are to avert catastrophe and world destruction!

Further Suggestions:

Each nation's representative in the UN General Assembly to

1. DEMAND an end to all weapons of mass destruction, nuclear weapons in particular (to include testing, manufacture and storing of these weapons)

2. DEMAND the destruction of delivery systems capable of reaching far beyond a nation's border (e.g ICBMs).

3. DEMAND a strict limitation to the possession of conventional armaments and military hardware by any nation.

4. DEMAND strict limitations on the manufacture of armaments and military hardware solely for the purpose of selling to other nations for profit.

5. DEMAND stringent rules on the selling or trading of armaments and military hardware.

6. DEMAND punitive measures, to be of an economic nature, against nations that disregard the UN General Assembly's rulings on these issues of disarmament.

In case of occurrence of war between nation states:

1. A United Nation's Force to participate to bring hostilities to an end.

2. These UN Forces to be created on a regional basis with nations of each region providing equitable resources to maintain such a UN Force:

    Africa

    Europe

    Middle East

    Far East

Unwarranted Influence

Australasia/South East Asia/Pacific

North and Central America

South America

3. Dispute to be resolved ONLY by nations in the region where hostilities have commenced and by its UN Force in accordance with directives from the General Assembly.

4. National Defence Forces of all other nations not involved in original dispute to remain neutral and uninvolved.

5. Temporary omission of warring states from the UN General Assembly whilst any belligerent actions are taking place.

6. Compulsory reparations to be borne by both states after the ceasing of hostilities.

The prevention of wars is to be seen as a safeguard against the trespass of human rights. Nations or groups that collectively wage war are in contravention of humanitarian rights and as such are liable to punishment by the International Community and International Criminal Court. This may take the form of economic restrictions and/or incarceration of those leaders found to be guilty of seeking violent solutions to conflict.

The General Assembly must adhere to the principle of 'simplicity of language and comprehension' and steer away from complex legalise that leads to confusion or worse, sterility and inaction.

War is not to be entered into or encouraged as a means to profiteering by individuals or corporations. Evidence of 'seeding a war' for financial gain by an entity must be presented to the relevant International Criminal Court as determined by the International Community through its representatives at the General Assembly.

No nation has a 'power of veto' at the UN General Assembly and all nations must recognise and respect the will of the Assembly via those successful motions placed before it and brought into International Law.

You, the Individual: The logo represents 'DEMAND NUCLEAR DISARMAMENT' and it is now up to every individual to make such a demand to their respective national representative at the United Nations General Assembly. It remains abhorrent and totally disgusting that a far away nation possesses a nuclear weapon atop an ICBM that can reach my house and city if that nation so desires. It is a gross infringement of my right to safety and wellbeing; it transgresses my right to life as a human and similarly to my family, friends and neighbours. It contravenes International Humanitarian Law which needs to be applied to have such a weapon and delivery system completely dismantled. I protest the UN General Assembly to enact such laws so that ALL these weapons disappear from off the face of the planet. AND YOU MUST DO THE SAME. There is a pro-forma of such a petition provided in the Appendix which you may copy. Alternatively you may download the same from either of the websites:

https://demandnow.org

or   https://longership.com

Whether you reside in London, Berlin, Paris, Rome, Moscow, New York, Beijing or some small remote village in Africa, Australia or South America it is *vital* that you make an effort to GET YOUR VOICE HEARD! It is the author's dream and hope that all this may be accomplished before the close of the year 2025. BUT, Tom Law cannot do it alone. It can and will only be achieved by the combined efforts of a majority of citizens of planet Earth!

It may be that the politicians holding power in your country are in the pockets of the international armaments moguls. If so, they will be of no assistance and may even go out of their way to block your intention!

My personal complaint to the Human Rights Council of the United Nations is given here:

Human Rights Council

Complaint Procedure Form

- **You are kindly requested to submit your complaint in writing in one of the six official UN languages (Arabic, Chinese, English, French, Russian and Spanish) and to use these languages in any future correspondence;**
- **Anonymous complaints are not admissible;**
- **It is recommended that your complaint does not exceed eight pages, excluding enclosures.**
- **You are kindly requested not to use abusive or insulting language.**

I. Information concerning the author (s) of the communication or the alleged victim (s) if other than the author

---

Individual ☒   Group of individuals ☐   NGO ☐
Other ☐

Last name: LAW
First name(s):   THOMAS JOHN
Nationality: AUSTRALIAN

Address for correspondence on this complaint: LAKESIDE AVENUE, MT. BEAUTY, AUSTRALIA, 3699.

Tel and fax: +61461257429

email: tomjlaw987@gmail.com

Website: demandnow.org

Submitting the complaint:

On the author's own behalf: ☒

On behalf of other persons: ☐

II. Information on the State concerned

Name of the State concerned and, as applicable, name of public authorities responsible for the alleged violation(s): ALL STATES IN POSSESSION OF NUCLEAR WEAPONS, WHICH ARE CURRENTLY: Russia, China, United States of America, France, United Kingdom, Pakistan, India, North Korea and Israel. Addressed to the National Government of each of these states.

III. Facts of the complaint and nature of the alleged violation(s)

The complaint procedure addresses consistent patterns of gross and reliably attested violations of all human rights and all fundamental freedoms occurring in any part of the world and under any circumstances.

Please detail, in chronological order, the facts and circumstances of the alleged violations including dates, places and alleged perpetrators and how you consider that the facts and circumstances described violate your rights or that of the concerned person(s).

During the time period since the 1st January 1945 until present, each of the above nation states has developed, tested and stored nuclear weapons, atomic and/or thermonuclear. Some of the said nations have also developed missile delivery systems able to bring these weapons many thousands of kilometres from the launching site. As a weapon of mass destruction, it is evident that even a single detonation upon a perceived enemy would wrought unacceptable destruction to civilian populations and be followed by consequential environmental damage lasting decades or centuries to soil, water and the atmosphere. Under International Law, possession of such a weapon infringes upon the human rights of all peoples upon the Earth by virtue of an ever present threat to life and limb. Further, such a threat bears heavily on the human psyche in such a profound way as to render constant fear and stress. The knowledge of the existence of these weapons takes away all possibility of leading a safe, happy and normal creative existence for humans. In fact, normality of life, taken to be a fundamental freedom and right for all humans, is severely compromised.

I herewith beg that the Human Rights Council consider this complaint and, if in agreement to its content, forward to the General Assembly a motion demanding an end to nuclear weapons based on humanitarian argument and that all nation states currently in possession of such weapons proceed to a complete dismantling of such by midnight GMT of 31st December 2025 at latest.

IV. Exhaustion of domestic remedies

1- Steps taken by or on behalf of the alleged victim(s) to exhaust domestic remedies– please provide details on the procedures which have been pursued, including recourse to the courts and other public authorities as well as national human rights institutions[1], the claims made, at which times, and what the outcome was:

---

[1] National human rights institutions, established and operating under the Principles Relating to the Status of National Institutions (the Paris Principles), in particular in regard to quasi-judicial competence, may serve as effective means of addressing individual human rights violations.

The best that some of the above nation states have agreed upon in the past is to curb the maximum number of weapons held (e.g USA-Russia agreements on total number of nuclear weapons in their respective arsenals).

A summary of the Russian-USA arms control agreements (from SALT I through to New START) is provided in the document at:

https://www.armscontrol.org/factsheets/USRussiaNuclearAgreemen tsMarch2010

Although the public of many nations have called for a total ban on these weapons (see other organisations such as CND, ICAN, DND etc. and list at: **https://en.wikipedia.org/wiki/Anti-nuclear_organizations**),
In fact no national government of a state in possession of nuclear weapons has made any effort to completely ban such weapons.
2- If domestic remedies have not been exhausted on grounds that their application would be ineffective or unreasonably prolonged, please explain the reasons in detail:

All public attempts at scientific and logical arguments placed before national governments have come to no avail. In fact, either there has been no discussion by said governments or excuses of national security have been proffered as a justification for the continued ownership and possession of nuclear weapons.

> ## V. Submission of communication to other human rights bodies

1- Have you already submitted the same matter to a special procedure, a treaty body or other United Nations or similar regional complaint procedures in the field of human rights?

No

2- If so, detail which procedure has been, or is being pursued, which claims have been made, at which times, and the current status of the complaint before this body:

VI. Request for confidentiality

In case the communication complies with the admissibility criteria set forth in Council resolution 5/1, kindly note that it will be transmitted to the State concerned so as to obtain the views of the latter on the allegations of violations.

Please state whether you would like your identity or any specific information contained in the complaint to be kept confidential.

Request for confidentiality:

Yes ☐   No ☒

Please indicate which information you would like to be kept confidential

Date: 09 August 2018   Signature:

VII. Checklist of supporting documents

Please provide copies (not original) of supporting documents (kindly note that these documents will not be returned) in one of the six UN official languages.

- Decisions of domestic courts and authorities on the claim made (a copy of the relevant national legislation is also helpful): ☐

- Complaints sent to any other procedure mentioned in section **V** (and any decisions taken under that procedure): ☐

- Any other evidence or supporting documents deemed necessary: ☐

VIII. Where to send your communications?

Office of the United Nations High Commissioner for Human Rights

Human Rights Council Branch-Complaint Procedure Unit
OHCHR- Palais Wilson

United Nations Office at Geneva
CH-1211 Geneva 10, Switzerland
Fax: (+41 22) 917 90 11
E-mail: CP@ohchr.org

Website:
http://www.ohchr.org/EN/HRBodies/HRC/Pages/HRCIndex.aspx

As mentioned earlier, there is a blank copy of this form in the Appendix or you may get one from the above website. Good Luck! And remember … the planet and future generations depend on your actions taken now!

One of the most disappointing aspects of the superpowers is that although these major nuclear powers have agreed to stop live testing, they are using simulated experiments to develop the next generation of nuclear weapons! This is WHY they must ALL be held to account by way of the application of international law!

This is the Earth- it is our home and the only fertile planet in our Solar System

Chelsea Elizabeth Manning, born Bradley Edward Manning, is an American activist, politician and former United States Army soldier. She was convicted by court-martial in July 2013 of violations of the Espionage Act and other offenses, after disclosing to WikiLeaks nearly 750 000 classified sensitive military and diplomatic documents and was imprisoned between 2010 and 2017.

Awards: National Defense Service Medal, Global War on Terrorism Service Medal, Army Service Ribbon, Overseas Service Ribbon, Iraq Campaign Medal.

Great Battles of Antiquity

Before launching into modern wars and those where definitive war crimes have taken place we will mention a few of the great battles of the past, particularly where many soldiers fought and died:

Battle of Kadesh 1274 BC

Between: Egypt and Hittite Empire

Egyptian Leader: Ramesses II

Hittite Empire Leader: Muwatalli II

Location: Orontes River near Kadesh

The Battle of Kadesh is the oldest ever recorded military battle in history in which the details of formations and tactics are known. The battle took place in present day Syria between the Egyptians and Hittite Empire. It is believed to have been the largest chariot battle ever fought, involving between 5 000 and 6 000 chariots in total. Ramesses, along with his bodyguard, arrived from the north to join the Amun division and to set up a fortified camp to await the Ra division, who were marching from the North. They captured two Hittite spies who, after being tortured, revealed the true location of Muwatalli's army. After learning the location, Ramesses summoned the remainder of the army and planned to attack. When Muwatalli saw an approaching army, he sent his chariot force south of Kadesh to attack the approaching Ra division army. The Hittite army was ultimately forced to retreat, but the Egyptians were unsuccessful in capturing Kadesh.

Battle of Gaugamela 331 BC

Location: Tel Gomel (near current day Mosul)

Persian Army: 100 000

Alexander's Army: 35 000

The decisive battle between Alexander the Great and the Persian Achaemenid Empire. Despite his small military force compared to that of the Achaemenid Empire, Alexander's tactics worked effectively. The two great armies met near Gaugamela (present day city of Mosul in Iraq). Alexander's ingenious tactics worked so effectively that the battle led to the fall of the Achaemenid Empire.

Third Servile War 73 BC – 71 BC

Battle Between: Roman Republic and Army of escaped slaves

Slaves Leaders: Spartacus, Crixus, Oenomaus, Castus, Gannicus

Roman Leaders: Gaius Claudius Glaber, Publius Varinius, Lucius Furius, Lucius Cossinius, Gnaeus Cornelius Lentulus Clodianus

Lucius, Gellius Publicola, Gaius Cassius Longinus, Gnaeus Manlius, Marcus Licinius Crassus (leader).

Slaves Army: 120 000 (approximate) escaped slaves and gladiators
Roman Army: 8 Roman legions of 4 000-6 000 Infantrymen + auxiliaries 32 000-48 000 Infantry + auxiliaries, 12 000 garrison troops.

The Third Servile War was the last in a series of slave rebellions against the Roman Republic lead by the rebellious Roman slave Spartacus. The small group of 78 slaves and escaped gladiators grew into a massive army consisting of 120 000 men, women, and children. With the growing alert from the slave rebellions, the Romans formed an army of eight legions under the leadership of Marcus Licinius Crassus. The war ended in 71 BC with the decisive Roman victory. Of the survivors, some 6 000 were crucified along the Appian Way.

Battle of Plataea 479 BC

Battle Between: Persia and Greece

Greek Leaders: Generals Pausanias and Aristides

Persian Leaders: Xerxes and Mardonius

Victory: Greece

Location: Plataea, Greece

Greek Army: 40 000 men

Persian Army: 70 000-120 000 men

Although the above might be an exaggeration, the overall battle may
have still involved around 200 000 men in total! The large Persian force
lead by King Xerxes invaded Greece. The Greeks tried to hold the
Persian force with 300 Spartans and 7000 Hoplites under the leadership
of King Leonidas in a narrow pass. Despite the gallant efforts of the
Spartans, Persia conquered Thermopylae and achieved several victories
in Artemisium, Thessaly, Boeotia, Euboea, and Attica. However, they
lost the Battle of Salamis. Xerxes then retreated and returned to Asia
with half of his army. He put Mardonius in charge in Boeotia.

The 60 000 Hoplites, under the command of the Spartan King Pausanius
marched towards Boeotia to seek battle with the Persians. The Historic
battle took place near Plataea (modern Plataiai) in Boeotia. A huge
portion of the Persian army was trapped in the camp and slaughtered.
This battle allegedly happened on the same day as the Battle of Mycale
and marked the end the Persian invasion.

Battle of Thermopylae- none shall pass! 480 BC

Battle Between: Persia and Greece

Greek Leaders: King Leonidas I, Demophilus

Persian Leaders: King Xerxes I of Persia, Mardonius, Hydarnes

Location: Thermopylae, Greece

Unwarranted Influence

An unparalleled Greek force of 7 000 men led by King Leonidas of Sparta blocked the outnumbered Persian army at a pass. The Greeks held off the Persians for 7 days with 3 vicious battles epitomized as famous 'last-stand' battles in history. Leonidas blocked the road with his force for two days being the only way for the Persian army to pass. After the continuous two day battle, Greek resident Ephiatles revealed a secret pass where the Persian army could enter. Leonidas with his 300 Spartans and several other Thespians and Thebans died a glorious death at the pass.

Battle of Red Cliffs 208 AD
Between: Southern warlords Liu Bei and Sun Quan against Northern warlord Cao Cao
Southern Leaders: Zhou Yu, Cheng Pu, Liu Bei
Northern Leader: Cao Cao
Location: Yangtze River China
Southern Warlords Army: 50 000
Northern Warlord Army: 800 000

The Han dynasty ruled China for around four centuries, dividing the kingdom into its Western and Eastern Province. A decisive battle took place between the two southern warlords, Liu Bei and Sun Quan against Cao Cao, who had control over the north. Cao Cao assembled his 800 000 soldiers and attacked his southern rivals swiftly with a mission to unify China. Southern warlords had altogether 50 000 soldiers, including 30 000 trained naval soldiers led by Zhou. Despite having low numbers of soldiers, Zhou Yu and Lu Su were able to analyze the disadvantages of Cao's army. Cao Cao was faced with an unstable rear supply as well as the fact that many of his soldiers were inexperienced in battles on water.

50

Battle of Changping 262 BC - 260 BC

Between: State of Qin and State of Zhao

State of Zhao Leaders: Lian Po, Zhao Kuo

State of Qin Leaders: Wang He, Bai Qi

Location: Northwest of Gaoping, Shanxi

Zhao Army: 450 000

Qin Army: 550 000

The Battle of Changping took place during the Warring States period in China between the State of Qin and Sate of Zhao. Qin won a decisive victory. Qin attempted to invade Zhao in 262 BC but was forced back. Zhao, with his 400 000 man force attacked the Qin camp. However, before reaching the camp, Qin's army ambushed the Zhao force in the mountains. After 46 days without supplies Zhao finally surrendered.

Battle of Gaixia 202 BC

Between: Han and Western Chu

Han Leader: Liu Bang

Western Chu leader: Xiang Yu

Location: Gaixia (present-day Suzhou, Anhui)

Han Army: 600 000-700 000

Western Chu Army: 100 000

The decisive battle between Liu Bang and Xiang Yu ended with the victory of Liu Bang. Liu Bang later proclaimed himself Emperor of China and founded the Han Dynasty. Xiang Yu committed suicide after the battle. During the battle, Han troops captured Xiang Yu's wife. Yu sent most of his army to the capital to save her and thus dividing his force. Liu Bang snared Xiang Yu's 100 000 army with his prodigious 300 000 force at night. When Xiang Yu saw his army crumbling he had no choice but to take his own life with a sword.

Battle of Cannae 216 BC

One of the most famous battles of the Punic Wars was the Battle of Cannae which took place in Apulia, southeastern Italy. It was fought between the Roman Republic and the allied soldiers of Carthage made up of African, Spanish, and Gallic contingents under General Hannibal. The battle was a complete tactical victory achieved by one side and accounting as one of the worst defeats of Rome. According to Polybius the Romans fielded over 80 000 men whilst the Carthaginian forces were significantly outnumbered fielding around 50 000. Never the less, by military stratagem, Hannibal's army proved victorious!

Battle of Kalinga   261 BC

Describes an important battle of the Maurya Empire which covered present day India, Pakistan, Afghanistan and parts of Iran. The Battle of Kalinga was fought between the vastly numbered Mauryan forces of

Emperor Ashoka and the yet unconquered feudal republic of Kalinga (now the state of Odisha, in eastern India).

It was a significant event in Indian history with the Greek traveller Megasthenes describing the Kalinga forces as fielding more than 60 000 soldiers and 700 elephants along with a large number of armed civilians. The Mauryan army was thought to have been in excess of 100 000 soldiers. Total fatalities brought on by the battle were an astronomical 100 000 entailing a hard-won victory by the Mauryans.

Battle of Watling Street 61 AD

Boudicca, Warrior Queen of the Iceni

This battle was fought in Britain between the Roman forces under Suetonius combining Legio XIV Gemina with a part of the XX Valeria Victrix against the Iceni under Queen Boudicca. The precise location of the Watling Street battle varies according to different sources, but approximately between Londinium and Viroconium, Manduessedum near Atherstone in Warwickshire, to a small site near Lactodorum in Northamptonshire.

Tacitus and Cassius Dio gave varying numbers on participants. According to Tacitus, the Romans fielded around 10 000 men while the Iceni forces brought forth 100 000 people to the battlefield. Cassius Dio cites this number as being 230 000, probably a greatly inflated figure! One thing is for certain, the Romans were vastly outnumbered, while the battle in itself was one the largest ever fought in ancient Britain. With unflinching discipline, the Romans defeated the Iceni who fled the field after heavy losses of its warriors.

Battle of Adrianople 378 AD

Probably the worst Roman defeat since the Battle of Cannae, the Battle of Adrianople was the 4th century nadir of a declining Roman Empire. Fought between the Romans led by Emperor Valens and the Goths led by Fritigern, the battle occurred eight miles to the north of Adrianople (now Edirne, Turkey). Some sources put the Roman force at around 30 000 to 40 000 men which included cavalry. The Goths on the other hand fielded an estimated complement between 50 000 and 80 000 also including cavalry.

Genghis Khan and Mongol Empire 1206-1368 AD

The Mongol Empire emerged from the unification of several nomadic tribes in the Mongol homeland under the leadership of Genghis Khan, who was proclaimed ruler of all the Mongols in 1206. The empire grew rapidly under his rule and that of his descendants after invasions in every direction. Genghis quickly came into conflict with the Jin dynasty of the Jurchens and the Western Xia of the Tanguts in northern China. He also had to deal with two other powers, Tibet and Qara Khitai.

Towards the west he moved into Central Asia, devastating Transoxiana and eastern Persia, then raiding into Kievan Rus' (an earlier state of Russia, Belarus, and Ukraine) and then the Caucasus.

Mongols invade Baghdad- Staatsbibliothek, Berlin

He encouraged literacy, adopting the Uyghur script which became the Uyghur-Mongolian script of the empire.

Before his death, Genghis Khan divided his empire among his sons and immediate family, making the Mongol Empire the joint property of the entire imperial family. Genghis Khan died in August 1227, by which time the Mongol Empire ruled from the Pacific Ocean to the Caspian Sea, an empire twice the size of the Roman Empire! By 1294, the Mongol Empire had fractured into four separate khanates.

Though the Mongols launched many more invasions of the Levant, briefly occupying it and raiding as far as Gaza after a decisive victory at the Battle of Wadi al-Khazandar in 1299, they withdrew and from this time on the empire diminished.

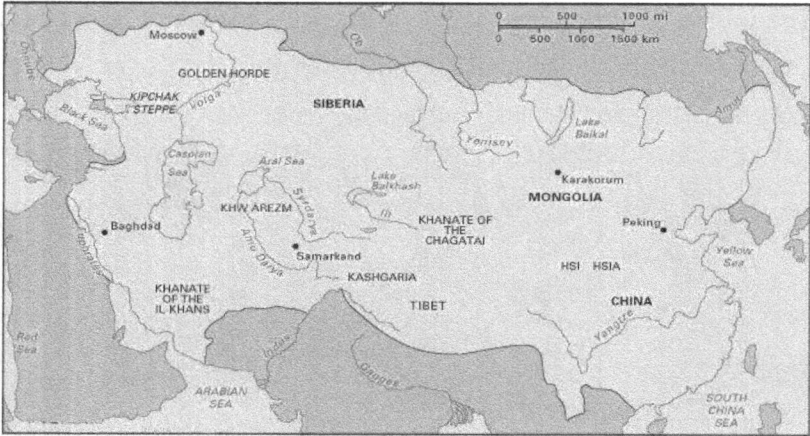

Extent of Mongol Empire 1259

Greatest conquerer of all time:

Genghis Khan conquered around 12 million square miles of territory i.e 20% of the known world and more than any individual in history.

Historians put the number of deaths attributed to the Mongol invasions at as many as 40 million but more likely half of this. The Mongols may have reduced the earth's population by as much as 10%.

By the time of his death, Kahn's Mongol army was four times that of Alexander the Great and twice that of the Roman Empire at its height.

The Mongol Empire enveloped Asia, Southern Russia, Eastern Europe, Persia, Afghanistan, and China.

Unwarranted Influence

Human Population upon the Earth Last 100 000 Years

It is estimated that in the last 100 000 years of human history, 112 billion human beings have been born. There are approximately 7.5 billion alive today. In the same time period around 250 million have died from war and conflict and around 500 million dying before adulthood due to disease. The Toba event 75 000 ya (largest volcanic eruption in the world occurring in Sumatra, Indonesia) is thought to have reduced the world population to some 100 000 or less, predominantly surviving in Africa.

HUMAN POPULATION

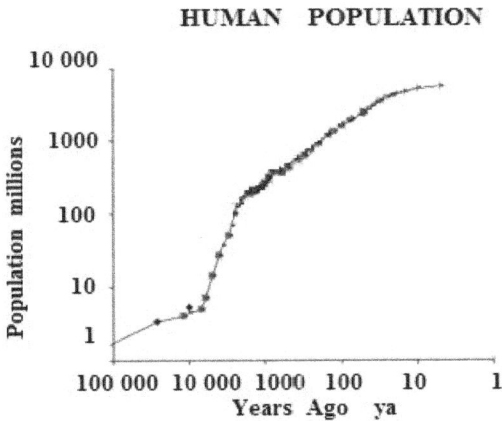

The diaspora of humans started some 60 000 years ago out of Africa to all parts of the globe. Although predominantly homo sapiens, a minimal genetic variation appears due to some cross breeding with earlier more primitive sub species of humans such as homo sapiens sapiens, homo sapiens neanderthalensis and homo sapiens idaltu.

War Crimes- a Brief History

There is no beginning to the history of war crimes. The further we go back in time we always find evidence of horrific murder by kings, tribal chiefs and generals. Where do we start? With Qin Shi Huang the first emperor of China, bloody Alexander or Gaius Julius Caesar and his mass murder of the Gauls and German tribes? War and murder seem to have been part of the human condition since Cain and Abel; and today it is achieved on a scale never before experienced!

Definition: Provided initially by the words of Raphael Lemkin at the 1948 Convention on the Prevention and Punishment of the crime of Genocide.

Any of the following acts committed with intent to destroy, in whole or in part, a national, ethnic, racial or religious group as such:

A   Killing members of the group

B   Causing serious bodily or mental harm to members of the group

C   Deliberately inflicting on the group the conditions of life calculated to bring about physical destruction in whole or in part.

D   Imposing measures intended to prevent births within the group

E   Forcibly transferring children of the group to another group

Chinese Civil War 1850-1864 I was recently in Jakarta, Indonesia visiting my wife's family and where her younger sister is married to a Japanese business man.. a very nice fellow I might add. Anyhow, I was in a conversation with this man and referred to a comment from a book I was currently reading: 'Mandarin' by Robert Elegant. It said that over the fourteen year period of the civil war in China between the armies of the Emperor and the rebels, the Taipings, it was estimated that in excess of 20 million persons had died, many of them civilians of various cities such as Shanghai, Suzhou and Nanjing to name a few. To my surprise he responded in an abrupt manner "You know Tom that in Japan many people do not accept that number!"

I was rather taken aback at that moment and made no reply. On later consideration I thought that, being a most sensitive man to anything about Japanese adventurism in the 20th Century he had mistakenly thought I was referring to Manchuria and China during the 1930s when in fact I was talking about the 1850s, a period in which there was no Japanese presence. I felt extremely sorry for a considerable time after as my host is always a most generous and considerate person and a wonderful family man. I had inadvertently touched a sensitive nerve by means of a lack of language skills on both sides.

It is said that the estimate of total war dead (the majority ordinary citizens) by contemporary historians is anything between 20 and 100 million.

The Taiping Civil War was a massive rebellion or civil war in China fought between the established Manchu Emperor of the Qing dynasty and the Christian millenarian movement of the Taiping Heavenly Kingdom from 1850 to 1864.

The Taiping Rebellion began in the southern province of Guangxi when local officials launched a campaign of religious persecution against a millenarian sect known as the God Worshipping Society led by Hong Xiuquan, who believed himself to be the younger brother of Jesus Christ. The goals of the Taipings were religious, nationalist, and political in nature; they sought the conversion of the Chinese people to the Taiping version of Christianity, the overthrow of the ruling Manchus (whom they did not accept as being Chinese in any case) and a reformation of the state. More than just getting rid of the ruling classes, the Taipings sought to replace the moral and social order of China by invoking Christianity. The war was mostly fought in the provinces of Jiangsu, Zhejiang, Anhui, Jiangxi and Hubei. In particular, this war was the largest in China since the Qing conquest in 1644, and it also ranks as one of the *bloodiest wars in human history*, the bloodiest civil war, and the largest conflict of the 19th century, with estimates of the war dead, as said, ranging from 20 million to as high as 100 million, with millions more displaced. Cities were sacked by armies with theft, murder and rape on a grand scale! But then nearly all wars between humans end with what we consider as war crimes. This war severely damaged the Chinese perception of Christianity, a value which many hold to the present!

European mercenaries assist Manchu Qing dynasty forces against the Taiping Heavenly Kingdom forces under Hong Xiuquan at the walls of Nanking.

WWI

This was described naively as 'the War to End War'. It raged through Europe for five years with horrific battles costing millions of young lives. The combatants were Germany and elements of the old Austrian-Hungarian Empire versus Western European nations along with the British Empire and later America. Many battles were fought in trenches with machine guns, tanks and bombs dropped from aeroplanes. Mechanised war was a new concept that brought about both heroic and futile foolish deeds from both sides. For the first time poisonous gases were introduced onto the field of battle producing undignified choking death to combatants and outrage by the public at home. The total death toll of the war was horrendous. Some of the worst battles are described below:

First Battle of the Marne, Sept 6th - 10th , 1914
Germany's 'Schlieffen Plan' to bypass French border fortifications by passing through Belgium and Luxembourg and swiftly defeating the French Army worked well initially. German soldiers were within 50 miles (80 km) of Paris. Their commander in chief, General Helmuth von Moltke, then changed the Schlieffen Plan; instead of going to the west of Paris to encircle the French capital, he sent his forces east to meet what he thought was a nearly defeated army head-on, giving the French and a British Expeditionary Force (Britain entered the war after Germany invaded Belgium) to strike the German western flank in the Valley of the Marne Both sides suffered heavy casualties and began digging trenches that would define warfare in the Great War.
Allied casualties: 263000
German casualties: 263000 (estimate)

Battles of Tannenberg and Masurian Lakes, Aug-Sept, 1914

In August, a German army encircled Russia's Second Army near Tannenburg, East Prussia. The manoeuvre was so well planned and executed that only about 10 000 of the Second Army's 150 000 men escaped and some 500 Russian artillery pieces were captured. The Russian commander, Gen. Alexander Samsonov committed suicide. The following month, German forces enveloped Russian general Pavel Rennenkampf's First Army in the Masurian Lakes area near East Prussia's border with Russia and dealt the Czar's troops another staggering defeat. The architects of the German plans, Gen. Paul von Hindenburg and his chief of staff Erich Ludendorff, were hailed as German heroes. After Russia was knocked out of the war in 1917, they were brought to the Western Front to take command there and were given extraordinary control.

Tannenberg
Russian Casualties: 122 000 some 92 000 of which were taken prisoner
German Casualties: 13 000

Masurian Lakes

Russian Casualties: 125 000
German Casualties: 40 000

Gallipoli, Feb 1915-Jan 1916
Britain's First Lord of the Admiralty, Winston Churchill, developed a plan to attack the Central Powers through their "soft underbelly" in Turkey and reopen the Dardanelles Straight between the Black and Aegean seas to Russian ships. The Gallipoli Peninsula jutted like the toe

of a shoe between the Dardanelles to its south and east and the Aegean Sea to the west. In April, British, Australian and New Zealand troops landed, mostly on the Aegean coast. The landings were largely unopposed, but British officers didn't move their troops from the exposed beach to the heights above upon landing. By the next day Turkish soldiers and their German advisors poured down a murderous fire on the invaders, who would never penetrate far inland during the campaign.

British & Commonwealth Forces casualties: 214 000

Turkish casualties: 300 000

Battle of Verdun, Feb-Dec 1916

The German offensive began against French fortifications anchored at the town of Verdun and stretching to the Swiss border. Three forts were captured, but not the fortifications at Verdun where the French commander, General Henri Philippe Petain, had declared "They shall not pass!" The Germans opened the offensive by firing 2 million shells against a front of just eight miles. A British attack on the Somme Front and a Russian offensive on the Eastern Front forced the Germans to pull troops away from Verdun. The final German offensive took place there on July 21. During autumn, having gained artillery superiority, the French began counterattacks. By December 15 they had regained all the ground previously lost, leaving the lines as they had been before the German attack began the previous February.

Allied casualties: 400 000
German casualties: 340 000

Battle of the Somme, Jul-Nov 1916

This was the British offensive to break through German lines near the Somme River in north eastern France and relieve pressure on Verdun to the south. It was intended to be 'the big push' that would end the war. A week of bombardments sent 1.6 million shells screaming into the German lines, but their damage was insignificant. When British troops attacked on July 1, they suffered the greatest single-day loss in all of Britain's history: 60 000 casualties, one-third of which were killed (approx 20 000). As the offensive dragged on, French troops came to reinforce the British. When the battles ended in mid-November, the Allies had won just five miles (eight km) of ground, but attrition was high among the German defenders, including a large number of junior officers and NCOs, which would affect their army's effectiveness during the remaining years of the war.

Allied casualties: 615 000 approximately two-thirds British
German casualties: 650 000

Tommies in Flanders   1916

Third Battle of Ypres (Passchendaele), Jul-Nov 1917

The area around Ypres, Belgium, had already witnessed two bloody struggles during the war, one of which saw the Germans first use of poison gas. Before launching the July 1917 offensive, British guns hurled 4.5 million artillery shells against the German position, but fortifications protected the defenders. The first waves of attacking British were mowed down. The months of August and October saw some of the heaviest rains in 30 years which turned the battlefield into a quagmire. Attacking soldiers at times found themselves in knee-deep mud as enemy machine-gun bullets whistled toward them. Some men and animals literally drowned in the mud of the fields that had been churned up by the extensive artillery barrage and soaked with rain. The offensive gained just five miles (eight km), which included the village of Passchendaele.

Allied casualties: 325 000

German casualties: 260 000

Spring Offensive-Ludendorff Offensive, Kaiser Battle Mar-Apr 1918

The German offensive on the Western Front was intended to win the war before American troops that had begun arriving in France could be fully deployed. Planned by General Paul von Hindenburg's Chief of Staff, Erich Ludendorff, the main offensive was to be against the British forces on the Somme Front and accompanied by three diversionary attacks. Initially the offensive sent the Allied troops reeling back, but the Germans advanced so quickly their supplies could not keep up in the muddy terrain pockmarked with shell craters. The attack fizzled out with the Germans in a weak defensive position. However they had inflicted severe losses that were only made up by the arrival of the American troops.

Allied casualties: 850 000

German casualties: 650 000

Hundred Days Offensive Jul-Nov 1918

This was the allied (American, British, French) offensive on the Western Front against the German Second Army. It included the battles of Amiens, Second Somme, Second Noyons, Second Arras and Meuse-Argonne Offensive. The allied forces pushed the Germans back to the Hindenburg Line of fortifications which protected Germany. The offensive continued eventually breaking through the Hindenburg Line resulting in Germany's surrender and thus ending the war.

Allied casualties: 1 070 000

German casualties: 786 000

Total Deaths of World War One:

Total Allied Powers Military Combatant Deaths: **4 834 000**

Total Allied Powers Military Deaths from Other Causes: **916 000**

Grand Total Allied Powers Military Deaths: **5 750 000**

Total Central Powers Military Combatant Deaths: **3 209 000**

Total Central Powers Military Deaths from Other Causes: **691 000**

Grand Total Central Powers Military Deaths: **3 900 000**

Dresden Germany 1945

Hiroshima, Japan   August 6th 1945

Total Wounded of World War One:

Total Military Wounded World War One:
Total Allied Powers Military Wounded:	**12 200 000**
Total Central Powers Military Wounded:	**8 570 000**

Total Civilian Deaths of World War One:
Total Allied Powers Civilian Deaths:	**627 000**
Total Central Powers Civilian Deaths:	**1 621 000**

The combined total number of military and civilian casualties in World War I was more than 41 million. There were over 18 million deaths and 23 million wounded, ranking it the deadliest conflict in human history.

The total number of deaths includes from 9 to 11 million military personnel and about 5 to 6 million civilians. The Allies lost about 6 million military personnel while the Central Powers lost about 4 million. At least 2 million died from diseases and 6 million went missing, presumed dead.

Turkey's Armenians

Sultan Abdul Hamid II obsessed with loyalty and infuriated by the Armenian campaign to win basic civil rights declared that he would solve the "Armenian question" once and for all. "I will soon settle those Armenians," he told a reporter in 1890. "I will give them a box on the ear which will make them relinquish their revolutionary ambitions." Between 1894 and 1896, this took the form of a state-sanctioned pogrom. Turkish military officials, soldiers and ordinary men sacked Armenian villages and cities and massacred their citizens. It is believed that hundreds of thousands of Armenians were murdered. Although Hamid was never directly implicated, it is believed that the massacres had his tacit approval.

MILLION ARMENIANS KILLED OR IN EXILE

American Committee on Relief Says Victims of Turks Are Steadily Increasing.

POLICY OF EXTERMINATION

More Atrocities Detailed In Support of Charge That Turkey Is Acting Deliberately.

Headline of *The New York Times*, 15 December 1915

The Armenian community was made up of three religious denominations: Armenian Catholic, Armenian Protestant, and Armenian Apostolic- the Church of the majority of Armenians. Under the millet system, the Armenian community was allowed to rule itself under its own system of governance with fairly little interference from the Ottoman government.

Tehcir Law of Armenian Expulsion

In 1914, the Turks entered World War I on the side of Germany and the Austro-Hungarian Empire. As the war intensified, Armenians organized volunteer battalions to help the Russian army fight against the Turks in the Caucasus region. These events led the Turkish government to push for the "removal" of the Armenians from the war zones along the Eastern Front. Minister of War Enver Pasha publicly blamed defeat on Armenians in the region having actively sided with the Russians. In November 1914 Shaykh ul-Islam proclaimed Jihad or Holy War against the Christians. On April 24, 1915, the Armenian genocide began. That day, the Turkish government arrested and executed several hundred Armenian intellectuals. After that on 29 May 'Tehcir Law' was enacted demanding expulsion; ordinary Armenians were turned out of their homes and sent on death marches through the Mesopotamian desert without food or water. Frequently, the marchers were stripped naked and forced to walk under the scorching sun until they dropped dead. People who stopped to rest were shot.

At the same time, the Young Turks organized "killing squads" to carry out, as one officer put it, "the liquidation of the Christian elements." These killing squads were often made up of murderers and other ex-convicts. They drowned people in rivers, threw them off cliffs, crucified them and burned them alive, littering the countryside with Armenian corpses. An estimated 1.5 million Armenians died. By 1923 there were just 388 000 Armenians remaining in the Ottoman Empire.

On his return home in 1924 after thirty years as a US Consul in the Near East, and most of the preceding decade as Consul General at Smyrna, George Horton wrote his own account of the "Systematic Extermination of Christian Populations by Mohammedans and of the Culpability of Certain Great Powers; with a True Story of the Burning of Smyrna". Horton's account quoted numerous contemporary communications and eyewitness reports including one of the massacre of Phocea in 1914 by a Frenchman and two of the Armenian massacres of 1914/15 by an American citizen and a German missionary. It also quoted US businessman Walter M. Geddes regarding his time in Damascus:

"Several Turks whom I interviewed told me that the motive of this exile was to exterminate the race."

Since that time successive Turkish governments have denied that genocide took place. Also, it wasn't until March 2010 that a US Congressional panel finally voted to recognize the genocide!

The Armenian Genocide Memorial on the hill of Tsitsernakaberd , Yerevan

The Protocols of Zion
by French Priest at the Vatican c1600

The International Jew
by Henry Ford c1920

Two books distributed in Germany in the 1930s on anti-semitism

WWII

Coventry England 1940

Victoria Station London 1941

Unwarranted Influence

It is February 2018 and the Polish Government have just introduced laws placing any person in prison for daring to suggest that any Pole was associated with Nazis during the second world war! Why they would open themselves to such ridicule by other nations is unfathomable? Certainly there were many Poles that were compliant either for reasons of fear or because they supported Nazi ideals, especially the 'final solution' in doing away with the Jewish people. It must be eternally remembered that extermination camps in Poland were the busiest and most efficient in Europe and to suggest that Poles played no part is a naïve and insulting view point! Sadly, there was no country invaded by Nazi Germany that had no keen accomplices to the evil perpetrated. The Nazis always found 'willing hands' to assist them in rounding up and murdering people based purely on their religion. Such is the nature of the lowest elements of human kind!

World War II is seen to have been the deadliest military conflict in human history to date in absolute terms of total casualties. A staggering figure of over 60 million people were killed (about 2.6% of the 1940 world population of 2.3 billion). Fatality statistics vary, with estimates of total deaths ranging from 50 million to more than 80 million. The higher figure includes deaths from war-related diseases and famine. Civilians killed totalled between 50 and 55 million, including around 25 million from war-related disease and famine. Military deaths from all causes totalled around 25 million, including deaths in captivity of about 5 million prisoners of war. Civilian deaths from bombing of cities together with extermination of Jews plus the high number of deaths in captivity point to an almost unbelievable scale of war crimes during this abominable world conflict.

Recent research has shed new light on the topic of Second World War casualties. Since the collapse of the Soviet Union there has been a revision of estimates of Soviet WW2 fatalities. According to Russian government figures, USSR losses within post-war borders now stand at 26.6 million, including 8.5 million due to war related famine and disease.

Further, in August 2009 the Polish Institute of National Remembrance has now estimated Poland's dead at between 5.6 and 5.8 million. Historian Rüdiger Overmans of the Military History Research Office, Germany, published a study in 2000 that estimated the German military dead and missing at 5.3 million, including 900 000 men conscripted from outside of Germany's 1937 borders. These were from Austria and east and central Europe.

The People's Republic of China now puts its war dead at 20 million, while the Japanese government estimates its casualties due to the war at 3.1 million. (The Japanese figure is difficult to validate as Imperial Japanese Forces were serving outside of Japan from as early as 1905).

Total Deaths of World War Two:

Total Allied Powers Military Deaths from all Causes: 17 600 000
Total Axis Powers Military Deaths from all Causes: 7 595 000
Total Deaths Military   25 195 000

Total Allied Powers Military Wounded: 16 000 000
Total Axis Powers Military Wounded: 7 500 000
Total Military Wounded World War Two: 23 500 000

Total Allied Powers Civilian Deaths from all Causes: **50 895 000**

Total Axis Powers Civilian Deaths from all Causes: **4 105 000**

Total Civilian Deaths of World War Two: **55 000 000**

Total Deaths Military + Civilian   **80 000 000**

Of the Allied Powers, Russia (as the USSR) and China suffered the most significant number of deaths:

Russian Military deaths: 10 600 000

Russian Civilian deaths: 16 000 000

Chinese Military deaths: 3 500 000

Chinese Civilian deaths: 15 000 000

[One study of the Chinese population concluded that a conservative estimate puts the total human casualties directly caused by the war of 1937-1945 at between 15 000 000 and 20 000 000. It cited a Chinese Nationalist source placing the total civilian casualties at 2 144 048

(i.e 1 073 496 killed; 237 319 wounded; 71 050 captured by Japanese; 335 934 killed in Japanese air raids; 426 249 wounded in air raids), and military casualties at 6 750 000 from 1937-1943 (1 500 000 killed;

3 000 000 wounded; 750 000 missing; 1 500 000 deaths caused by sickness.)

In addition 960 000 collaborator forces and 446 736 Communists were killed or wounded.]

Holocaust Deaths

The Holocaust is the term generally used to describe the genocide of European Jews, Roma (Gypsies), Homosexuals, Handicapped persons, Ethnic Poles and Slavic persons during World War II.

Jews: Martin Gilbert estimates 5.7 million (78%) of the 7.3 million Jews in German occupied Europe were Holocaust victims. Estimates of Holocaust deaths range between 4.9 and 5.9 million Jews.

Statistical breakdown of Jewish dead:

In Nazi extermination camps: according to Polish Institute of National Remembrance (IPN) researchers, 2 830 000 Jews were murdered in the Nazi death camps*:

500 000	Belzec
150 000	Sobibor
850 000	Treblinka
150 000	Chełmno
1 100 000	Auschwitz
80 000	Majdanek

In the USSR by the Einsatzgruppen: Raul Hilberg puts the Jewish death toll by mobile killing groups at 1.4 million.

Emaciated survivers at Ebensee, Austria May 1945

Aggravated deaths in the Ghettos of Nazi-occupied Europe: Raul Hilberg puts the Jewish death toll in the Ghettos at 700 000.

[* for a complete list of Nazi death camps and work camps see Appendix M]

Up to 250 000 handicapped persons were killed. The German Federal Archive has estimated the total murdered during the Action T4 and Action 14f13 programs at 200 000.

POW deaths in Nazi captivity totalled 3.1 million which included between 2.6 to 3 million Soviet prisoners of war.

According to the United States Holocaust Memorial Museum it is estimated that the Germans killed at least 1.9 million non-Jewish Polish civilians during World War II. The Polish government affiliated Institute of National Remembrance (IPN) estimates that around 2 770 000 ethnic Polish deaths were due to the German occupation.

According to Nazi ideology Slavs were useless sub-humans (untermensch). As such, their leaders, the Soviet elite, were all to be killed and the remainder of the population enslaved or expelled further eastward. As a result, millions of civilians in the Soviet Union were deliberately killed, starved, or worked to death. Contemporary Russian sources use the terms 'genocide' and 'premeditated extermination' when referring to civilian losses in the occupied USSR. Civilians killed in reprisals during the Soviet partisan war and wartime-related famine account for a major part of the huge toll. The *Cambridge History of Russia* puts overall civilian deaths in the Nazi-occupied USSR at 13.7 million persons including 2 million Jews. There were an additional 2.6 million deaths in the interior regions of the Soviet Union. The authors maintain 'scope for error in this number is very wide'. At least 1 million perished in the wartime GULAG camps or in deportations. Other deaths occurred in the wartime evacuations and due to war related malnutrition and disease in the interior. The authors also maintain that both Stalin and Hitler 'were both equally responsible but in different ways for these deaths.' Bohdan Wytwycky maintained that civilian losses of 3.0 million Ukrainians and 1.4 million Belarusians 'were racially motivated'. According to Paul Robert Magocsi, between 1941 and 1945, approximately 3 million Ukrainian and other non-Jewish victims were killed as part of Nazi extermination policies in the territory of modern Ukraine. Dieter Pohl puts the total number of victims of the Nazi policies in the USSR at 500 000 civilians killed in the repression of

President Roosevelt and Churchill, Casablanca Jan. 1943

partisans, 1 million victims of the Nazi Hunger Plan, circa 3 million Soviet prisoners of war and 1 million Jews (in pre-war borders). Soviet author Georgiy A. Kumanev put the civilian death toll in the Nazi-occupied USSR at 8.2 million (4.0 million Ukrainians, 2.5 million

Belarusians, and 1.7 million Russians). The Russian Academy of Sciences in 1995 put the death toll due to the German occupation at 13.7 million civilians (including Jews): 7.4 million victims of Nazi genocide and reprisals; 2.2 million persons deported to Germany for forced labour; and 4.1 million famine and disease deaths in occupied territory with sources published in the Soviet Union cited to support these figures.

The United States Holocaust Memorial Museum states that between 1933 and 1945 German police arrested an estimated 100 000 men for being homosexuals. Most men sentenced by the courts spent time in regular prisons and between 5 000 and 15 000 were interned in concentration camps. There seems to be no factual statistics for the number of homosexuals who died in these camps however other anecdotal evidence suggests that many were hanged.

Around 1 500 Roman Catholic clergy, 1 000 Jehovah Witnesses, and an unknown number of Freemasons perished in Nazi prisons and camps.

The fate of black people from 1933 to 1945 in Nazi Germany and in German-occupied territories ranged from isolation to persecution, sterilization, medical experimentation, incarceration, brutality and murder. During the Nazi era Communists, Socialists, Social Democrats and trade union leaders were victims of Nazi persecution.

The numbers of Serbs murdered by the Croatian Ustashe is estimated to have been over 500 000 with a further 250 000 expelled and 200 000 forcibly converted to Catholicism. The estimate of the United States Holocaust Memorial Museum is that the Ustashe murdered between 320 000 and 340 000 ethnic Serbs in the Independent State of Croatia between 1941 and 1945, with roughly 45 000 to 52 000 murdered at the Jasenovac concentration camp alone. According to the Wiesenthal Center at least 90 000 Serbs, Jews, Muslims, Gypsies and anti-fascist Croatians perished at the hands of the Ustashe at the camp at Jasenovac. According to Yugoslav sources published during the Tito era, estimates of the number of Serb victims range from 200 000 to at least 600 000 persons.

The author has not detailed here Hitler and the Nazi relationship to the Roman Catholic Church. The reader is referred to Chapter 8 of the earlier book 'Return to Animalia' which poses the question: "... *did Hitler envisage that one day he himself might be crowned Emperor of the Holy Roman Empire?"*

Interior of the courtroom of the Nuremberg War Crimes Trials in 1946

Nuremburg Trials: Major war criminals included here: Hermann Goering, former leader of the Luftwaffe, Rudolf Hess, former Deputy Fuhrer of Germany, Joachim von Ribbentrop, former Nazi Minister of Foreign Affairs, Wilhelm Keitel, former leader of Germany's Supreme

Command and Ernst Kalterbrunner, the highest ranking surviving SS leader. Goering, von Ribbentrop, Keitel, and Kaltenbrunner were sentenced to death by hanging along with eight others. Goering committed suicide the night before his execution. Hess was sentenced to life imprisonment which he served at Spandau Prison Berlin until his death in 1987.

General Charles de Gaulle shaking hands with children two months after the German capitulation in Lorient, France   July 1945.

Jews deported from Prague, Czechoslovakia, move their belongings through the streets of the Lodz ghetto in occupied Poland. November 20, 1941. USHMM

The entrance to the former Nazi concentration camp Auschwitz-Birkenau with the lettering 'Arbeit Macht Frei' … work will make you free!

Japanese War Crimes

R. J. Rummel estimates the civilian victims of Imperial Japanese Forces democide at 5 424 000.

By country:

China	3 695 000
Indochina	457 000
Korea	378 000
Indonesia	375 000*
Malaya	283 000
Philippines	119 000
Burma	60 000
Pacific Islands	57 000

*As seen later, a gross underestimate

Rummel estimates POW deaths in Japanese custody at 539 000

By country of origin:

China	400 000
French Indochina	30 000
Philippines	27 300
Netherlands	25 000
France	14 000
Britain	13 000
British Colonies	11 000
US	10 700
Australia/New Zealand	8 000

Singapore:

Out of 60 000 Indian Army POWs taken at the Fall of Singapore, 11 000 died in captivity. There were 14 657 deaths among the total 130 895 western civilians interned by the Japanese due to famine and disease.

Imperial Japanese Soldiers in Nanjing, China   1932

Leonard Siffleet was an Australian Special Forces radio operator, sent to Papua New Guinea to establish a coast watching site monitoring the movements of Japanese forces. He and two Ambonese comrades, H. Pattiwal and M. Reharing, were discovered and detained by local tribesmen loyal to the Japanese. After the Japanese had interrogated them for two weeks, all three were beheaded on Aitape Beach on 24th October 1943 (Japanese execution by beheading is referred to as Bushido.)

Beheadings of Chinese soldiers, Nanjing 1932

84

Unwarranted Influence

Beheading of Australian Leonard Sifleet   **Attrocities, Nanjing 1930s**

Indonesia

Ranryō Higashi Indo   蘭領東印度

The Japanese Empire occupied the Dutch East Indies, now Indonesia, during World War II from March 1942 until after the end of the War in 1945. Initially, most Indonesians joyfully welcomed the Japanese as liberators from their Dutch colonial masters. This sentiment soon changed however as Indonesians were expected to endure more hardship for the war effort.

Experience of the occupation varied considerably, depending upon where one lived and one's social position. Many who lived in areas considered important to the war effort experienced torture, sex slavery, arbitrary arrest and execution and other war crimes. Many thousands of people were taken away from Indonesia as forced labourers, the so called *romusha*, for Japanese military projects including the Burma-Siam and Saketi-Bayah railways and suffered or died as a result of ill-treatment and starvation. Between 4 million and 10 million *romusha* in Java were forced to work by the Japanese military. About 270 000 of these Javanese labourers were sent to other Japanese-held areas in South East Asia; only 52 000 were repatriated to Java meaning that there was a death rate of around 80% !

Japanese troops took control of government infrastructure and services such as ports and postal services. In addition to the 100 000 European (and some Chinese) civilians interned, 80 000 Dutch, British, Australian, and US allied troops went to prisoner-of-war camps where the death rates were between 13% and 30%. Later a United Nations report stated that four million people died in Indonesia as a result of famine and forced labour during the Japanese occupation, including 30 000 European civilian internee deaths. A Dutch government study described how the Japanese military recruited women as prostitutes by force in Indonesia. In 1943 the Japanese beheaded Tengku Rachmadu'llah, a member of the royal family of the Sultanate of Serdang. In the 1943-1944 Pontianak incidents (also known as the Mandor Affair), the Japanese orchestrated a mass arrest of Malay elites and Arabs, Chinese, Javanese, Manadonese, Dayaks, Bugis, Bataks, Minangkabau, Dutch, Indians, and Eurasians in Kalimantan, including all of the Malay Sultans. They were accused of plotting to overthrow Japanese rule and for this, they were duly massacred. The Sultans of Pontianak, Sambas, Ketapang, Soekadana, Simbang, Koeboe, Ngabang, Sanggau, Sekadau, Tajan, Singtan, and Mempawa were all executed by the Japanese, which included many of their family members.

The Japanese occupation officially ended with the Japanese surrender in the Pacific and two days later Soekarno declared Indonesian Independence. However Indonesian forces would spend the next four years fighting the Dutch for independence as Dutch troops assisted by a contingent of British troops returned to Indonesia.

The Soekarno government of Indonesia demanded $10 billion from the government of Japan for reparation against their estimate of the loss of 4 million lives under the romusha program. The Japanese government rejected the claim, citing a lack of evidence, as they had done repeatedly in the instance of the *Comfort Women.* The government of Japan formally apologized to those women in the 1990s. However some Japanese nationalists today are seen to campaign for the withdrawal of the apology, citing a lack of evidence. Romusha survivors from the many hundreds of work sites all across the Japanese Empire described essentially similar experiences. They had been held captive at gunpoint in guarded compounds. At 'Klender 129' they were given grossly inadequate rations, no medical attention whatsoever, forced to perform backbreaking labour, routinely beaten for the slightest offense and summarily executed for insubordination, theft or attempted escape. Infections like malaria, dengue, typhus and enteric diseases went

Japanese Soldiers after surrender, Dili, East Timor   **Sept 1945.**

untreated as did serious nutritional deficiencies like beriberi and scurvy. Each of these maladies came with very high rates of mortality.

General Suharto managed to squeeze out Soekarno to become dictator of Indonesia. With the rise of the PKI, the communist party in Indonesia, Suharto and his fellow generals saw a need for a military response, also encouraged by the West including Australia. By the mid 1960s a pogrom commenced resulting in the execution of hundreds of thousands of Indonesian communists and in excess of 1 million ethnic Chinese, many of which were shop owners and business persons with no connection to PKI. Sadly, the communist purge had become an excuse for ethnic cleansing of Chinese Indonesians!

Japanese businesses now flourish in Indonesia in the 21st Century with corporate investments at a staggering $15 billion and expanding by 30% per annum in the country- their greatest in South East Asia!

The International Military Tribunal for the Far East, Tokyo. May 1946. The Allies began the trial of 28 Japanese civilian and military leaders for war crimes. Seven were hanged and the others sentenced to prison terms.

Unwarranted Influence

An Allied War Crime: The Bombing of Dresden

In four raids between 13 and 15 February 1945, 722 heavy bombers of the British Royal Air Force and 527 of the United States Army Air Force dropped more than 3 900 tons of high-explosive bombs and incendiary devices on the city of Dresden, capital of the German state of Saxony. The resulting firestorm destroyed over 1 600 acres (6.5 km^2) of the city centre. An estimated 25 000 people were killed, although larger casualty figures have been claimed over the years. (However, subsequent investigations support the 25 000 figure, including a 2010 study commissioned by the Dresden city council.) Three more USAF air raids followed, two occurring on 2 March aimed at the city's railway marshalling yard and one smaller raid on 17 April aimed at industrial areas.

Critics of the bombing have claimed Dresden was a cultural landmark of little or no strategic significance and that the attacks were indiscriminate area bombing and not proportionate to any significant military gain. Some have gone so far as to suggest it as a war crime.

In response to international concern about the bombing, the US Air Force wrote a report (which remained classified until December 1978). It declared that there were 110 factories and 50 000 workers in the city supporting the German war effort at the time of the raid. According to the report, there were aircraft components factories; a poison gas factory (Chemische Fabrik Goye and Company); an anti-aircraft and field gun factory (Lehman); an optical goods factory (Zeiss Ikon AG); as well as factories producing electrical and X-ray apparatus (Koch & Sterzel AG); gears and differentials (Saxoniswerke); and electric gauges (Gebrüder Bassler). It also said there were barracks, hutted camps, and a munitions storage depot.

The USAF report also states that two of Dresden's traffic routes were of military importance: north-south from Germany to Czechoslovakia, and east-west along the central European uplands. The city was at the junction of the Berlin-Prague-Vienna railway line, as well as the Munich-Breslau, and Hamburg-Leipzig lines.

Colonel Harold E. Cook, a US POW held in the Friedrichstadt marshalling yard the night before the attacks, later said that "I saw with my own eyes that Dresden was an armed camp: thousands of German troops, tanks and artillery and miles of freight cars loaded with supplies supporting and transporting German logistics towards the east to meet the Russians."

Other raids were carried out that night to confuse German air defences. Three hundred and sixty heavy bombers (Lancasters and Halifaxes) bombed a synthetic oil plant in Böhlen, 60 miles from Dresden, while de Havilland Mosquito medium bombers attacked Magdeburg, Bonn, Misburg near Hanover and Nuremberg.

A witness of the bombing recounted:

"We saw terrible things: cremated adults shrunk to the size of small children, pieces of arms and legs, dead people, whole families burnt to death, burning people ran to and fro, burnt coaches filled with civilian refugees, dead rescuers and soldiers. Many were calling and looking for their children and families, and fire everywhere, everywhere fire, and all the time the hot wind of the firestorm threw people back into the burning houses they were trying to escape from.

I cannot forget these terrible details. I can never forget them."

An RAF assessment showed that 23 percent of the industrial buildings, and 56 percent of the non-industrial buildings, not counting residential buildings, had been seriously damaged. Around 78 000 dwellings had been completely destroyed; 27 700 were uninhabitable, and 64 500 damaged, but readily repairable. Between 100 000 and 200 000 refugees fleeing westwards from advancing Soviet forces were in the city at the time of the bombing. Exact figures are unknown, but reliable estimates were calculated based on train arrivals, foot traffic, and the extent to which emergency accommodation had to be organised.

1 858 bodies were discovered during the reconstruction of Dresden between the end of the war and 1966.

British historian Frederick Taylor wrote of the attacks: "The destruction of Dresden has an epically tragic quality to it. It was a wonderfully beautiful city and a symbol of baroque humanism and all that was best in Germany. It also contained all of the worst from Germany during the Nazi period. In that sense it is an absolutely exemplary tragedy for the horrors of 20th century warfare and a symbol of destruction".

The Hague Conventions, addressing the codes of wartime conduct on land and at sea, were adopted before the rise of air power. Despite repeated diplomatic attempts to update international humanitarian law to include aerial warfare, it was not updated before the outbreak of World War II. The absence of positive international humanitarian law does not mean that the laws of war did not cover aerial warfare, but there was no general agreement of how to interpret those laws.

[.. and as we shall see later, in the Middle East in the first two decades of the current 21st Century, aerial bombardment of cities by planes and missiles continues with no application of International Law. Consequently the deaths of hundreds of thousands of innocent civilians has occurred as definitive war crimes with no punishment to the perpetrators to date! But there remains hope of such!]

"Ever since the deliberate mass bombing of civilians in the Second World War, and as a direct response to it, the international community has outlawed the practice. It first tried to do so in the Fourth Geneva

Convention of 1949, but the UK and the US would not agree, since to do so would have been an admission of guilt for their systematic *area bombing* of German and Japanese civilians." *A.C. Grayling**

According to Dr. Gregory Stanton, lawyer and president of Genocide Watch: "Every human being has the capacity for both good and evil. The Nazi Holocaust was among the most evil genocides in history. But the Allies' firebombing of Dresden and nuclear destruction of Hiroshima and Nagasaki were also war crimes- and as Leo Kuper and Eric Markusen have argued, also acts of genocide. We are all capable of evil and must be **restrained by law** from committing it!"

Nuclear Attacks on Hiroshima and Nagasaki

Even before the surrender of Nazi Germany on May 8, 1945, plans were underway for the largest operation of the Pacific War, Operation Downfall- the Allied invasion of Japan. The operation had two parts: Operation Olympic and Operation Coronet. Set to begin in October 1945, Olympic involved a series of landings by the US Sixth Army intended to capture the southern third of the southernmost main Japanese island, Kyushu. Operation Olympic was to be followed in March 1946 by Operation Coronet, the capture of the Kanto Plain, near Tokyo on the main Japanese island of Honshu by the US First, Eighth and Tenth Armies, as well as a Commonwealth Corps made up of Australian, British and Canadian divisions. The target date was chosen to allow for Olympic to complete its objectives, for troops to be redeployed from Europe, and the Japanese winter to pass.

Secretary of War Henry L. Stimson was sufficiently concerned about high American estimates of probable casualties to commission his own

[*Anthony Clifford Grayling CBE, British philosopher & author born: April 1949]

92

study by Quincy Wright and William Shockley. Wright and Shockley spoke with Colonels James McCormack and Dean Rusk, and examined casualty forecasts by Michael E. DeBakey and Gilbert Beebe. Wright and Shockley estimated the invading Allies would suffer between 1.7 and 4 million casualties in such a scenario, of whom between 400 000 and 800 000 would be dead, while Japanese fatalities would have been around 5 to 10 million persons.

The Allies called for the unconditional surrender of the Imperial Japanese armed forces in the Potsdam Declaration on July 26, 1945, the alternative being *prompt and utter destruction*. The Japanese ignored the ultimatum and the war continued.

Under the Quebec Agreement with the United Kingdom, nuclear

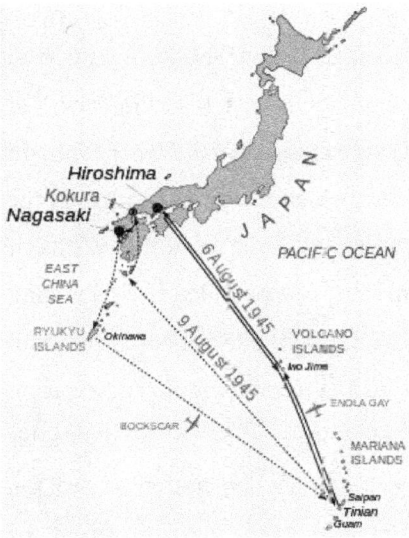

weapons would not be used against another country without mutual consent. Stimson therefore had to obtain British permission. A meeting of the Combined Policy Committee was held at the Pentagon on July 4, 1945. Field Marshal Sir Henry Maitland Wilson announced that the British government concurred with the use of nuclear weapons against Japan, which would be officially recorded as a decision of the Combined Policy Committee.

On August 6, *Enola Gay*, one of the US B-29s dropped *Little Boy*- a uranium gun-type bomb on the Japanese city of Hiroshima. Three days later on August 9, *Fat Man*- a plutonium implosion-type bomb was dropped by *Bockscar*, another B-29, on Nagasaki. The intended target was Kokura, but cloud and smoke resulted in 70% of the area over Kokura being covered, consequently obscuring the aiming point. After three runs over the city and with fuel running low because of a failed fuel pump, *Bockscar* headed for the secondary target, the city of Nagasaki.

On August 12, the Emperor informed the imperial family of his decision to surrender. One of his uncles, Prince Asaka, then asked whether the war would be continued if the *kokutai** could not be preserved. Hirohito simply replied, *"Of course"*. As the Allied terms seemed to leave intact the principle of the preservation of the Imperial Throne, Hirohito recorded on August 14 his capitulation announcement which was broadcast to the Japanese nation the next day despite a short rebellion by militarists opposed to the surrender.

 The bombs immediately devastated their targets. Over the next two to four months the acute effects of the atomic bombings killed in excess of 100 000 people in Hiroshima and in excess of 50 000 people in Nagasaki with roughly half of the deaths in each city occurring on the first day. Large numbers of people continued to die from the effects of burns, radiation sickness and other injuries, compounded by illness and malnutrition for many months afterward. In both cities most of the dead were civilians, although Hiroshima had a sizable military garrison. Japan announced its surrender to the Allies on August 15, six days after the bombing of Nagasaki and the Soviet Union's declaration of war. On September 2, the Japanese government signed the instrument of surrender, effectively ending World War II.

Many argue that both these nuclear attacks constituted a war crime. In view of the number of estimated deaths of American and allied service men and women that would have resulted from the planned military

[*kokutai: essentially meaning national identity, essence and character]

94

invasion of Japan, it must be an acceptable consideration that the nuclear strike saved these lives. However, one must consider the huge loss of civilian lives from the two attacks also when making such a judgement. After viewing the devastation of Hiroshima from the first bomb, one might state that the decision to attack Nagasaki with a second bomb was indeed wrong and thus a definitive war crime. The new American president Harry.S.Truman along with Winston Churchill should never have permitted the second bombing to occur. The fact that it was a military experiment is no justification to such an horrific and immoral act!

London 1942: British children depart the city for the safety of the countryside.

Bombing of Cities and Civilians in the 21st Century

Some interesting statistics:

American Service men and women killed in WWII: approx 417 000

American Service men and women killed since WWII: 153 000

This tally is from the Korean War, the Vietnam War, the Gulf Wars and the current war on terror (Afghanistan, Iraq and Syria)

Americans killed by gun deaths at home since WWII: 600 000+

Americans killed in the American Civil War: 750 000

THE GALLANT CHARGE OF THE FIFTY FOURTH MASSACHUSETTS (COLORED) REGIMENT,

Union and Confederate soldiers engaged in combat during the attack of the Massachusetts 54th Infantry Regiment on Fort Wagner, South Carolina, July 18, 1863 by Currier & Ives. (Library of Congress)

As we can see, deaths of Americans by firearms at home since 1946 have been **greater** than **ALL** deaths in every war aggregated since the end of WWII (… tell that to Trump and the NRA !)

Incidentally, America has been involved in nineteen wars since World War II and has been responsible for an estimated 12 million+ deaths!

The essence of this chapter however, is the continual application of aerial bombings of cities and civilians in war carried over into the 21st Century. It was the hallmark of World War II and was again applied in Korea, Vietnam and Laos during the latter half of the 20th Century (see later chapters). In the current century we saw the US and its allies bombing cities and civilians in the Gulf wars and those wars against the Taliban in Afghanistan and ISIS in Syria and Iraq. Israel has bombed various nuclear facilities of neighbouring Middle East countries and in 2014 made a most horrific bombing attack on Gaza. The Russians have continued to bomb civilian areas whilst assisting the Syrian regime against rebel forces. They are also responsible for bombings in eastern Ukraine. Saudi Arabia and the United Arab Emirates have bombed cities and civilian areas in Yemen.

Bombs, missiles and heavy artillery are still being applied as part of the landscape of war with devastating outcomes to civilian populations suffering underneath them. This author states that: " **... in the modern era these methodologies of fighting wars are against humanitarian law and as such ALL nations that have participated in such tactics have broken the rules and must be charged and punished under international criminal law for war crimes!"**

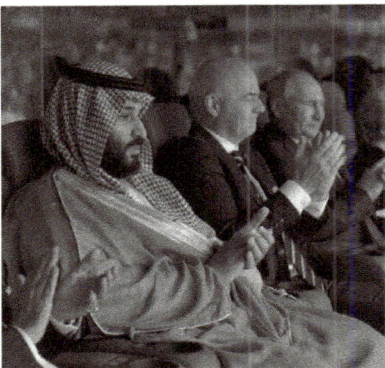

July 2018: While Saudi Arabia's Crown Prince Mohammed Bin Salman al-Saud laughed and joked with Putin in Moscow's Luzhniki Stadium, 2 800 miles away Saudi led forces were launching one of the largest attacks on Yemen since the war began in 2015. International monitors warned that the assault could result in the deaths of tens of thousands of people and create a humanitarian catastrophe. 'Save The Children' estimated at least 48 000 children died in Yemen in 2017, an average of 130 every day! In August 2018 this figure has climbed to

Israel bombs Gaza July 2014

A Palestinian searches for salvageable items from the rubble of his home 2014

https://www.pri.org/stories/2014-07-09/these-are-images-gaza-are-too-graphic-many-us-news-outlets-publish-day-31

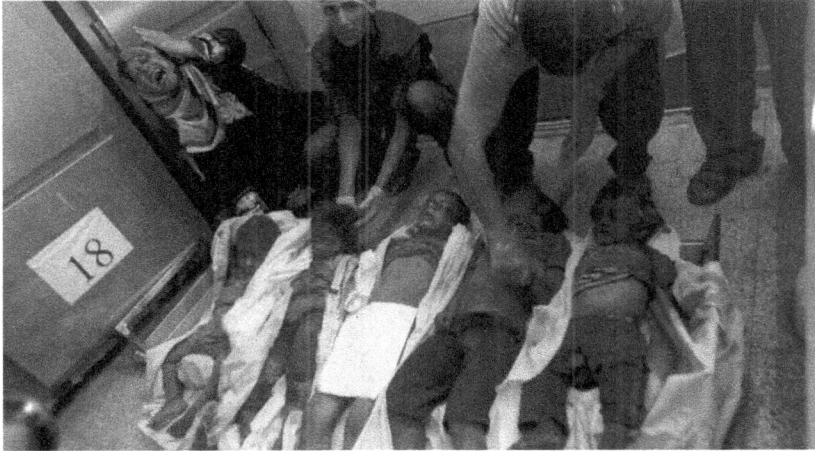

Dead children in Gaza after Israeli air strikes   **July 2014**

180 deaths of children per day!

Monday 3 April 2017: More civilians caught up in the Syrian conflict were killed by the US-led coalition than by ISIS or Russian led forces in the last month, according to figures by a human rights organisation.

Kobane 2015

Kobane 2015

Queuing for food Yarmouk Camp Syria 2015

Brig. Gen. Matthew Isler stated that since the Mosul battle began the coalition has released 8 700 precision-guided munitions "every one

approved by an Iraqi general officer or a Kurdish leader." -well that's
OK then! On a typical day, the coalition flew A-10 Warthogs, Navy

Mosul 2015

Mosul July 2017

Before ...

... and after ...   well done boys!

F/A-18s, Marine Corps Harriers, French Rafale fighters, Belgian F-16s, British Typhoons, and US Air Force B-52 Stratofortresses to support the fight as well as unmanned drones, some of which were armed.

Old City of Mosul Iraq July 2017

Devastation of Raqqa

"We need surgical, accurate operations to target terrorists without causing collateral damage among residents." ... what a load of crap! Interesting that the US and its allies claimed there were only up to 200

Devastation of Resafa, neighbourhood of Aleppo by murdering Russian Air Force ... before

... and after ! December 2016

civilian casualties from this constant bombing. You may draw your own conclusions from the images. The Daily Telegraph claimed that over 8 000 Iraqi civilians were killed during the Mosul battle, mainly by airstrikes conducted by the US led coalition.

From March 2015, the US led 'Global Coalition to Counter the Islamic State of Iraq and the Levant' (comprising over sixty countries)

Homs, Syria 2018

Homs, Syria 2018

contributed in various ways (including cutting off financing and funding and exposing ISIL's true nature) to degrade and eliminate the enemy.

The United States first supplied the rebels of the Free Syrian Army with non-lethal aid but later began providing training, cash, and intelligence to selected Syrian rebel commanders. During the Syrian Civil War, which began in 2011, two US programs attempted to assist the Syrian rebels. One was a military program that planned to train and equip 15 000 Syrian rebels, cancelled in 2015 after spending $500 million and producing only a few dozen fighters. A $1 billion covert program run by the CIA was more successful, but decimated by Russian bombing and hence cancelled in mid-2017 by the Trump administration.

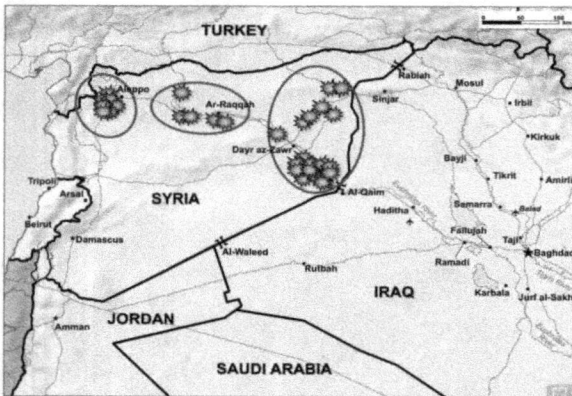

Beginning of US and coalition air strikes in Syria December 2015

A man carries an infant rescued from the rubble of buildings after government and Russian bombing in the rebel held town of Hamouria, in the besieged Eastern Ghouta region, the outskirts of the capital Damascus. Almost 300 people were killed in the three day bombing of Eastern Ghouta; warplanes bombing densely populated areas and helicopters dropping barrels packed with shrapnel and crude explosives. As the conflict escalated, international powers, including the United

Hamouria in Ghouta region February 2018   Syria's bloodiest day

States, Russia, Turkey and Iran all scrambled for influence. In Eastern Ghouta the final pocket of rebels around the capital was finally extinguished by Syrian government forces.

Syrian government and Russian bombing in Hamouria, Eastern Ghouta
A 'White Helmet' carries an injured child rescued from the rubble.

February 2017: The Syrian Network for Human Rights (SNHR), found ISIS killed 119 civilians in Syria in March, including 19 children and 7 women, with Russian forces believed to have killed 224 civilians in the

Attack on Hamouria, Eastern Ghouta, February 2018

same month, including 51 children and 42 women. However, for the same month they found the international coalition forces, led by the US, had killed 260 civilians, including 70 children and 34 women.

As of August 9, 2017 the coalition's 'Operation Inherent Resolve' had conducted 13 331 strikes in Iraq and 11 235 strikes in Syria. According to the US Air Force, the coalition fired well over 100 000 weapons as part of the operation. Especially concerning is the fact that they caused a high number of civilian casualties. It is likely that from August 2014 until March 2018 in excess of 10 000 civilians were killed by coalition strikes. However, Russia's track record of bombing in Syria was no better than the US led coalition's and probably worse. All participants were in breach of UN and International Humanitarian law and have committed despicable war crimes which need to be addressed!

Unwarranted Influence

The United Nations General Assembly needs to discuss, pass and enact new International laws banning the destruction of cities and towns by bombs, missiles or super cannon, all of the conventional kind, notwithstanding the possibility of the application of nuclear weapons.

Unilateral decision making to join a war by a member state must also be rendered an illegal act. Only the UN General Assembly can direct a UN Force to quell a war between states or sides within a state in future.

As mentioned elsewhere, serious rules regarding the manufacture and sale of armaments and military hardware for profit by private corporations must also be reined in with heavy economic punishments to those that flaunt relevant international laws. All these things need to be framed and written into 'international law' for a safe future of all peoples on this planet. The world is at a crossroads where it can move along to a more peaceful era or slide into chaos and total destruction of humanity and modern society. You, my reader, have an obligation to petition and demonstrate until all this is met and fulfilled. Do it for your family, your children, for your country and for the world!

Saudi Arabia and UAE jets bombing Yemen 2017 and 2018

Saudi Arabia, the United Arab Emirates, the US and Iran taking sides in the Yemen civil conflict have brought the country to its knees with millions at starvation point and thousands of child deaths.

Devastation in Yemen due to Saudi Arabia and UAE Air Forces

... and more destruction in Yemen

Nothing to do with me you say? Well note this: 'your government, through taxation of large munitions and military hardware companies, has made millions of pounds sterling or dollars through the sales of weapons to participating states in this war and other wars! Further, your relatively high standard of living has relied upon the murder, suffering and starvation of millions living far beyond your shore together with the levelling of homes and whole cities.'

What do you intend doing about this situation? If you do nothing, say nothing then this author assures you of this fact:

"At some point in the not too distant future, the same will be meted out to you arriving at your doorstep: devastation of your city, your home, your family and the civilisation of which you are a part of, all in the name of profit and monetary gain of a few madmen that control the nature of world economics and power. As individuals, you do have the power to change this, especially if you act along with your fellow humans in all parts of the world. Do not delay!"

Evil personified- Putin and al Assad embrace on a 'job well done' ! The ICC at The Hague awaits them!

Communist Revolutions:

Russia

The February Revolution of 1917 had toppled Tsar Nicolas II of Russia, and replaced his government with a weak Provisional Government. Russia continued with World War I which became increasingly unpopular with the death of millions. A nationwide crisis developed affecting social, economic, and political relations. Disorder in industry and transport had intensified with difficulties in obtaining provisions increasing. Gross industrial production in 1917 had decreased by over 36% from what it had been at the beginning of the war. By the end of August as much as 50% of all enterprises were closed down in many of the country's industrial centres, leading to mass unemployment. At the same time, the cost of living increased sharply. Real wages had fallen about 50%. Russia's national debt in October 1917 had risen to 50 billion roubles with debts to foreign governments more than 11 billion roubles. The country was facing financial bankruptcy.

The Bolshevik Coup was a revolution in Russia led by the Bolsheviks and Vladimir Lenin that was instrumental in the larger Russian Revolution of 1917. It took place with an armed insurrection in Petrograd (now St. Petersburg) on 25 October 1917.

Members of the Bolsheviks and other leftist groups such as the Left Socialist Revolutionaries were placed in important positions within the new state, that is the establishment of the Russian Socialist Federation or Soviet Republic (USSR), the world's first self-proclaimed socialist state. Queen Victoria's cousin, the Tsar, together with his entire family were executed on 17 July 1918.

Unwarranted Influence

A coalition of anti-Bolshevik groups attempted to unseat the new government in the Russian Civil War from 1918 to 1922. In an attempt to intervene in the civil war after the Bolsheviks' separate peace with the Central Powers, the Allied powers (United Kingdom, France, Italy, United States and Japan) occupied parts of the Soviet Union for over two years before finally withdrawing. The European powers recognized the Soviet Union in the early 1920s and began to engage in business with it. However, the United States did not recognize the new Russian government until 1933.

How many people died in the revolution and subsequent civil war? Documents with objective assessment are classified. Until now, Russia holds a vast amount of Soviet era documents which remain classified. Some estimate around ten million. The late Rudolph Rummel, the demographer of government mass murder estimated the human toll of twentieth-century socialism to be about 61 million in the Soviet Union, 78 million in China, and roughly 200 million worldwide. These victims perished during state-organized famines, collectivization, cultural revolutions, purges, campaigns against "unearned" income, and other experiments in social engineering.

Lenin's decree of January 20, 1918: Nationalization of church property began: cathedrals, churches, church grounds, and all buildings owned by churches were looted, and valuables (gold, silver, platinum, paintings, icons, and historical artefacts) were either stolen or sold to the West. Then again in 1935, Stalin introduced Article 12 of the USSR Criminal Code, which permitted that children age twelve and older be sentenced to death or imprisonment as adults. This "law" was directed at the orphans of victims of the regime. The total number of deaths under Stalin alone is estimated to be between 20 and 30 million persons.

The dissolution of the Soviet Union occurred on December 26, 1991, officially granting self-governing independence to the Republics of the former Soviet Union and forming the new Russian Federation.

China

解放战争

Jiěfàng Zhànzhēng, The War of Liberation, commenced in 1946 by the Chinese Communist Party which was initially formed in 1921. The party was weakened by the Nationalists in the late 1920s under leader Chiang Kai Shek. During the Japanese invasion and occupation, however, the Communists built more localized bases in Japanese occupied zones (1937 – 1945).

Under Mao Zedong, the Communists forced the Nationalists to capitulate. Under agreement, the Nationalists were permitted to retreat to the island of Formosa (now named Taiwan). This second great Chinese Civil War (1945-49) officially ended in October 1949, when Mao Zedong and the Chinese Communist Party proclaimed the People's Republic of China.

In the 1960s, Chinese Communist Party leader Mao Zedong came to feel that the current party leadership in China, as in the Soviet Union, was moving too far in a revisionist

中国人民解放军是毛泽东思想大学校

direction, with an emphasis on expertise rather than on ideological purity. Mao's own position in government had weakened after the failure of his "Great Leap Forward" (1958-1960) and the economic crisis that followed. Mao gathered a group of radicals, including his wife Jiang Qing and defence minister Lin Biao, to help him attack current party leadership and reassert his authority.

He shut down the nation's schools, calling for a massive youth mobilization to take current party leaders to task for their embrace of bourgeois values and lack of revolutionary spirit. In the months that followed, the movement escalated quickly as the students formed paramilitary groups called the Red Guards and attacked and harassed members of China's elderly and intellectual population. The rich and powerful soon found themselves alongside peasants and workers tilling the fields in the countryside if they survived execution. Famine and murder took its toll with estimates of between 60 and 100 million persons dying over the decade 1966 to 1976. Many of the Red Guard groups formed opposing factions and fought with each other. Fourteen year old high school girls would beat a University Physics lecturer to death for teaching Einstein's theories "Down with reactionary doctrine… Einstein's theories are purely capitalistic and must be replaced by revolutionary science!"

Jiang Qing had political ambitions and allied herself with Wang Hongwen together with propaganda specialists Zhang Chunqiao and Yao Wenyuan, forming a political clique later dubbed as the "Gang of Four".

On January 8, 1976, Zhou Enlai died. Years of resentment over the Cultural Revolution, the public persecution of Deng Xiaoping and the prohibition against public mourning of Zhou led to a rise in popular discontent against Mao and the Gang of Four.

Mao Zedong died on September 9, 1976 ending a significant chapter of the communist regime.

In August, the Party's Eleventh Congress was held in Beijing, officially naming Hua Guofeng, Ye Jianying, Deng Xiaoping, Li Xiannian, and Wang Dongxing as new members of the Politburo Standing Committee.

At the Fifth Plenum held in 1980, Peng Zhen, He Long and other leaders who had been purged during the Cultural Revolution were politically rehabilitated. Formal power was transferred to a new generation of pragmatic reformers, who reversed Cultural Revolution policies almost in their entirety.

Public discussion of the Cultural Revolution is still limited in China. The Chinese government continues to prohibit news organizations from mentioning details of the Cultural Revolution; online discussions and books about the topic are subject to official scrutiny. The focus of the Chinese government on maintaining political and social stability has been a top priority since the Tiananmen crackdown on reformers on June 4, 1989 in which hundreds of students were murdered by the police and military. The current government has no interest in re-evaluating any issue which might polarize the Party on ideological grounds. Interesting that in March 2018, President Xi Jin Ping achieved (as with his ancient Roman counterpart Julius Caesar) the status: "Leader for Life".

Xi Jin Ping now China's President for Life!

Amending the constitution to allow Mr Xi such an honour has stirred worries of China's return to an era of autocratic rule not seen since Chairman Mao. Typical of a dictatorship (or even Emperor ?) his image dominates hours of state television broadcasts, the front pages of state newspapers, magazine covers, billboards around parks, signs posted along footpaths and roads as well as posters sold at markets. However, it is Mao's countenance that still adorns the paper currency!

Cuba

In 1952, when it became apparent that he would lose, military figure Fulgencio Batista seized power cancelling the imminent elections. The people of Cuba were disgusted by this power grab, preferring Cuba's democracy, as flawed as it was. One such person was the rising political star Fidel Castro.

After the failed attack on the isolated Moncada army barracks, Castro, his

Che Guevara, Fidel Castro 1961

brother Raol and many of his socialist rebels were arrested and put on trial. Sentenced to 15 years in prison Fidel had become a nationally recognized figure and hero to many Cubans. Then in 1955, the Batista government, bending to international pressure to reform, released many political prisoners including Fidel and Raol. They went to Mexico to regroup and plan the next step in their revolution. Among new recruits were charismatic Cuban exile Camilo Cienfuegos and Argentine doctor Ernesto (Ché) Guevara. In November 1956, 82 men crowded onto the tiny yacht Granma and set sail for Cuba.

In the impenetrable highlands the rebels regrouped, attracting new members, collecting weapons and staging guerrilla attacks on military targets. Try as he might, Batista was not able to demolish the socialist rebels. Towards the end of 1958 Castro sent Cienfuegos and Guevara into the plains with small armies. Castro followed them with the remaining rebels capturing towns and villages along the way, where they were greeted as liberators. Guevara and 300 weary rebels defeated a much larger force at the city of Santa Clara on December 30th, capturing valuable munitions in the process. Cienfuegos and Guevara entered Havana on January 2nd 1959 disarming the remnants of the government military. Fidel finally entered Havana on January 5th to a hero's welcome, Batista having fled the country. Although Castro initially declared himself as a nationalist, he soon gravitated toward communism and openly courted the leaders of the Soviet Union. Communist Cuba would be a thorn in the side of the United States for decades, triggering international incidents such as the Bay of Pigs and the Cuban Missile Crisis. The United States imposed a trade embargo in 1962 that led to years of hardship for the Cuban people.

The Cuban revolution inspired revolutionaries throughout Latin America as idealistic young men and women took up arms to try and oust repressive hated governments. Across South America, Marxist revolutionary groups such as Chile's MIR and Uruguay's Tupamaros led to right-wing military governments seizing power (and assisted by the CIA). During the ensuing years these Marxist rebellions were mainly eradicated, but many innocent civilians died also during these conflicts.

Under the presidency of President Barack Obama, the US began to engage Cuba and by 2015 announced that the long-standing embargo would gradually be loosened. This announcement resulted in a surge of

Map of Cuba showing the location of the arrival of the rebels on the *Granma* in late 1956, the rebels' stronghold in the Sierra Maestra, and Guevara and Cienfuegos' route towards Havana via Las Villas Province in December 1958.

travel between the US and Cuba resulting in cultural exchanges between the two nations.

Korea

Korea was a part of the Japanese Empire from 1910 (but being a protectorate since 1905) until the end of World War II. In August 1945 the Soviet Union declared war on Imperial Japan, as a result of an agreement with the United States, liberated the northern part of Korea with US forces moving into the south. Thus Korea was split into two regions with separate governments, a democratic south and communist north. Both claimed to be the legitimate government of all Korea with neither accepting the border as permanent. The disagreement escalated into open warfare when North Korean forces supported by the

119

communist countries the Soviet Union and China, broke through the border invading the south on 25 June 1950. Thousands of Koreans had served in the Chinese People's Liberation Army (PLA) during the Chinese civil war in the late 1940s. The North Korean contributions to the Chinese Communist victory were not forgotten after the creation of the People's Republic of China in 1949. As a token of gratitude, around 60 000 Korean veterans that served in the PLA were sent back along with their weapons to play a significant role in the initial invasion of South Korea.

In Russia, Stalin promised economic and military aid to China through the Sino-Soviet Treaty of Friendship, Alliance, and Mutual Assistance. Soviet generals with extensive combat experience from the Second World War were sent to North Korea as the Soviet Advisory Group. The Russians later provided jet fighters with Russian pilots, but no ground troops. Some estimate that there were more than 50 000 Russians in North Korea performing various tasks to assist the North Korean forces.

During October 1950 the police of South Korea executed people who were suspected to be sympathetic to North Korea. Similar massacres were carried out until early 1951. With the advent of UN troops entering the war, a surprise Chinese intervention and mass movement of Chinese troops, around 200 000, triggered a retreat of UN forces which continued until mid 1951. China poured in more troops (> 500 000) and equipment into Korea resulting in a great loss of Chinese lives. The war had become a war between China and the Western combined forces!

On again, off again armistice negotiations continued for the next two years. On 2nd December 1952, the newly elected US president Eisenhower went to Korea to learn what might end the Korean War. North Korea was subjected to a massive bombing campaign after which fighting ended on 27 July 1953. The United Nations had accepted India's proposed 'Korean War Armistice' and hence the KPA, the PVA and the UN Command ceased fire with the battle line approximately at the 38th parallel. Upon agreeing to the armistice, the belligerents established the Korean Demilitarized Zone (DMZ), which has since been patrolled by the North and South forces as well as the United States and Joint UN Commands. Despite this armistice being signed, creating the Korean Demilitarized Zone separating North and South Korea, no peace treaty was ever signed leaving the two Koreas technically still at war!

Bombing: Almost every substantial building in North Korea was destroyed as a result of bombing with the majority of North Korean cities and villages reduced to rubble. As a consequence, North Korean factories, schools, hospitals and government offices were forced to move underground. The North claimed that the US used chemical and biological weapons. These claims were denied. There were fears that the US might make use of its nuclear arsenal but 'The Joint Chiefs of Staff' advised their allies that the United States would use nuclear weapons only if necessary to prevent a major military disaster! When Eisenhower succeeded Truman he was similarly cautious about using nuclear weapons in Korea to avoid a major conflict with China.

Casualties of the war:

South Korea	North Korea
Military Casualties:	
180 000 killed	>600 000 killed
600 000 wounded	750 000 wounded
Civilian Casualties:	
1 000 000 killed or wounded	1 500 000 killed or wounded

Combined North and South Korean Civilian

2 000 000 killed (approx)

Specific:

Military Casualties

US 36 500 killed	Chinese ~400 000 killed
103 000 wounded	600 000 wounded
~8 000 unaccounted	Russia ~300 killed

Other UN:

UN Country	Dead	Wounded	Missing	POW
United Kingdom	710	2 278	1 263	766
Turkey	717	2 246	167	217
Australia	297	1 240	43	23
Canada	309	1 055	30	2
France	288	818	18	11
Thailand	114	794	5	0
Greece	169	543	2	1
The Netherlands	111	589	4	0
Columbia	140	452	65	29
Ethiopia	120	536		
Philippines	92	299	57	40
Belgium and Luxemburg	97	350	5	1
New Zealand	34	80		1
South Africa	20		16	6

War Crimes: There were numerous atrocities and massacres of civilians throughout the Korean War committed by both the North and South Koreans. Many started on the first days of the war.

> Bodo League massacre
> Seoul National University Hospital massacre
> No Gun Ri Massacre
> Sinchon Massacre
> Ganghwa massacre
> Sancheong-Hamyang massacre
> Geochang massacre   to name a few!

South Korean President Syngman Rhee ordered the Bodo League massacre on 28 June, beginning numerous killings of more than 100 000 suspected leftist sympathizers and their families by South Korean officials and right wing terror groups. North Korean Army political officers purged South Korean society of its intelligentsia by executing every educated person, academic, governmental and religious, who might lead a resistance against the North. US troops acted under a 'shoot-first-ask-questions-later' policy against any civilian refugee approaching US battlefield positions, a policy that led US soldiers to kill an estimated 400 civilians at No Gun Ri (26-29 July 1950) in central Korea.

In 2005, the South Korean Truth and Reconciliation Commission has investigated numerous atrocities committed by the Japanese colonial government, North Korean military, US military, and the authoritarian South Korean government. It has investigated atrocities before, during and after the Korean War. They verified that in excess of 14 000 civilians were killed in the Jeju uprising (1948-49) that involved South Korean military and paramilitary units against pro-North Korean guerrillas.

At Geoje prison camp on Geoje Island, Chinese POWs experienced anti-communist lecturing by agents from the US and Taiwan in No. 71, 72 and 86 camps. Pro-Communist POWs experienced torture, the cutting off of limbs, or executed in public!

The United States Senate 'Subcommittee on Korean War Atrocities of the Permanent Subcommittee of the Investigations of the Committee on Government Operations' reported that 'two thirds of all American prisoners of war in Korea died as a result of war crimes'. The Chinese rarely executed prisoners like their North Korean counterparts; however mass starvation and diseases swept through the Chinese run POW camps during the winter of 1950-1951. About 43 percent of US POWs died during this period along with dozens of British POWs.

Out of 80 000 South Korean POWs held by the Communists, when ceasefire negotiations began in 1951, they reported that only 8 000 South Koreans were being held!

Murdering their own: In the winter of 1951, around 70 000 South Korean National Defence Corps soldiers starved to death while marching southward during the Chinese offensive when their commanding officers embezzled funds earmarked for their food!

Peace in Our Time? Post war, about 100 000 North Koreans were executed in purges; forced labour and concentration camps were responsible for over one million deaths in North Korea between 1945 and 1987. Estimates based on the most recent North Korean census suggest that in excess of 300 000 people died as a result of the 1990s North Korean famine and that there were 750 000 unnatural deaths in North Korea between 1993 and 2008. A study by South Korean anthropologists of North Korean children who had defected to China found that 18 year old males were 13 centimetres shorter than South Koreans their age due to the effects of malnutrition. In the decades after the war, South Korea transformed into an economic powerhouse with many of its citizens knowing little about the conflict. Meanwhile, North

Korea became a most retrograde imprisoned state boasting the fourth largest army in the world.

May/June 2018: North Korean leader Kim Jong Un and South Korean President Moon Jae-in pledged to work towards a complete denuclearisation of the Korean peninsula. With the attendance of US diplomats it is envisaged that peace will at last arrive. Whether a unified Korea is possible in the future remains to be seen. Can a 'one nation two systems' be mapped to raise the standard of living of the peoples in the North? Certainly a new and prosperous Korea is possible if all parties see the benefits of peace and cooperation. Looking back at all the deaths and destruction from political differences of the past, its people deserve a new way for secure and safe lives!

The two Koreas are committed to work with the United States and

China to declare an official end to the Korean War and seek an agreement to establish a permanent peace.

May 2018: North Korean leader Kim Jong Un and South Korean President Moon Jae-in meet to discuss denuclearisation. All things are possible!

Vietnam, Laos and Cambodia

Indochina was a French colony from the 19th century to 1950. The Japanese invaded during World War II and were strongly opposed by the Viet Minh. They acquired some remnant Japanese arms after the Japanese surrender. The Viet Minh under the leadership of Ho Chi Minh then initiated an insurgency against French rule. Hostilities escalated into the First Indochina War beginning in December 1946. In January 1950 the People's Republic of China and the Soviet Union recognized the Viet Minh's Democratic Republic of Vietnam, based in Hanoi, as the legitimate government of Vietnam. The following month the United States and Great Britain recognized the French-backed State of Vietnam in Saigon, led by former Emperor Bảo Đại, as the legitimate Vietnamese government.

There soon followed a conflict that spilled over from Vietnam into Laos, and Cambodia from 1st November 1955 to the fall of Saigon on 30th April 1975. It was the second of the Indochina Wars and was officially fought between North Vietnam and the government of South Vietnam. The North Vietnamese army was supported by the Soviet Union, China and other communist allies and the South Vietnamese army was supported by the United States, South Korea, Australia, New Zealand, Thailand, Philippines, Taiwan and other anti-communist allies. Britain and Canada did not take part officially. However around 30 000 Canadians volunteered to join the American forces in Vietnam. Britain had assisted France in 1945-1946 but had no intention to return to Vietnam.

The domino theory, which argued that if one country fell to communism then all of the surrounding countries would follow, was first proposed as policy by the Eisenhower administration. John F. Kennedy, a Senator at the time, said in a speech to the American Friends of Vietnam: "Burma, Thailand, India, Japan, the Philippines and obviously Laos and Cambodia are among those whose security would be threatened if the Red Tide of Communism overflowed into Vietnam."

This was a major war for the West not seen since the Korean war with total dead in excess of four million and the United States and allies losing some 65 000 military personnel. The majority of those killed were civilians, almost two million from Vietnam.

Deaths in Vietnam War (1954–75) per R. J. Rummel

	Middle estimate
North Vietnam/Viet Cong military and civilian war dead	1 062 000
South Vietnam/US/South Korea military and civilian war dead	741 000
Democide by North Vietnam/Viet Cong	214 000
Democide by South Vietnam	89 000
Democide by the United States	6 000
Democide by South Korea	3 000
Subtotal Vietnam	2 115 000
Cambodians	273 000
Laotians	62 000
Grand total of war deaths: Vietnam, Cambodia, and Laos (1954–75)	2 450 000

Beginning in 1950, American military advisors arrived in what was then a colony named French Indochina with most of the funding for the French war effort being provided by the United States. This involvement rapidly escalated in the early 1960s with troop levels tripling in 1961 and again in 1962. Following the 1964 Gulf of Tonkin incident in which a US destroyer clashed with North Vietnamese fast attack craft the President gave authorization to further increase the US military presence. Regular combat units were deployed beginning in 1965. Operations crossed bordering areas of Laos and Cambodia which were being used by North Vietnam as supply routes and were heavily bombed by US forces. In 1968 the communists launched the Tet Offensive which aimed to overthrow the South Vietnamese government. Although a failure, it became the turning point in the war where a large segment of the American civilian population became disillusioned, rejecting their government's claims of progress toward winning the war. The deaths of so many young Americans coupled with the cost were just too much!

Gradual withdrawal of forces and decline in American involvement in the war followed, with the transfer of fighting the communists to the South Vietnamese alone. In America and the Western world a large anti-Vietnam War movement developed as part of a larger counterculture.

Direct military involvement ended on 15 August 1973 followed by the capture of Saigon by the North Vietnamese Army in April 1975. North and South Vietnam were reunified the following year to form the Socialist Republic of Vietnam.

Chemical Warfare

The widespread use of chemical defoliants between 1961 and 1971 were used to defoliate large parts of the countryside to prevent the Viet Cong from being able to hide their weapons and encampments under the foliage. These chemicals continue to change the landscape, cause diseases and birth defects and poison the food chain. Dow Chemical Company and Monsanto were given the task of developing herbicides for this purpose many of which contained 2,4,5-T, 2,4-D and the extreme poison dioxin. About 11-12 million gallons (41.6-45.4 million L) of Agent Orange were sprayed over southern Vietnam between 1961 and 1971. Between 1961 and 1967, the US Air Force sprayed 20 million gallons (75 700 000 L) of concentrated herbicides over 6 million acres (24 000 km^2) of crops and trees, affecting an estimated 13% of South Vietnam's land. As of 2006, the Vietnamese government estimated that there were over 4 000 000 victims of dioxin poisoning in Vietnam, although the United States government denies any conclusive scientific links between Agent Orange and the Vietnamese victims of dioxin poisoning.

The US Veterans Administration has listed the following post war medical conditions among veterans: prostate cancer, respiratory cancers, multiple myeloma, Diabetes mellitus type 2, B-cell lymphomas, soft-tissue sarcoma, chloracne, porphyria cutanea tarda, peripheral neuropathy, and spina bifida in children of veterans exposed to Agent Orange.

Vietnamese victims affected by Agent Orange attempted a class action lawsuit against Dow Chemical and other US chemical manufacturers, but District Court Judge Jack B. Weinstein dismissed their case. They appealed but the dismissal was cemented in February 2008 by the Court of Appeals for the Second Circuit. (.. and hardly independent! Ed)

Support by China and Russia

Between 1953 and 1991, the hardware donated by the Soviet Union included 2000 tanks, 1700 APCs, 7000 artillery guns, over 5000 anti-aircraft guns, 158 surface-to-air missile launchers and 120 helicopters. During the war the Soviets sent North Vietnam annual arms shipments worth $450 million. From July 1965 to the end of 1974 fighting in

Vietnam was said to have been observed by some 6500 officers and generals as well as more than 4500 soldiers and sergeants of the Soviet

Military aid given to North Vietnam by the People's Republic of China 1964 to 1975								
Guns	Artillery pieces	Bullets	Artillery shells	Radio trans-mitters	Telephones	Tanks	Planes	Auto-mobiles
1,922,897	64,529	1,048,207,000	17,074,000	30,808	48,922	560	164	15,771

Armed Forces. In addition, Soviet military schools and academies began training Vietnamese soldiers.

Both North Korea and Cuba provided substantial aid and military personnel to assist the Viet Cong.

War Crimes

According to political scientist R.J. Rummel, US troops murdered about 6000 Vietnamese civilians during the war. The use of free-fire zones i.e rules of engagement where civilians who ran from soldiers or helicopters could be viewed as Viet Cong. Further, a widespread disdain for Vietnamese civilians led to massive civilian casualties and endemic war crimes inflicted by US troops. The infamous My Lai Massacre being just one of many such incidents (later, we see similar disdain against Muslims when America entered wars in Afghanistan and the Middle East). Over 800 alleged atrocities were investigated, but only 23 soldiers were ever convicted on charges and most of these served sentences of less than a year.

During the Diem era, 1954-1963, R.J. Rummel estimated that 16 000 to 167 000 South Vietnamese civilians were killed in democide. From

Unwarranted Influence

1964-1975, Rummel* estimated a total of 42 000 to 128 000 were killed in democide. The total for 1954-1975 was between 57 000 and 284 000 deaths caused by South Vietnam. Torture and ill-treatment were frequently applied by the South Vietnamese to POWs as well as civilian prisoners.

Notable Viet Cong atrocities include the massacre of over 3000 unarmed civilians at Huế during the Tet Offensive and the incineration of hundreds of civilians at the Dak Son massacre with flamethrowers. Up to 155 000 refugees fleeing the final North Vietnamese Spring Offensive were killed or abducted on the road to Tuy Hòa in 1975. According to Rummel, North Vietnamese and Viet Cong troops murdered between 106 000 and 227 000 civilians in Vietnam.

In the Cambodian Civil War, Khmer Rouge insurgents reportedly committed atrocities during the war. These include the murder of civilians and POWs by slowly sawing off their heads a little more each day, the destruction of Buddhist wats and the killing of monks, attacks on refugee camps involving the deliberate murder of babies and bomb threats against foreign aid workers, the abduction and assassination of journalists and the shelling of Phnom Penh for more than a year. Journalist accounts stated that the Khmer Rouge shelling "tortured the capital almost continuously", inflicting random death and mutilation on 2 million trapped civilians. The Khmer Rouge forcibly evacuated the entire city after taking it in what has been described as a death march. Under the leadership of Pol Pot the Khmer Rouge would eventually kill between 1 and 3 million Cambodians out of a population of around 8 million in one of the bloodiest genocides in history.

[*STATISTICS OF DEMOCIDE: Genocide and Mass Murder Since 1900 by R.J. Rummel, School of Law, University of Virginia, 1997 and Transaction Publishers, Rutgers University]

United States expenditures in South Vietnam (SVN) (1953–1974)				
U.S. military costs	U.S. military aid to SVN	U.S. economic aid to SVN	Total	Total
$111 billion	$16.138 billion	$7.315 billion	$134.53 billion	$1.020 trillion

Laos

From 1964 to 1973 the US dropped more than two million tons of ordnance on Laos during 580 000 bombing missions. This is the equivalent of a planeload of bombs every 8 minutes, 24 hours a day for 9 years, making Laos the most heavily bombed country per capita in all of history. The bombings were part of the 'Secret War in Laos' to support the Royal Lao Government against the Pathet Lao and to interdict traffic along the Ho Chi Minh Trail where the Vietcong brought supplies into North Vietnam. The bombings destroyed many villages and displaced hundreds of thousands of Lao civilians during the nine year period.

Up to a third of the bombs dropped did not explode, leaving Laos contaminated with vast quantities of unexploded ordnance. Over 20 000 people are believed to have been killed or injured by these unexploded bombs in Laos since the bombing ceased. But the wounds of war are not only felt in Laos. When the Americans withdrew in 1973, hundreds of thousands of refugees fled the country with many of them ultimately resettling in the United States.

March 1971: Navy personnel wheel out 500 lb. bombs to be dropped on Laos

Launched from the ground or dropped from the air, cluster munitions consist of containers that open and disperse sub-munitions indiscriminately over a wide area. Many explosive sub-munitions, also

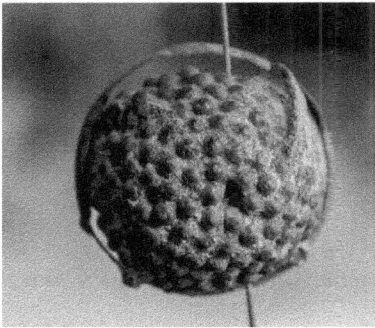

known as bomblets, fail to detonate as designed, becoming landmines that kill and maim indiscriminately. They are difficult to locate and remove, posing a danger to civilians long after a conflict ends. Children are particularly at risk, as they are

A cluster bomb   attracted to the bombs' toy-like appearance.

The *Convention on Cluster Munitions* bans the stockpiling, use and transfer of virtually all existing cluster bombs and also provides for the clearing up of unexploded munitions.

It has been adopted by 108 states with the exception of the USA which, according to some estimates, spent as much on clean-up efforts in Laos between 1995 and 2013 as it spent in three days of bombing during the war.

Laos is likely to ask for an extension to its commitment to get rid of unexploded ordinance when Convention member states next meet in August 2020.

Facts:

- Over 270 million cluster bombs were dropped on Laos during the Vietnam War with up to 80 million not detonating.
- Less than 1% of these munitions have been destroyed to date. More than half of all confirmed cluster munitions casualties in the world have occurred in Laos.
- Each year there are now just under 50 new casualties in Laos, down from 310 in 2008. Close to 60% of the accidents result in death and 40% of the victims are children.
- Between 1993 and 2016 the US contributed on average $4.9 million per year for UXO clearance in Laos; the US spent $13.3 million per day during the nine years whilst bombing Laos.
- In just ten days of bombing Laos, the US spent $130 million which computes to more than it has spent in clean up over the past 24 years- $118 million.

"Given our history here, I believe that the United States has a moral obligation to help Laos heal"

Barack Obama visited Laos, as US president in September 2016. He pledged $90 million in aid to Laos for clearance. It seems not to have been paid yet, due to disagreement between the United States and Laos about how to spend it. Also, $90 million doesn't sound quite as impressive when you realise that the US was already paying Laos $15 million a year for clearance.

"What Obama pledged was to double this for three years but, of course, we're not sure if we will ever get those payments for three years, given the incumbent president!"

It was noted that the president made no apology for all the damage done!

Joshua Kurlantzick, a senior fellow at the Council on Foreign Relations and a former newspaper contributor, enriches this study even further by connecting the CIA's unprecedented paramilitary activities in Laos to the secret wars of today in Yemen, Somalia and elsewhere!

[Read: **A Great Place to Have a War: America in Laos and the Birth of a Military CIA** by Joshua Kurlantzick, *Simon & Schuster*]

Yei Yang with two of his children

Cambodia

In 1970 President Richard Nixon issued orders to National Security Advisor and later Secretary of State Henry Kissinger:

"They have got to go in there and I mean really go in. I don't want the gunships, I want the helicopter ships. I want everything that can fly to go in there and crack the hell out of them. There is no limitation on mileage and there is no limitation on budget. Is that clear?"

Kissinger relayed these orders to his military assistant General Alexander Haig: "He wants a massive bombing campaign in Cambodia. He doesn't want to hear anything. It's an order, it's to be done. Anything that flies on anything that moves."

Just how many people the United States killed and injured will never be known precisely. In his book *Ending the Vietnam War*, Kissinger himself cites an apparent memo from the Historical Office of the Secretary of Defense stating there were 50 000 Cambodian casualties. The leading Cambodian Genocide scholar, Ben Kiernan, estimates the likely number to be between 50 000 and 150 000. However, as many as 500 000 people may have died as a result of the

April 1970:   President Nixon announces attack on Cambodia

136

bombings coupled with the effects of displacement, disease or starvation during this period.

The Khmer Rouge, previously a marginalized guerrilla group, propagandized the bombing campaign to great effect. By the CIA's own intelligence estimates, the bombing campaign was a key factor in the increase in popular support for the Khmer Rouge rebels. After their victory in 1975, the Khmer Rouge oversaw a period in which between one and two million Cambodians died from execution, hunger and forced labour. The United States dropped upwards of 2.7 million tons of bombs on Cambodia, exceeding the amount it had dropped on Japan during WWII -including Hiroshima and Nagasaki- by almost a million tons. During this time, about 30 per cent of the country's population was internally displaced.

Murder of University Protesters: The Kent State shootings were the shootings on May 4 1970, of unarmed college students by members of the 'Ohio National Guard' at Kent State University in Ohio during a mass protest against the bombing of Cambodia by United States military forces.

Total number of deaths: 4

Non-fatal injuries: 9

Weapons: M1 Garand, M1911 pistol, Shotgun.

No criminal convictions were obtained against any National Guardsman for this heinous crime!

Reparation and the Building of a New Country:

Unexploded ordnance continues to detonate and kill people today. The Vietnamese government claims that unexploded ordnance has killed some 42 000 people since the war officially ended. The United States has spent over $65 million since 1998 in an attempt to make Vietnam safe. Agent Orange and other chemical substances (defoliants) applied during the war have also caused a considerable number of deaths and injuries over the years, including members of US military personnel that handled

them. The government of Vietnam estimates that 4 million of its citizens were exposed to Agent Orange with 3 million having suffered consequential related illnesses. The Red Cross of Vietnam estimates that as many as a million people have disabilities or other health problems associated with Agent Orange - approximately 100 000 of them being disabled children. Every year, particularly in the areas heavily sprayed with Agent Orange, thousands of children are born with illnesses and birth deformities.

From August 2012, the United States and Vietnam began a cooperative cleaning up of toxic chemicals in an area of Da Nang International Airport (Da Nang was the primary storage site of these chemicals). Other cleanup sites include Biên Hòa Air Base and Phù Cát Air Base. According to a local newspaper report, the US government is providing $41 million to the project to reduce soil contamination at these and other sites. But this is small fish and mere gesture when compared to the billions of dollars spent on the war!

[See Notes on Presidents Dwight Eisenhower and John F Kennedy later in the Chapter: War Industries East and West]

Military Deaths and Casualties US and Allies:

US Armed Forces

- 58 318 killed in action (also includes missing & deaths in captivity)
- 1 598 Missing in action
- 153 303 Wounded
- 115 died in captivity

[Note that during the Vietnam War approximately 30% of wounded service members died of their wounds.]

South Korea

- 5 099 killed in action
- 14 232 wounded
- 4 missing in action

Australia

- 426 killed in action, 74 died of other causes
- 3 129 wounded
- 6 missing in action (later accounted for and repatriated)

Thailand

- 351 killed in action
- 1 358 wounded

New Zealand

- 37 killed in action + 2 Civilians
- 187 wounded

Philippines

- 9 killed in action
- 64 wounded

Taiwan

- 25 killed in action

Military Deaths and Casualties for Countries Supporting the Vietcong:

People's Republic Of China

- 1 446 killed in action

Soviet Union

- ~16

Nick Ut famous image of a 9 year old girl running from a napalm attack AP

Anti-war demonstrators face off National Guard   c 1974

Balkan Wars

My friend Izzy is a fairly prosperous man
with a business in Melbourne and a sheep and
cattle farm here in the hills of East Gippsland.
I believe when he was a boy his family were
middle class in Bosnia and completely
unprepared for the death of socialist dictator
Tito in 1980 and the consequential racism
and frenetic slide into ethnic wars that followed
Josep Broz Tito
(despite historical tensions between Serbs and ethnic Albanians for in
excess of a hundred years!). He is a tall and affable man and you would
hardly suspect the pain he carries in his heart due to the slaughter of
cousins and uncles for no other reason other than that they were Muslim.
Having said this, his grandparents witnessed village people being
dragged away to concentration camps by the enthusiastic Croatians
(Ustase) to be murdered alongside Jews, socialists, Serbs and Roma
under Hitler's Reich in the 1940s.

Bosnia: The war in Bosnia and Herzegovina (1992-1995) came about as
a result of the breakup of the Socialist Federal Republic of Yugoslavia.
A crisis emerged as a result of the weakening of the confederation at the
end of the Cold War. The League of Communists of Yugoslavia was
losing its ideological potency as ethnic nationalism experienced a
renaissance in the 1980s, after violence broke out in Kosovo. While the
goal of Serbian nationalists was the centralisation of Yugoslavia, other
nationalities in Yugoslavia aspired to the federalisation and the
decentralisation of the state. Bosnia and Herzegovina was historically a
multi-ethnic state. In the 1991 census, 44% of the population considered
themselves Muslim or Bosniak (ethnic Albanians), 32.5% Serb, 17%
Croat with 6% describing themselves as Yugoslav. Formally

autonomous and independent, under Slobodan Milosevic, Serbia sought control of the region. In early 1991 meetings between the leaders of the

six Yugoslav republics and the two autonomous regions discussed the ongoing crisis. On 25 June 1991, both Slovenia and Croatia declared independence leading to wars between members of the different ethnic groups. In September 1991, the United Nations Security Council passed a resolution imposing an arms embargo on all of the former Yugoslav

Slobodan Milošević

territories which, as we shall see, was ignored by many nations which supported the various factions and their armies, particularly Albania. The Croatian National Guard and the Yugoslav National Army were soon firing upon the Bosniaks and Albanians (and later the Kosovo Liberation Army in Kosovo) some seven months before the start of the Bosnian War and causing the first casualties.

Then the RAM plan arrived: all Serbs with their territories were to live together in the same state. A meeting of Serb army officers in Belgrade in 1991 adopted an explicit policy to target women and children as the most vulnerable portion of the Muslim religious and social structure to achieve the plan's goals.

The Croat leadership organized autonomous communities in areas with a Croat majority which covered eight municipalities in northern Bosnia. At the end of February 1992, a referendum proposal for independence was adopted in the form as proposed by Muslim deputies in the absence of Serb and Croat members, placing the Bosnian government and the Serbs on a collision course! Violence and killings soon commenced.

The three factions in the Bosnian War:

Bosnian (or Bosniak), loyal to the Republic of Bosnia and Herzegovina.

Croat, loyal to the Croatian Republic of Herzeg-Bosnia and Croatia.

Serb (or Yugoslav), loyal to the Republika Srpska and FR Yugoslavia.

The three ethnic groups predominantly supported their respective ethnic or national faction. Bosniaks mainly the ARBiH, Croats the HVO, Serbs the VRS. It is noted that there were foreign volunteers in each faction. The Serbs commenced systematic ethnic cleansing within Bosnia.

The cities Sarajevo and Mostarwere turned to **General Ratko Mladic** rubble and war atrocities occurred in Srebrenica and elsewhere as Bosniak women were systematically raped by Serbian soldiers with men and young boys massacred.

Bodies of people killed in April 1993 around Vitez, Bosnia and Herzegovina

In Croatia, the Serbs created an enclave, Krajina, supported by the Serbian army. A conflict soon erupted with thousands of Croat civilians being massacred and later discovered in mass graves. Eventually the Croatian army, after being better armed, ensured that some half a million Serbs were either killed or forced out of Croatian territory.

Casualties of Bosnian Conflict (approximate figures):

Bosniaks	62 000	64.5%
Serbs	25 000	26.0%
Croats	8 500	8.8%
Other ethnicities	600	0.6%
Total dead or disappeared:	**96 100**	

Kosovo: It was argued that Kosovo Serbs were being subjected to "physical, political, legal and cultural genocide in an open and total war" that had been ongoing since the spring of 1981. Claims were that Kosovo's status in 1986 was a worse historical defeat for the Serbs than any event since liberation from the Ottoman Empire in 1804 and that some 200 000 Serbs had moved out of the province over the previous twenty years. The perceived remedy was for genuine security and equality for all peoples living in Kosovo and Metohija to be established and for the return to a greater Serbian nation [cf Tito's Yugoslavia].

United Nations Special Rapporteur, Tadeusz Mazowiecki, reported on 26 February 1993 that the police had intensified their repression of the Albanian population since 1990, including depriving them of their basic rights, destroying their education system as well as large numbers of political dismissals of civil servants.

A policy of passive resistance succeeded in keeping Kosovo quiet during the wars in Croatia and Bosnia during the early 1990s. However, continuing repression convinced many Albanians that only armed resistance would change the situation and the Kosovo Liberation Army was formed. The Yugoslav government considered the KLA to be terrorists who indiscriminately attacked police and civilians, while most Albanians saw them as freedom fighters. Author Alastair MacKenzie claimed that the KLA received training from covert UK military in 1998 at a training camp in the Albanian mountains whilst at the same time the US regarded them as terrorists! Attacks and reprisals increased throughout the province with murders of civilians on both sides.

Hence the incursion of more Yugoslav and Serbian troops with tanks heralded the commencement of the Kosovo war in earnest!

By October 1998 it was estimated that 250 000 displaced Albanians,

30 000 of whom were out in the woods, were without warm clothing or shelter with winter fast approaching. On 13 October 1998, NATO was ordered to execute limited air strikes and a phased air campaign in

Yugoslavia. On 15 October an agreement for a ceasefire was signed. A Serbian withdrawal commenced around 25 October 1998. Fighting resumed in December 1998 after both sides broke the ceasefire! After evidence of massacres, it was decided that the conflict could only be settled by introducing a NATO military peacekeeping force.

On 18 March 1999, the Albanian, American, and British delegations signed what became known as the 'Rambouillet Accords' with the Yugoslav and Russian delegations refusing to sign. The accords called for a NATO administration of Kosovo as an autonomous province within Yugoslavia. The Serbian assembly accepted the principle of autonomy for Kosovo and non-military part of the agreement, while rejecting a NATO troop presence. As all else had failed to satisfy an aggressive Milošević, on 24 March NATO started its bombing campaign against Yugoslavia. On 12 June, after Milošević accepted conditions, the NATO multinational peacekeeping Kosovo Force (KFOR) began entering Kosovo. Interestingly, Russian forces operated as a unit of KFOR but not under the NATO command structure!

Published in 2000 in the medical journal the Lancet, it was estimated that 12 000 deaths in the total population were attributed to the war. The highest mortality rates were in men between 15 and 49: 5 500 victims of war as well as for men 50 and over: 5 000 victims.

In 2001 a United Nations administered Supreme Court based in Kosovo, found that there had been a systematic campaign of terror, including murders, rapes, arsons and severe maltreatments. After the war a list was conducted which documented that 13 500 people were killed or went missing in the conflict. The Yugoslav and Serb forces caused the displacement of around 1.4 million Kosovo Albanians. After the war, around 200 000 Serbs, Romani and other non-Albanians fled Kosovo.

The NATO bombing of the Serbian army and later Belgrade itself did not gain the approval of the UN Security Council. It caused around 500 Yugoslav civilian deaths which included substantial numbers of Kosovar refugees!

It was accused that the US and NATO made use of spent uranium shells in the Balkans as they also did during the Gulf War!

Milošević was sent to The Hague in the Netherlands to stand for criminal charges in 2001. After 5 years of deliberation he was found dead in his cell and thus never convicted!

In November 2017 Ratko Mladić, Bosnian Serb and former general, was found guilty of committing war crimes and genocide by the International Criminal Tribunal and jailed for life. The crimes against humanity included the slaughter of 8 000 Muslim men and boys at Srebrenica and the siege of the Bosnian capital Sarajevo, in which more than 11 000 civilians were killed by shelling and sniper fire over almost four years.

Afghanistan

Mistrust and pathological animosity between America and Russia commenced after the Russian invasion of Afghanistan in nineteen seventy nine. The Russians suffered some 14 500 deaths and around 54 000 wounded. The Mujahedeen suffered around 80 000 killed and a similar figure wounded. But ... wait for it... **in excess of 1 500 000 civilians were killed, 3 million wounded with another 5 million leaving the country as refugees to Pakistan, Iran and elsewhere. And all this my reader BEFORE the US, NATO and its allies arrived!**

The material loss of the Russian forces was astronomical running into the billions of dollars.

The Soviet war in Afghanistan lasted over nine years from December 1979 to February 1989. Part of the Cold War, it was fought between Soviet-led Afghan forces against multi-national insurgent groups called the Mujahedeen, mostly composed of two alliances – the Peshawar Seven and the Tehran Eight. The Peshawar Seven insurgents received military training in Pakistan and China, as well as weapons and billions of dollars mainly from the United States, the United Kingdom and Saudi Arabia. The Shia groups of the Tehran Eight alliance received support from the Islamic Republic of Iran. Early in the rule of the PDPA government, the Maoist Afghanistan Liberation Organization also played a significant role in opposition, but its major force was defeated by late 1979, prior to the Soviet intervention.

But why did they go there? Since 1947, Afghanistan had been under the influence of the Soviet government and received large amounts of aid, economic assistance, military equipment training and military hardware from the Soviet Union. They were lulled into Afghanistan by the government at the time that failed utterly to control the country and had tens of thousands of dissidents executed at the notorious Pul-e-Charkhi prison, including many village mullahs and headmen. As well as the Western supported Mujahedeen, over ten years the Russians faced contingents of foreign fighters who wished to wage jihad against the atheist communists. Notable among them was a young Saudi Arabian named Osama bin Laden, whose Arab group eventually evolved into al-Qaeda (the Base).

So were al-Qaeda solely responsible for the 9/11 destruction of the twin towers in New York City and the attack on the Pentagon? The Russians had been more than a little pissed off with the West for some time. The fact that they were more restrained, being a nuclear power, is quite remarkable in hindsight. But the West has never given up on pushing and punishing the Russians and thwarting them in many ways. Now in 2018 one feels it is coming to a head with possible horrific consequences. The conflict against a bunch of crazy Arabs wanting a middle-ages styled caliphate will *pale into insignificance* when the final fuse is lit!

US Invasion, Operation Enduring Freedom: The US in their 2001 invasion was supported initially by the United Kingdom and Canada and later by a coalition of over 40 countries, including all NATO members. The war's intended aims were to dismantle al-Qaeda and to deny it a safe base of operations in Afghanistan by removing the Taliban from power. The War in Afghanistan is the longest war in United States history, now into its 18th year!

On September 11, 2001, nineteen members of al-Qaeda carried out four simultaneous attacks in the United States after hijacking four commercial passenger jet airliners. Two were deliberately crashed into the Twin Towers of the World Trade Center in New York City, killing everyone on board and more than 2000 people in the buildings. Both buildings collapsed within two hours. A third airliner was purposefully crashed into the Pentagon in Arlington, Virginia. The fourth plane crashed into a field near Shanksville, in rural Pennsylvania. Total deaths were 2996, which included the hijackers, firefighters, police, workers and other civilians on the ground. Another 6000 were injured.

Initially the combined forces had success in driving al-Qaeda and the Taliban out of Afghanistan but with few actual killings. In the elections of 2004, Hamid Karzai was elected president of the country, now named the Islamic Republic of Afghanistan. However, the Afghan Army was poorly trained and lacked military fighting skills. To complicate matters, the Taliban and al-Qaeda were now back in the country with greater numbers and re-equipped with hardware, mainly from Pakistan.

In 2006, a multinational force started to replace US troops in southern Afghanistan. The British 16 Air Assault Brigade, later reinforced by Royal Marines, formed the core of the force accompanied by troops and helicopters from Australia, Canada and the Netherlands. NATO achieved many tactical victories but the Taliban were not completely defeated and were able to regroup. Mistakes in civilian killings produced resentment and growing hostility to foreigners in Kabul and across the country.

By 2007 it was apparent that 'mission creep' ensued with the deployment of more troops from the US, Britain and other supporting countries. Analysts estimated the strength of Taliban forces at about 10 000 fighters fielded at any given time. Up to 300 full-time combatants were foreigners, many from Pakistan, Uzbekistan, Chechnya, Western China and various Arab countries.

US and coalition forces peaked from 2010 until 2013 with a total of around 165 000. Further deaths of civilians continued in various operations including cross-border attacks into Pakistan. These later included drone attacks to the anger of the Pakistani government.

Due to increased use of IEDs by insurgents the number of injured coalition soldiers, mainly Americans, significantly increased. Beginning in May 2010 NATO Special Forces began to concentrate on operations to capture or kill Taliban leaders. By March 2011 the US military claimed that this strategy had resulted in the capture or killing of more than 900 Taliban commanders.

The release of Wikileaks (by Julian Assange at left) classified documents on US military incidents and intelligence reports described sanitized and covered up accounts of civilian casualties caused by Coalition Forces. They also contained reports of Pakistan collusion with the Taliban and that the Pakistani intelligence agency Inter-Services Intelligence ISI was the most important accomplice to the Taliban outside of Afghanistan! Further, the American Government in the 1980s flooded al-Qaeda and the Taliban via Pakistan's ISI with **billions of dollars** to fight the Russians! On 2nd May 2011, US officials announced that al-Qaeda leader Osama bin Laden had been killed in Operation Neptune Spear conducted by the US Navy SEALs in Pakistan.

2014: Despite some attempts to secure a peace with the Taliban, Afghanistan was shaken with a new spate of suicide bombings, particularly in Kabul. After 13 years Britain and the United States officially ended their combat operation in Afghanistan in October 2014. Britain handed over its last base in Afghanistan, Camp Bastion and the United States handed over its last base, Camp Leatherneck to Afghan forces.

Canadian servicemen carry fallen comrades

Unwarranted Influence

On December 28, 2014 NATO officially ended combat operations in a ceremony held in Kabul. However, NATO and US troops continue in Afghanistan in essentially non-combat roles, assisting Afghan security and the Afghan National Army. The Quadrilateral Coordination Group-consisting of Afghan, American, Chinese and Pakistani officials have attempted peace talks with the Taliban since January 2016, but to no avail. Suicide bombings in the capital Kabul and sporadic attacks continue to the present.

In January 2016, the US government sent a directive to the Pentagon granting new authority for the US military to go on the offensive against ISIL-KP (Islamic State of Iraq and the Levant – Khorasan Province), designated a foreign terrorist organisation.

As well as suicide bombings, bus hijackings on highways followed by executions were a new strategy by the insurgents. Once again the US military invoked greater use of air power to assist the Afghan Army. In July 2016 *Time Magazine* estimated that at least 20% of Afghanistan was under Taliban control with southernmost Helmand Province as the major stronghold. In April 2017 the Taliban announced the beginning of their spring offensive. In August 2017, US President Donald Trump stated that he would expand the American presence in Afghanistan. The *New York Times* reported that the CIA was seeking authority to conduct its own drone strikes in Afghanistan and other war zones!

In January 2018 the *BBC* reported that the Taliban were openly active in 70% of the country, supported by ISIS! A UN report demonstrated the failure of peace talks with both the Taliban and the US government focused on victory rather than settlement. More airstrikes will result in more suicide bomb attacks promoting an intensification of the war rather than an end to it!

It is probable that in excess of 200 000 civilians have died in Afghanistan since 2001.

War Crimes

It is claimed that ALL parties in the fighting in Afghanistan have been involved in unlawful killings and massacres. It has been counter claimed that the US government in some cases blocked investigations into such incidents, notably the Dasht-i-Leili massacre in 2001.

The cost of involvement to the American taxpayer since 2001 is estimated to be well above one trillion US dollars.

Coalition Fatalities 2001 to end 2016

Total:	3 406
United States:	2 271
United Kingdom:	456
Canada:	158
France:	89
Germany:	57
Italy:	53
Australia:	41
Others:	281
Wounded	
Total	24 000
United States:	20 000
United Kingdom:	2 200
Canada:	635
Australia:	261

Contractors

Killed: 2 000   Wounded: > 15 000

Afghan Forces

Killed: 40 000

Civilians

Killed: > 35 000

Wounded: > 40 000

Enemy (Taliban, ISIS and other militants)

Killed: c 50 000

Wounded: c 75 000

Estimates by Brown University:

The combined, cumulative death toll of war in Afghanistan and Pakistan 2001 to 2016 was 173 000 with 183 000 others seriously injured, according to a new study by the 'Costs of War' project based at Brown University's Watson Institute for International and Public Affairs.

April 2018: Islamic State and the Taliban in Afghanistan continue to murder people, especially in Kabul, by suicide bombers. Similar for May, June and July!   ... and so it goes on!

This author's final analysis is that the country Afghanistan and its society has been systematically destroyed jointly by the two superpowers Russia and America over the last forty years*. Will there be retribution?

Restating the effects on civilians during the Russian occupation 1979 until 1988:

In excess of 1 500 000 civilians were killed, 3 million wounded with another 5 million leaving the country as refugees to Pakistan, Iran and elsewhere.

During this period, Dec 1979 until Feb 1989, it is to be noted that the US, Saudi Arabia and Western allies provided excessive amounts of cash and equipment to the Mujahedeen and other international fighters. It is without doubt that Osama bin Laden's al-Qaeda managed to embrace a reasonable slice of this! The Pakistani secret service ISI also received large amounts of cash from America part of which also found its way into the hands of Muslim extremist groups in the country.

[* For a clearer picture of all that went on read the two books 'Ghost Wars' and 'Directorate S' by Steve Coll, Penguin Press 2018]

The Middle East

Iran-Iraq War

The armed conflict between Iran and Iraq began on 22 Sept 1980 when Iraq invaded Iran, and ended on 20 Aug 1988 when Iran accepted the UN ceasefire. A range of reasons included: fear that the 1979 Iranian Revolution would lead Iraq's Shi'ite majority to rebel against the Ba'athist government; a long history of border disputes plus the Iraqi intention to annex the oil-rich Khuzestan Province and east bank of the Shatt al-Arab. Ayatollah Ruhollah Khomeini called on Iraqis to overthrow the Ba'ath government wanting an Islamic revolution bringing anger to Baghdad and its ruler, Saddam Hussein. A successful invasion of Iran would enlarge Iraq's petroleum reserves and make Iraq the region's dominant power. In 1979-80, Iraq was experiencing an oil boom, allowing the government to go on a spending spree of which the military was no mean recipient. Iraq's leaders decided to carry out a surprise airstrike against the Iranian air force's infrastructure prior to the main invasion. In Iran, by Sept 1980, the government had purged 12 000 army officers with many executed. These purges resulted in a drastic decline in the Iranian military's operational capacities.

Saddam Hussein of Iraq and adversary Ruhollah Khomeini of Iran

157

The mountainous border between Iran and Iraq made the task of a ground invasion impossible. Air strikes were used instead, targeted at Iranian airfields and Iran's capital, Tehran. Iraq launched a full-scale invasion on 22 Sept 1980, but with hardened aircraft shelters where most of its combat aircraft were stored, the Iranian airforce remained largely intact. A ground invasion followed the next day. Four divisions were sent to Khuzestan, which was located near the border's southern end, to cut off the Shatt al-Arab from the rest of Iran. Two more divisions invaded across the northern and central part of the border with the strategy of preventing an Iranian counter-attack. The first chemical weapon attack by Iraq on Iran probably took place during this early fighting. Iranian Army helicopter gunships began attacks on the advancing Iraqi divisions, along with F-4 Phantoms armed with Maverick missiles. They destroyed numerous armoured vehicles and slowed the Iraqi advance. On 24 Sept the Iranian Navy attacked Basra, Iraq, destroying two oil terminals near the Iraqi port of Faw, immediately reducing Iraq's ability to export oil. Further, on 30 Sept Iran's air force struck and badly damaged the almost complete Osirak Nuclear Plant near Baghdad (later to be bombed again in a surprise Israeli air strike carried out on 7 June 1981).

An estimated 200 000 fresh Iranian troops arrived at the front by November. On the 28th Iran launched a combined air and sea attack destroying 80% of Iraq's navy and all of its radar sites in southern Iraq. The war developed into World War I style trench warfare with an admixture of tanks and modern weapons. Iraq also began firing Scud missiles into Iranian cities plus bombing, bringing the war to Iranian civilians.

Human wave attacks by the Iranians were extremely bloody, costing the lives of tens of thousands of troops. When applied in combination with infiltration and surprise, however, the result was often a major Iraqi defeat.

All in for Their Cut!

In April 1982 Syria closed the Kirkuk-Baniyas pipeline leaving Iraq with the pipeline to Turkey as the only means of exporting oil. With a capacity of only 500 000 barrels per day, it was insufficient to pay for the ongoing war. Saudi Arabia was said to have provided Iraq with $1 billion per month starting in mid-1982. American President Reagan removed Iraq from the list of countries supporting terrorism and began selling it weapons such as howitzers via Jordan and Israel. France sold Iraq millions of dollars worth of weapons, including Gazelle helicopters, Mirage F-1 fighters, and Exocet missiles. Both the United States and West Germany sold Iraq pesticides and poisons that would later be used to create chemical weapons (under the guise of dual purpose!)

The Iraqi military was bolstered with Soviet, Chinese, and French fighter jets and helicopters. Iraq also rebuilt stocks of small arms and anti-tank weapons (AK-47s and rocket-propelled grenades). Tank forces were replaced with more from Russia and China. Iran was now portrayed as the aggressor, and would remain so until the Gulf war when Iraq would be the new bad boy!

And so ALL the great powers of the world poured in military materials to make huge profits from Saudi, Iraqi and Iranian oil dollars fuelling the death and destruction of hundreds of thousands of Muslims willy-nilly! What did they care then and what do they care now almost forty years on? Niente!

An estimated 95 000 Iranian child soldiers were made casualties during the Iran-Iraq War, mostly about the age of 16 but a few even younger! Through the 1980s, Saddam had commenced a policy of total war, preparing for an Iranian invasion and spending around 50% of the country's GDP on military equipment. Saddam had also more than

Child Soldiers of the Iranian Army

doubled the size of the Iraqi army from 200 000 soldiers to 500 000. By 1988 Iraq would have 1 million soldiers, giving it the fourth largest army in the world!

Bringing the war into Iraq, with fewer soldiers and equipment, Iran hoped to defeat Iraq by strategy. Some of the biggest land battles since WWII occurred with huge casualties on both sides around Basra.

In 1984 Iraq made use of F-1 Mirage, Super Etendard, Mig-23, Su-20/22, and Super Frelon helicopters armed with Exocet anti-ship missiles as well as Soviet made air-to-surface missiles to enforce a blockade in the Persian Gulf, repeatedly bombing Iran's main oil export facility on Kharg Island. In retaliation, Iran attacked tankers carrying Iraqi oil from Kuwait and later attacking tankers from any Persian Gulf state that supported Iraq.

As early as May 1985, anti-war demonstrations took place in 74 cities throughout Iran but soon crushed by the regime with some protesters being shot dead.

On 28 June 1987 Iraqi bombers attacked the Iranian town of Sardasht near the border using chemical mustard gas bombs. Iraq also increased their airstrikes against Kharg Island and Iranian oil tankers. With their allies tankers now protected by US warships in the Gulf, the Iraqi airforce could operate with virtual impunity. Also, the West had supplied laser-guided smart bombs, allowing attacks on economic targets while evading anti-aircraft defences (as well as experimenting for the West to see how effective these weapons were!)

In southern Iraq a new force attacked the Iranian positions around Basra. One of the most successful Iraqi tactics was the use of chemical weapons. They would saturate the Iranian front line with rapidly dispersing cyanide and nerve gas, with mustard gas launched via fighter-bombers and rockets against the Iranian rear, blocking any reinforcements.

In retaliation against Iran for damaging a US warship with a mine, Iran lost oil platforms, destroyers, and frigates to **US air-launched missiles and bombs!**

Saddam sent a warning to Khomeini in mid-1988, threatening to launch a new and powerful full-scale invasion and attack Iranian cities with weapons of mass destruction i.e. predominantly chemical weapons. Both Iran and Iraq had accepted Resolution 598 by the UN but this did not deter a continuation of hostilities. The last combat action of the war took place on 3 Aug 1988 in the Persian Gulf when the Iranian navy fired on a freighter and Iraq launched chemical attacks on Iranian civilians. Iraq spent the rest of August and early September clearing Kurdish resistance in the north, using troops, helicopter gunships, chemical weapons and mass executions. Many Kurdish civilians fled to Iran. By 3 Sept 1988 the campaign ended with an estimated 50 000 Kurdish civilians and soldiers killed.

The Bankers Arrive:

Iraq's debt to the Paris Club amounted to $21 billion, 85% of which had originated from the combined inputs of Japan, the USSR, France, Germany, the United States, Italy and the United Kingdom. The largest portion of Iraq's debt, amounting to $130 billion, was to its former Arab backers, with $67 billion loaned by Kuwait, Saudi Arabia, Qatar, UAE, and Jordan. After the Kuwait invasion, Iraq was placed under a complete international embargo pushing its external debt to private and public sectors to more than $500 billion by the end of Saddam's rule. This produced a debt-to-GDP ratio of more than 1000%, making Iraq the most indebted developing country in the world! As well as the extensive damage to oil industries, both Iran and Iraq had spent some 500 billion dollars each on the war over an eight year period.

... and who profited ?

Estimates of Casualties:

Iran:

Soldiers	Killed	500 000+	Wounded	350 000+
Civilians	Killed	70 000	Wounded	85 000

Iraq:

Soldiers	Killed	375 000+	Wounded	450 000+
Civilians	Killed	50 000+	Wounded	75 000+

Kurds:

Soldiers + civilians killed   50 000

Totals:

Killed	1 045 000+
Wounded	960 000+

... and all these before the Gulf Wars I and II !

Unwarranted Influence

Countries which supported either or both combatant(s)   **ref: Wikipedia**

Country	Supplied to Iraq	Supplied to Iran
Argentina		Sales of uranium and arms
Austria	Sales of self-propelled artillery pieces	Sold 140 GHN-45 Howitzers along with significant stocks of ammunition
Belgium		Sold jet engines for F-4 Phantom aircraft
Brazil	Sale of ammunition, armoured cars, and tactical multiple rocket launcher	Major supplier (Sold 500 Cascavel and Urutu armored vehicles)
Canada	Sales of war material	
People's Republic of China	Some financial support and military exports	Sale of military equipment, including fighter aircraft, surface-to-air missiles, rocket launchers, tanks, and artillery
Denmark	Sales of military equipment	
Egypt	Military exports	
Ethiopia		Sold 12 F-5 Tiger IIs
France	Sale of high-tech military equipment and uranium	Covert sales of large quantities of artillery shells (delivered 500,000 155mm and 203mm shells)
East Germany	Sale of high-tech military equipment	
West Germany	Sale of high-tech military equipment	Chemical warfare defence equipment
Hungary	Sales of war material	
Israel		Clandestine support (of course!)
Italy	Several billion dollars in funding; sale of land and sea mines as well as uranium	Sale of land and sea mines
Japan	Engineering equipment such as	Engineering equipment such as trucks,

	trucks, caterpillars bulldozers etc.	and caterpillars and bulldozers etc.
Jordan	Acted as main supply line	
North Korea		Sold domestically-produced arms; acted as an intermediate for covert sales by the Soviet Union, Soviet satellites, and China
Netherlands		Funded Iran with a total of $5 billion. Sales of Chemical Warfare defence equipment.
South Korea		Sold 12 F-4 Phantom IIs as well as spare parts, artilleries such as KH-179, and other heavy weapons.
Kuwait	Financial support and conduit for arms sales.	
Libya		Armaments, munitions and ballistic missiles.
Pakistan		Sold shoulder-launched surface-to-air missile; unaccountable and covert financial support for Iran by Pakistan
Poland	Sales of military material	
Portugal	Sale of uranium and arms	Sale of ammunition and explosives
Qatar	Initial support, though not openly	
Romania	Sales of military material	
Saudi Arabia	$20 billion in funding	
Singapore	Provided chemical warfare precursors; acted as a transhipment point for weapons; was manufacturing site of foreign-designed	

	weapons	
South Africa	Sale of military armament (200 G5 155mm Artillery systems)	30 G5 155mm Artillery systems
Soviet Union	Military equipment and advisors	Covert military equipment sales
Spain	Sale of conventional and chemical weapons, especially ammunition and explosives	Sale of weapons, especially ammunition and explosives
Sudan	Sent troops to fight alongside Iraqi troops	
Syria		Armaments, munitions and ballistic missiles.
Sweden		Covert sales of RBS-70 surface-to-air missile system, facilities/equipment/explosives/materiel for local weapons manufacturing, and fast-attack boats.
Switzerland	Sales of war material and Sales of chemical warfare equipment	Chemical Warfare defence equipment Delivered 15 PC-6 propeller utility aircraft and 47 PC-7 propeller training aircraft, as well as Cryptology equipment, large quantities of ammunition, and electronic components for radars.
Turkey	Sales of arms.	Sales of arms.
United Arab Emirates	Financial aid	
United Kingdom	Weapons-related equipment and 'Sodium cyanide for chemical weapons and plutonium and gas	Sales of Chemical Warfare defence equipment.

	spectrometers'	
United States	Several billion dollars worth of economic aid; the sale of dual-use technology and non-US origin weaponry; military intelligence; Special Operations training	Secret arms sales (Iran-Contra affair)
Yugoslavia	Weapons sales (more than $2 billion worth)	

And so my reader, did you notice *your* country in the above listing and *what* was supplied? Are you not disgusted and horrified that governments and private companies made so much money out of this war and let it go on for eight years no less? Can you not see that these are the makings of **the last and final war** on this planet leading to its destruction and annihilation of all of humanity?

Well, the sale of 'dual purpose' materials certainly brought on the paranoia of the West by the end of the nineteen nineties with the rumours and accusations of Saddam's program in creating 'Weapons of Mass Destruction' (particularly by Tony Blair). Or was it simply that military corporations across many countries wanted to make even more money out of Iraq and therefore governments were just looking for any excuse to invade? The power, momentum and inertia of capitalistic military corporations are too great and virtually unstoppable in the world today! With a dysfunctional United Nations Security Council and the disproportionate clout of the US in world affairs, these have led to too many horrific wars with the loss and destruction of millions of lives. That is Tom's analysis! Only by a concerted effort by the UN General Assembly to severely curb armaments sales between countries by introduction of stricter rules and penalties can the world free itself of the current 'helter skelter' slide to total destruction of civilisation. Hypocrisy of the big powerful nations must be focussed upon and their current powers reduced in a democratic way with greater equality taking sway in the General Assembly. As pointed out elsewhere, the Security Council needs either to be made redundant completely or suffer drastic reform. Despite its evolution and all the good it has served the world community to date, the General Assembly needs more teeth!

With the continued rule of Iran by successive mullahs, we have seen 40 years of imprisonments and executions of left wingers, atheists, lawyers and judiciary, those leaving Islam and other political dissidents. Taken together, these sum to hundreds of thousands of persons murdered by a cruel regime clinging to an archaic system of religious government. The country needs a revolution to free its people of sustained repression and move to the 21st century! It does not need to embrace all the values of the West!

As pointed out earlier, it is exemplory of an Islamic country BUT with anti-Islamic values. It does not follow the true values laid down in the al Koran but is following the cruel and ancient values of pre-Islamic Arabian culture and law! All murder is punishable by God, NOT rewarded!

Gulf Wars

Gulf War One: Codenamed 'Operation Desert Shield' (2 Aug 1990 until 17 Jan 1991) for operations leading to the build-up of troops and defence of Saudi Arabia and 'Operation Desert Storm' (17 Jan 1991 until 28 Feb 1991) in its combat phase, was a war waged by coalition forces from 35 nations led by the United States against Iraq in response to Iraq's invasion and annexation of Kuwait.

The Iraqis had always considered Kuwait as the lost part of Iraq due to the manipulation and drawing up of boundaries by the British (after signing the Anglo-Ottoman Convention of 1913, the United Kingdom split Kuwait from the Ottoman territories into a separate sheikhdom). In 1990 Iraq accused Kuwait of stealing Iraqi petroleum through slant drilling. There were possibly other reasons for the Iraqi move, including Iraq's inability to pay Kuwait more than US$14 billion (as part of its total debt of $60 billion) that had been borrowed to finance the Iran-Iraq

war (fuelled, financed and weapons supplied by the West) plus the perception of Kuwaiti overproduction of petroleum, keeping oil revenue down for Iraq. Also, because the US appeared to give a tacit green light to do so! (see later: Seeding Wars).

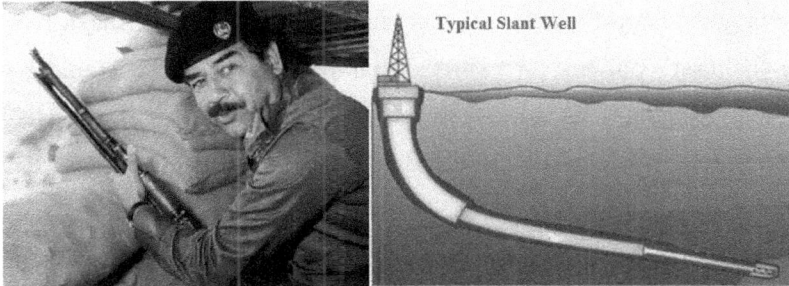

Typical Slant Well

1988: At the end of the war with Iran, the Iraqi Army was the fourth largest army in the world capable of fielding one million men and 850 000 reservists, 5 500 tanks, 3 000 artillery pieces, 700 combat aircraft and helicopters; and held 53 divisions, 20 special-forces brigades, and several militias.

The invasion started on 2 August 1990. Within two days of intense combat most of the Kuwait Armed Forces were soon overrun. Within hours of the invasion, Kuwait and US delegations requested a meeting of the UN Security Council, which passed Resolution 660, condemning the invasion and demanding immediate withdrawal of Iraqi troops. The Arab League passed its own resolution calling for a solution to the conflict from within the League and warned against outside intervention. On 29 November the Security Council passed Resolution 678 which gave Iraq until 15 January 1991 to withdraw from Kuwait and empowered states to use "all necessary means" to force Iraq out of Kuwait after the deadline.

The Kuwaiti oil fires were caused by the Iraqi military setting fire to 700 oil wells as part of a scorched earth policy while retreating from Kuwait in 1991 after being driven out by coalition forces. The fires started in January and February 1991 and the last one was extinguished by November. Somewhere around 6 million barrels of oil were lost each day. Eventually, privately owned contractors extinguished the fires at a total cost of US$1.5 billion to Kuwait.

Forming the largest military alliance since World War II, the majority of the coalition's military forces were from the US with Saudi Arabia, the United Kingdom, France, Italy, Australia and Egypt as leading contributors. It began with an aerial and naval bombardment on 17 Jan 1991, continuing for five weeks. This was followed by a ground assault on 24 Feb. It was a decisive victory for the coalition forces liberating Kuwait and then advancing into Iraqi territory. Coalition deaths amounted to 341 almost half of which were deemed accidental.

A few deaths occurred in Saudi Arabia and Israel from Iraqi Scud missiles, but these were minimal when compared to other theatres of the war.

The number of Iraqi combat casualties is believed to have been greater than 45 000 fatalities and around 75 000 wounded based on Iraqi prisoner of war reports. This is a vastly disproportionate number, suggesting a gross war crime on the part of the coalition forces! Iraqi civilian deaths were around 4 000 due to the bombing campaign with tens of thousands more dying of consequences of the war (possibly as many as 100 000 persons).

Around 4 000 Kuwaiti military personnel died during the Iraqi occupation together with around 1 000 civilians. When the US reinstalled the royal Sabah family as the government of Kuwait, the Sabahs proceeded to execute 628 Palestinians *while US troops were still present in the country*!

One of the most graphic and heinous crimes of Gulf War Operation Desert Shield/Storm occurred on the highway between Mutlaa, Kuwait and Basra, Iraq, also known as "The Highway of Death." As the US began its land assault, Iraq announced that it would comply with U.N.

resolution 660 and withdraw from Kuwait. Iraqi soldiers as well as Iraqi, Palestinian, Jordanian and other civilians piled into whatever vehicles they could commandeer and fled north towards Iraq. US planes then disabled vehicles at both ends of the convoy creating a seven mile long traffic jam. **US planes then began to bomb and strafe the entire line of some 2 000 vehicles for hours, killing tens of thousands of helpless soldiers and civilians while encountering no resistance and receiving no losses to themselves.** Another sixty mile stretch of road to the east was strewn with the remnants of tanks, armoured cars, trucks, ambulances and thousands of bodies following an attack on convoys on the night of Feb 25, 1991. One US commander said of the highway assault, "It's a turkey shoot". The US administration's attitude during the war was one that is more characteristic of the Nazi S.S. in their entire disregard for law, human decency and compassion. *Even as victors, the US government and its armed forces (and those of coalition partners) need to be held accountable for these war crimes and atrocities, regardless of the fact that this particular incident took place almost thirty years ago!*

The Jordanian Red Crescent Society estimated the civilian death toll in Iraq to be about 113 000 one week before the war ended, 60 percent of these children. When Air Force Chief of Staff General Michael J. Dugan hinted at US plans to destroy the Iraqi civilian economy on Sept 16, 1990, he was summarily fired from his job, even though that is exactly what the Bush administration planned and actually carried out.

The bombing of Iraqi civilians and infrastructure was in violation of the UN Charter, The Hague and Geneva Conventions, the Nuremberg Charter, and the laws of armed conflict.

Iraqi infrastructure and industry destroyed included: electric power stations (92 percent of installed capacity destroyed); refineries (80 percent of production capacity); petrochemical complexes; telecommunications centres (including 135 telephone networks); bridges (more than 100); roads, highways, railroads, hundreds of locomotives and boxcars full of goods; radio and television broadcasting stations; cement plants; factories producing aluminium, textiles, electric cables, and medical supplies; hospitals and schools.

Wholesale slaughter of defenceless Iraqi Troops: In the first hours of the allied air assault, most of Iraq's military communications were wiped out. In the subsequent forty-two days, "U.S bombing killed tens of thousands of defenceless soldiers, cut off most of their food, water and other supplies and left them in desperate and helpless disarray. Without significant risk to its own personnel, the US led in the killing of at least 100 000 Iraqi soldiers at a cost of 148 US combat casualties, according to the US government."

It has been suggested that both political leaders and military leaders of countries of the coalition forces should face the International War Crimes Tribunal, even if this means posthumously or in absentia! The fact that these crimes happened years ago is irrelevant. Justice must occur!

(General Norman Schwarzkopf, Desert Storm Commander died at age 78 in December 2012)

Among other illegal weapons used by the US during the Gulf War was a fuel air device known as the BLU-82, a 15 000-pound device capable of incinerating everything within hundreds of yards. Napalm and other phosphorus bombs were also used in violation of international law. One illegal fuel air device that was used is designed to consume all oxygen in a designated area, causing all personnel on the ground and within range to suffocate. The most horrific was the use of depleted uranium shells to destroy enemy tanks. US jets and tanks fired up to 10 000 depleted uranium rounds in Iraq during the war. Various cancers were reported in both Iraqis and returning coalition personnel long after the war and the finger has been pointed at the use of this material.

Films and romantic novels on the exploits of brave men (e.g. see SAS novels by Shaun Clark) do not impress where the enemy are reduced to inferior beings with total disregard to their humanity. Whilst it is true that some Iraqi military tortured POWs we cannot give this as an excuse for a disproportionate retaliation which can simply be described as mass murder by the coalition forces. The West will wait just ten years before making another inhuman strike at Iraq!

Gulf War II: Invasion of Iraq The 2003 invasion of Iraq lasted from 20 March to 1 May 2003 called 'Operation Iraqi Freedom'. The invasion consisted of 21 days of major combat operations, in which a combined force of troops from the United States, the United Kingdom, Australia and Poland invaded Iraq and deposed the Ba'athist government of Saddam Hussein. Under US President George W. Bush and UK Prime Minister Tony Blair the coalition aimed "to disarm Iraq of weapons of mass destruction, to end Saddam Hussein's support for terrorism, and to free the Iraqi people." According to Blair, the trigger was Iraq's failure to disarm itself of alleged nuclear, chemical, and biological weapons that officials called a threat to world peace. Also, the 9/11 attacks on New York were said to have played a significant role on the psyche of the American administration and the American people at the time (... somebody has to pay and suffer; it must be Muslims somewhere or anywhere!) However it is important to note that:

(i) there was no cooperation between Saddam Hussein and al-Qaeda.

(ii) the invasion was strongly opposed by some US allies, notably France, Germany, and New Zealand.

(iii) it was argued that there was no concrete evidence of weapons of mass destruction in Iraq and hence an invasion was not justified.

In fact during February 2003, the IAEA found no evidence of the revival of a nuclear weapons program. Also, UNMOVIC did not find evidence of the resumption of programs of weapons of mass destruction, chemical or biological! Amusingly in hindsight, the US government had engaged in elaborate domestic public relations campaigns to market the war to its citizens. Americans overwhelmingly believed Saddam did have weapons of mass destruction: 85% said so, even though the inspectors had not uncovered those weapons. President Bush had said "we know that Iraq, in the late 1990s, had several mobile biological weapons labs" ... (in fact so mobile they were never seen or captured! -author) He further added "The stated policy of the United States is regime change". .. (again see in later years the same arguments for Libya, Egypt, Syria and Iran! - author) In contrast, September 2002, Tony Blair in an answer to a parliamentary question stated " a regime change in Iraq would be a wonderful thing. However that is not the purpose of our action; our purpose is to disarm Iraq of weapons of mass destruction..."

This rationale for the invasion was presented in detail by US Secretary of State Colin Powell to the United Nations Security Council in February 2003. However, US government statements concerning Iraqi weapons programs and links to al-Qaeda were later discredited!

Meanwhile, the Iraq Liberation Act by the US government provided $97 million for Iraqi 'democratic opposition organizations' with the intent to destabilise the regime of Sadcam Hussein.

The invasion thus was carried out on a false premise presented to the American people and the world. Might is Right?

[It is now common practice for Western Governments to hire private think tank companies to mould propaganda for public digestion supporting unpalatable policies!]

Casualties of Invasion:

Coalition Forces:

Deaths: **around 200**   **Wounded:**   **around 600**

Iraqi Military:

Deaths: **estimates between 15 000 and 40 000**

Wounded: **estimates between 10 000 and 30 000**

Iraqi Civilian:

Deaths   **8 000+**   **Injured: estimates 12 000+**

Massive air strikes across the country and against the Iraqi command threw the defending army into chaos. The Iraqi military was quickly defeated and the coalition occupied Baghdad on 9 April 2003. The occupation would last until 2011. Details of the invasion and the dozens of heroic battles can be found elsewhere; needless to say that the combined forces involved billions of dollars worth of modern and sophisticated weaponry and support logistics in an overwhelming display force. The small country of Iraq smashed by a leviathan of Western power! The Iraqi army, armed mainly with older Soviet and Eastern European built equipment together with remnants from the First Gulf War, was overall ill-equipped but in many battles fought hard to defend their country.

The fall of Baghdad saw the outbreak of regional, sectarian violence throughout the country. Sunni groups were to bomb market places and mosques almost daily for the next eight years with many thousands of civilians maimed or killed. If the aim of the exercise was to destroy a country and its infrastructure, plus create a prolonged sectarian conflict, the job was well done! Saddam Hussein himself was captured on 13 December 2003, tried and executed by hanging. Saddam was convicted of crimes against humanity by the Iraqi Special Tribunal for the murder of 148 Iraqi Shi'ites in the town of Dujail in 1982, in retaliation for an assassination attempt against him. As supreme commander of the Iraqi military he should have been executed by shooting which is what he requested. The execution took place on 30th Dec 2006 at the joint Iraqi-American military base Camp Justice, located in Kazimain, a north-eastern suburb of Baghdad. His co-defendants Barzan Ibrahim al-Tikriti and Awad Hamed al-Bandar were executed on 15 January 2007. Saddam's cousin Ali Hassan al-Majid was hanged on 25 Jan 2010.

Despite war crimes inflicted by coalition forces (responsible to their individual national leaders and governments) during each of the Gulf wars, no state leader or high ranking military leader has been indicted to face trial for such crimes and certainly no trial leading to an execution. It seems that the righteous West can do no wrong!

War Crimes: Several American and British combatants were executed by Iraqi forces after capture.

Again, the US Airforce and tanks made use of depleted uranium shells. Despite the smartest of smart missiles, many buildings other than legitimate military targets were destroyed causing civilian deaths, particularly in Baghdad. Hospitals, schools, drinking water reservoirs, power stations and other societal infrastructures were indeed destroyed in the bombings.

Despite the high number of civilian deaths, the Prosecutor of the International Criminal Court in 2006, Luis Moreno-Ocampo, came to the conclusion: "The available information does not indicate intentional attacks on a civilian population." And further: "while many facts remain to be determined, the available evidence did not allow for the conclusion that there was a reasonable basis to believe that a clearly excessive attack within the jurisdiction of the Court had been committed."

It is just as well that Germany under Hitler did not win the Second World War !!

Legality of the Iraq Invasion: Robin Cook, the leader of the UK House of Commons and a former foreign secretary, resigned from Tony Blair's cabinet in protest over the UK's decision to invade without the authorization of a U.N. resolution. He said "In principle I believe it is wrong to embark on military action without broad international support. In practice I believe it is against Britain's interests to create a precedent for unilateral military action."

The UN Secretary-General Kofi Annan said in an interview with the BBC in September 2004, "from our point of view and from the Charter point of view, this war was illegal."

In 2010, a Dutch commission concluded that the 2003 invasion violated international law, saying: "UN resolution 1441 cannot reasonably be interpreted as authorising individual member states to use military force to compel Iraq to comply with Security Council resolutions."

Refugees: By 2008 there were over 4 million Iraqi refugees around the world, including 2 million in Iraq, 2 million in neighbouring Middle Eastern countries and around 250 000 in countries outside the Middle

East. Since the more recent war against ISIS and the Syrian conflict, this figure has increased to more than 5.5 million persons in total.

Interesting that the Baku-Tbilisi-Ceyhan oil pipeline of Azerbaijan to bring crude oil from the Caspian Sea to the Mediterranean was under way, opening in May 2006. It is partnered by BP, SOCAR, Chevron, Statoil, TPAO, Eni, Total S.A., Itochu, Inpex, ConocoPhillips, Hess Corporation and operated by BP plc. I mention this at the risk that you might think the author a cynic and holder of conspiracy theories!

Baku–Tbilisi–Ceyhan oil pipeline

Coalition Military Resources:

Person power, Coalition:

Australia:	2 000 invasion
Poland:	200 invasion (2 500 peak)
Spain:	1 300 invasion
United Kingdom:	46 000 invasion
United States:	150 000 to 250 000 invasion

About sixty other nations supported the coalition in various degrees from mere verbal support to some direct involvement with personnel

178

and equipment. Fifteen countries (including Israel) provided covert support.

Military Hardware: see Appendix C at rear of book.

The war was entered into illegally. The premises for this war were fragile and incorrect. The military might of the coalition and the damage done to Iraq can never and will never be justified. After 9/11 America wished to bully someone, specifically a Muslim country and Iraq was her choice (along with Afghanistan). Terrorism and hatred were exacerbated as was later experienced with the rise of al-Qaeda part of which morphed into Islamic State. There has, to date, been no punishment for war crimes committed by the coalition leaders and their military leaders involved in this second Gulf war or the first Gulf war apart from Saddam Hussein and the peoples of Iraq in their millions!

Author's Note: It is a common belief held in the West that Arabs and other Muslims are basically stupid and will never comprehend the 'colonial style wily games' played by the West, Russia and Israel over the last century or more. Further, that they will not ever understand how they are continually manipulated to make war upon each other by a sinister hand that aggravates and promotes the petty jealousies occurring between them i.e the Arab states and the Sunni-Shia schism in Islam. However, if this is a wrong assumption and ALL the Muslim nations of the world eventually come together with the intention of securing some almighty revenge, then we shall indeed pay dearly for our sins of the past! Let us pray that they are more civilised than we!

Islamic State of Iraq and the Levant and the Syrian Civil War

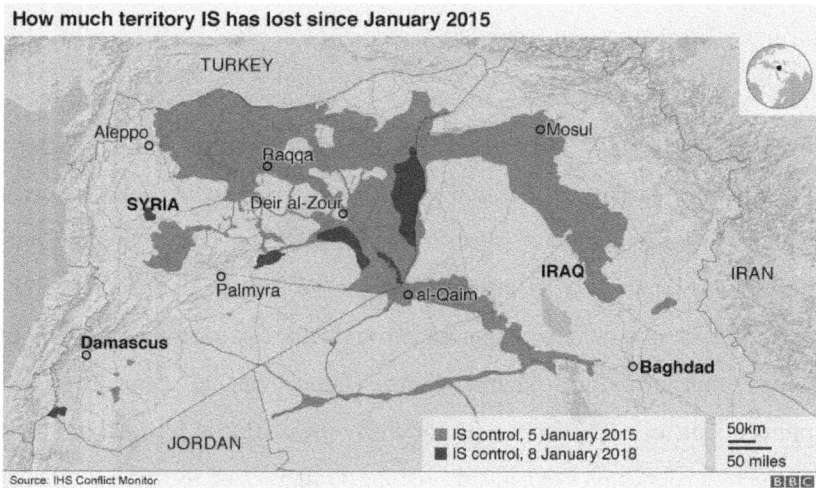

How much territory IS has lost since January 2015

It is recommended that this chapter be read in conjunction with the chapter titled **Khilafah Islam** for some understanding of Islam, its roots, its culture and dream of its future in the world. Having said this, it is an awesome task to jump into the mind of your average Muslim, let alone the extremist or fundamentalist adherent of that religion. In some ways, it is advantageous to have some knowledge of Christianity during the Middle Ages when Rome was absolute and the Inquisition was under way to rid the world of atheists, heretics and witches! In general terms we all struggle to understand our place in the scheme of things and, at moments, to wonder on the meaning of life, the universe and everything. In place of 42 we have God, Satan, Heaven and Hell or alternatively, nothingness stretching out forever. In this quest, humankind has constructed clubs (also referred to as religions, tribes and political groups) whose members must adhere to certain beliefs and follow certain rules. Some fear to diverge even in the slightest way whilst others accept the gist but neglect their duties and err and sin. But there is always forgiveness and rebirth to set our souls back on the correct road. The problem is, over the millennia several clubs have materialised which are occasionally in conflict of ideas. Schisms occur with variants of each club springing up causing further stress in the hearts and minds of the members. Some fall away. Some leave and join a new club. Where members of one group live among or adjacent to members of another group these accepted differences in belief systems sometimes lead to disharmony, detestation and even hatred and violence. Is it the fault of the club rules or the inherent nature of humankind to distrust those that are members of the other alternative club? The weakness of humans is that we generally fall into the trap of seeking out those differences between us instead of weighing the greater part i.e. the similarities. It is a failing and historically has lead to death, injury and great hurt to whole civilisations. If we were merely silica molecules, we could come together and form a beautiful quartz crystal and survive for millions of years. This analogy describes the most extreme of rules and behaviour with each entity absolutely identical to its neighbour. Perhaps this is a higher rule or law of evolution. Whatever, we must fight against it and not be humbled into such submissive extremes else we are then no longer human!

After the 2003 invasion of Iraq America and its allies found it costly to try to achieve some kind of democracy. Post-invasion Iraq was marked by a long and violent conflict between US led forces and Iraqi insurgents; firstly al-Qaeda and later ISIL plus Sunni extremists. Car bombings and suicide bombings against Shiite mosques, market places and any symbol of the Iraqi government: police, military, training camps etc. would go on for a decade and more! The coalition armed forces and private contractors assisting with the rebuilding program were also permanent targets.

The jihadists exploited the chaos and divisions within both Syria and Iraq. IS morphed out of what was al-Qaeda in Iraq and formed by Sunni militants after the US led invasion in 2003, becaming a major force in the country's sectarian insurgency. In 2011, the group joined the rebellion against President Bashar al Assad in Syria, where it found a safe haven and easy access to weapons. At the same time, it took advantage of the withdrawal of US troops from Iraq, as well as widespread Sunni anger at the sectarian policies of the country's Shia-led government. In 2013, the group began seizing control of territory in Syria and changed its name to Islamic State in Iraq and the Levant, ISIL. The following year it overran large swathes of northern and western Iraq, proclaiming the creation of a caliphate known as Islamic State.

Muslims have emigrated to western countries in large numbers because fellow Muslim countries generally do not accept them. In 2014, the self-appointed Caliph, Abu Bakr al Baghdadi, the leader of the Islamic State of Iraq and the Levant, took advantage of this resentment among some Muslims living in other Arab states and urged those Muslims to emigrate to the new Islamic caliphate promising all Muslim immigrants 'citizenship' immediately upon arrival.

A subsequent advance into areas controlled by Iraq's Kurds and the killing/enslaving of thousands of members of the Yazidi religious group, prompted a US led coalition to begin air strikes on IS positions in Iraq in August 2014.

With IS being slowly forced out of Iraq and Syria we saw the resurgence of hostilities between old rival groups. Already Iraqi forces have pushed the Kurds back from land they took during the fight against IS around

Kirkuk. Oppressed by Turkey, Iran, Iraq and Syria, will the Kurds ever see a homeland? It remains doubtful!

According to 'Iraq Body Count' the total number of civilian deaths in Iraq from Jan 2014 to the end of December 2017 was around 67 500. The true figure is more likely to be around 120 000. The US led coalition conducted more than 13 200 air strikes against IS targets in Iraq between August 2014 and end Dec 2017. Most attacks have been carried out by US aircraft, but those from Australia, Belgium, Denmark, France, Jordan, the Netherlands and the UK have also taken part. By the end of 2017, 74 countries were said to have joined the US led coalition fighting IS in Iraq and Syria which included Israel

US-led coalition strikes: **IRAQ: 13,260 SYRIA: 14,236**

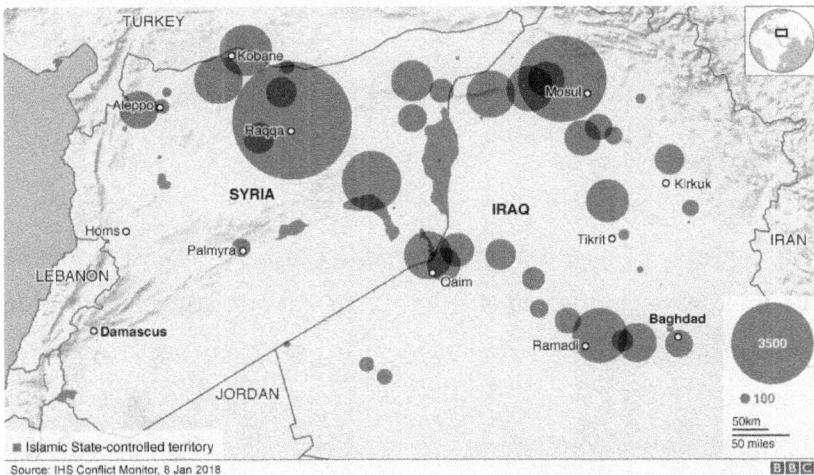

Islamic State-controlled territory

Source: IHS Conflict Monitor, 8 Jan 2018

An air campaign against IS targets in Syria began in September 2014. From then, more than 14 200 strikes were carried out by coalition forces 'til end December 2017. Main cities to be struck include Mosul, al Raqqa, Aleppo and Kobana. Israel has also joined in with more than 100 airstrikes, principally against Lebanese Hezbollah forces transporting weapons. Despite efforts to play down civilian casualties, these were thought to total in excess of 6 000 by end of 2015. By end 2017 that figure was in the vicinity of 20 000. But the total of civilian deaths in Syria since the uprising in 2011 is around 500 000+ with some 5 500 000 refugees having left the country and 6 million more displaced within the country.

The Syrian conflict was so complex, it beggars belief. Groups on the ground included:

Syrian Government Armed Forces
Islamic State of Iraq and the Levant
al Nusra Front
Free Syrian Army
al-Qaeda
Syria Revolutionaries
Army of Mujahedeen
Kurdish Forces
Iranian Special Forces
Cuban Special Forces
Turkish Armed Forces
Russian Armed Forces
US Coalition Forces

The Syrian conflict had its roots in protest marches against the ruling and oppressive government of al Assad. Similar protests had occurred in Tunisia and Egypt with a resulting toppling of governments. The army

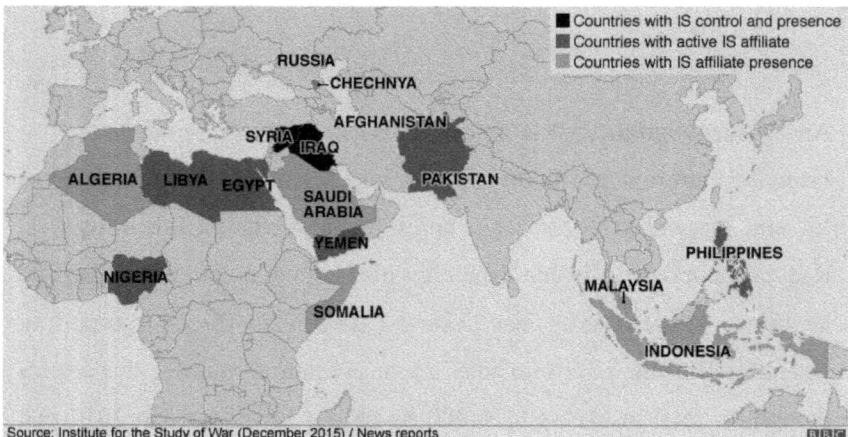

Source: Institute for the Study of War (December 2015) / News reports

and police fired on these demonstrations with guns, killing many and imprisoning many more. Defectors from the army helped rebel groups form the Free Syrian Army. Suburbs in Damascus and other cities became no go areas. The government responded with barrel bombs and even container bombs released from helicopters and levelling great areas to rubble. Poison gas was also used against the rebels. Thousands of prisoners are said to have been murdered. The internet played a vital role for communication and propaganda purposes leading to sectarian divisions. Governments of majority Shia adherents Iran and Iraq plus Lebanon based Hezbollah, supported Assad; while Sunni majority countries, including Turkey, Qatar, and Saudi Arabia supported anti-Assad rebels. The US assisted in arming the rebels. In 2013 the CIA had spent $500 million on a covert programme but only trained 60 fighters.. where did this money go? Israel carried out air raids inside Syria, reportedly targeting both Hezbollah and pro-government fighters and facilities.

Russia was not part of the coalition; it supported the regime of Bashar al Assad. Its jets began air strikes against what it labelled 'terrorists' in Syria in September 2015 including missile strikes launched from its warships on the Caspian and Black Seas. However it soon adopted a position where it saw the Free Syrian Army as also being a terrorist group (in line with the Syrian government's thinking) and consequently is responsible for the deaths of thousands of Syrian civilians. Turkey entered the war in Syria with Turkish troops advancing on Aleppo in Sept. 2016 primarily to attack the Kurdish YPG armed force which it regards as a terrorist organisation.

At UN Security Council meetings both Russia and China repeatedly vetoed Western backed resolutions on Syria (depicting their true colours as **enemy states** and again demonstrating the impotence of the Security Council!)

With the proclamation of a caliphate at the end of June 2014, IS signalled its intention to spread beyond Iraq and Syria. By August 2016, IS was operational in 18 countries across the world, including Afghanistan and Pakistan. It is also affiliated with groups in Mali, Egypt, Somalia, Bangladesh, Indonesia and the Philippines.

It has claimed attacks in a number of countries including Egypt, Turkey, Indonesia, France, Belgium, Germany, the US, Bangladesh and the UK as hailed in its online magazine Dabiq*.

It was suggested that a scientific station at Jamraya was used to produce chemical munitions in violation of a deal where Mr Assad had agreed to destroy his chemical arsenal after a deadly Sarin attack in Damascus in 2013. The Syrian army was again accused of using chlorine and sarin in

[* Note: al-Qaeda also had an online magazine called *Inspire*, both permitted !]

gas attacks against rebel forces in Damascus in April 2018 confirmed by the Organisation for the Prevention of Chemical Weapons, OPCW.

This was the second recent chemical attack following the OPCW determination that chlorine gas was released from cylinders operated by mechanical impact on February 4 which targeted civilians in Saraqeb in Idlib province. Despite their constant denials, the Russians and the Syrian Government must share responsibility for these attacks!

.

With strong assistance from Russia, Iran and other nations and organisations (some of which are designated as terrorist by the West) the Syrian armed forces mostly took back complete control of the West of the country (May 2018). This was a humiliation for the US that poured blame on Iran and Russia, the main allies of al Assad, throughout the civil war.

[Note: The tearing up of the 'Nuclear Deal' with Iran by President Trump in May 2018 signalled a new front in American foreign policy towards Iran despite a call for appeasement and calm from America's chief allies in Europe.]

Diaspora of Syrian Refugees (Wikipedia)	
Turkey	3 572 565 (registered April 2018)
Lebanon	2.2 million (estimated arrivals as of December 2015) 1 001 051 (registered)
Jordan	1 265 000 (census results as of November 2015) 661 114 (registered July 2017)
Germany	600 000 (2014 to late 2016) 429 000 (registered by late 2016) 456 023 (applicants by February 2016)
Saudi Arabia	500 000-2 500 000 (estimated overstays as of 2016)
United Arab Emirates	242 000 (estimated overstays as of 2015)

Iraq (incl. Iraqi Kurdistan)	230 836 (registered)
Kuwait	155 000+ (estimated overstays to June 2015)
Egypt	117 702 (registered by March 2016) 124 534 (UNHCR estimate as of September 2017) 500 000 (Egypt MFA estimate as of September 2016)
Sweden	110 333 (applicants to December 2015)
Sudan	100 000 (2016)
Yemen	100 000 (2015)
Hungary	72 505 (applicants to December 2015)
Canada	62 000+ (applicants to Feb 2017) 43 000+ (approved as of Feb 2017) 40 081 (resettled as of Feb 2017)
Croatia	55 000 (estimated as of September 2015) 386 (applicants to December 2015)
Greece	54 574 (estimated in country May 2016) 5 615 (applicants to December 2015)
Qatar	54 000 (estimated overstays 2017) 42 (registered)
Austria	45 827 (applicants to April 2017)
Algeria	43 000 (estimated as of November 2015) 5 721 (registered as of November 2015)
Netherlands	31 963 (applicants to July 2016)
Libya	26 672 (registered as of December 2015)
Armenia	22 000 (estimated as of January 2017)
Denmark	19 433 (applicants to December 2015)
Bulgaria	17 527 (applicants to December 2015)
United States	16 218 (resettled by November 2016)
Belgium	16 986 (applicants to July 2016)
Norway	13 993 (applicants to December 2015)
Singapore	13 856 (applicants to December 2015)
Switzerland	12 931 (applicants to July 2016)
Serbia	11 831 (applicants to February 2016)
France	11 694 (applicants to July 2016)

United Kingdom	9 467 (applicants to July 2016) 5 102 (resettled as of August 2015)
Brazil	9 000 (approved) 2 097 (as of November 2015)
Spain	8 365 (applicants to December 2015)
Russia	7 096 (overstays in residence to April 2016)
Australia	6 000 (resettled to Jan 2017) another 6000 to be taken
Malaysia	5 000 (estimated in August 2015) 1 980 (registered to May 2017)
Tunisia	4 000 (September 2015)
Cyprus	3 527 (applicants to December 2015)
Bahrain	3 500 (estimated June 2015)
Argentina	3 000 (approved)
Montenegro	2 975 (applicants to December 2015)
Italy	2 538 (applicants to December 2015)
Romania	2 525 (applicants to December 2015)
Macedonia	2 150 (applicants to December 2015)
Malta	1 222 (applicants to December 2015)
Somalia	1 312 (as of January 2016)
Finland	1 127 (as of December 2015)

However, as of June 2018, there remains more than one third of Syria under control of the Kurds and the Syrian Democratic Forces; also there are still pockets where ISIS is in control. With Saudi Arabia, Egypt and Russia in discussion, one still hopes for a political solution which will include an opposition party. But external forces East and West seem to have aggravated the sectarian dimension of this war as well as other conflicts in the Middle East. Muslims generally have been slow to put aside these differences and reflect on whom is it, their true enemy in the world?

War Crimes:

By the Syrian armed Forces and Police:

Use of barrel bombs and container bombs

Poison gas attacks using Chlorine and Sarin

Torture and murder of thousands of prisoners

By Russia:

Missile strikes on civilian areas in Damascus, Idlib and other cities

US and Coalition Air Forces:

Murder of thousands of civilians in bombing aimed at ISIS but mainly denied by Governments and military leaders

Use of torture by CIA agents e.g. water boarding of al-Qaeda prisoners.

Torture, rape and sodomy by US military personnel

ISIS:

Claims of up to 4 500 civilians murdered for a range of reasons .. but this figure unverified.

According to the Syrian Human Rights Network up to 15 000* persons have been murdered in al Assad's prisons, many of which underwent horrific torture first and/or rape followed by torture. Syrian Government forces with the assistance of Russian forces are responsible for the lion's share of civilian deaths, estimated to be around 200 000 to 250 000, mainly caused by bombing.

"I don't get how a pilot presses the button to bomb a hospital. How does he sleep, how does he eat? And then he comes back and bombs the people who are trying to help the victims"

Dr. Saoud Idlib

[* others have claimed in excess of 50 000 killed in Syrian prisons 2011-2017]

There is no doubt that ALL parties have committed war crimes in the Syrian conflict and that Russia has protected the Assad regime. Accountability and punishment should follow if the world is to remain with some semblance of civility and under the jurisdiction of International Law. This MUST come from the UN General Assembly. **One cannot rely upon the superpowers alone for execution of the law especially when we are straddled by a dysfunctional Security Council!**

Rewards for the Winners: Before the war, most of Syria's oil and gas went to Europe. With embargos remaining, Russian companies will step in. In accordance with an energy cooperation framework agreement signed in late January, Russia will have exclusive rights to produce oil and gas in Syria. The agreement encompasses the rehabilitation of damaged rigs and infrastructure, energy advisory support, and training a new generation of Syrian oilmen. Syria's offshore potential is still dubious, despite some seismic survey in the late 2000s; but is possibly as prolific as that of Israel, Egypt or Cyprus.

End Game of Syrian Conflict

Most of the remnants of rebel groups and their families from many cities in Syria found their way to the province of Idlib. Hundreds of thousands ended up camped in pathetic conditions at Atmeh refugee camp. Turkey's armed forces watched over the area as a final meeting between representatives of the Russians, the Iranians and the Turks came together to discuss the final conclusion to the seven years of armed conflict. Meanwhile the city of Idlib suffered more bombing raids by Russian and Syrian jets, killing more civilians including women and children. The US, British, French and allied coalition have ceased further strikes in the country. Al Assad accuses them of lies and a root cause of the misery of the civil war. Despite this, the white helmets and international observers confirmed the many strikes by the Assad regime using chemical weapons.

Idlib is the last rebel stronghold with fighters and residents having nowhere else to go. The Russian-backed Syrian government has trained its sights on the province and seems intent on crushing the rebels. Estimates put the population here at more than 3 million (July 2018) with most living in camps along the border with Turkey, a border closed to them at this time.

Atmeh, Idlib- a people awaiting their final destruction? August 2018

Anadolu Agency

August 2018

The Turks sent in a lot of humanitarian aid, set up military observation points and took on diplomatic efforts to sustain this area. People in Idlib knew that violence was closing in on them with no escape route available. "And where is the West now… what are *they* doing to help us?"

Nowhere to be seen!

An assault would result in very high casualties as the province is more densely populated than other areas in the country. Some internally displaced people in Idlib's tent cities live in a makeshift district called the Rahme Cluster. "Either we will die with honor or we will die with honor!"

"We left our home because of airstrikes. Our home is now gone, destroyed. This place is our last hope."

Syria's chemical attacks

Since 2013, hundreds of people have been killed and thousands affected by chemical attacks across rebel-held areas.

March 19, 2013	Khan al-Assal
March 19, 2013	al-Atebeh
March 24, 2013	Adra
April 29, 2013	Saraqeb, Idlib
August 21, 2013	Ghouta
April 11, 2014	Kafr Zita
April 11, 2014	Al-Temar'a, Hama, Idlib
April 21, 2014	Telmans, Idlib
August 2015	Marea
August 10, 2016	Aleppo
September 2016	Umm Hawsh
April 4, 2017	Khan Sheikhoun, Idlib
January 22, 2018	Douma
February 4, 2018	Saraqeb, Idlib
February 25, 2018	Al-Shifuniyah, eastern Ghouta
March 23, 2018	Irbín, eastern Ghouta
April 7, 2018	Douma, Eastern Ghouta

Marea
Aleppo
Khan al-Assal
Idlib
Saraqib
Kafr Zita
Khan Shaykhun
Hama
Douma
DAMASCUS
Adra
Atabeh
Irbin
Ghouta

Phosphorous bomb | **Chlorine gas bomb**
Mustard gas | **Unknown** | **Sarin gas**

@AJLabs

Source: Al Jazeera | Updated: April 14, 2018

ALJAZEERA

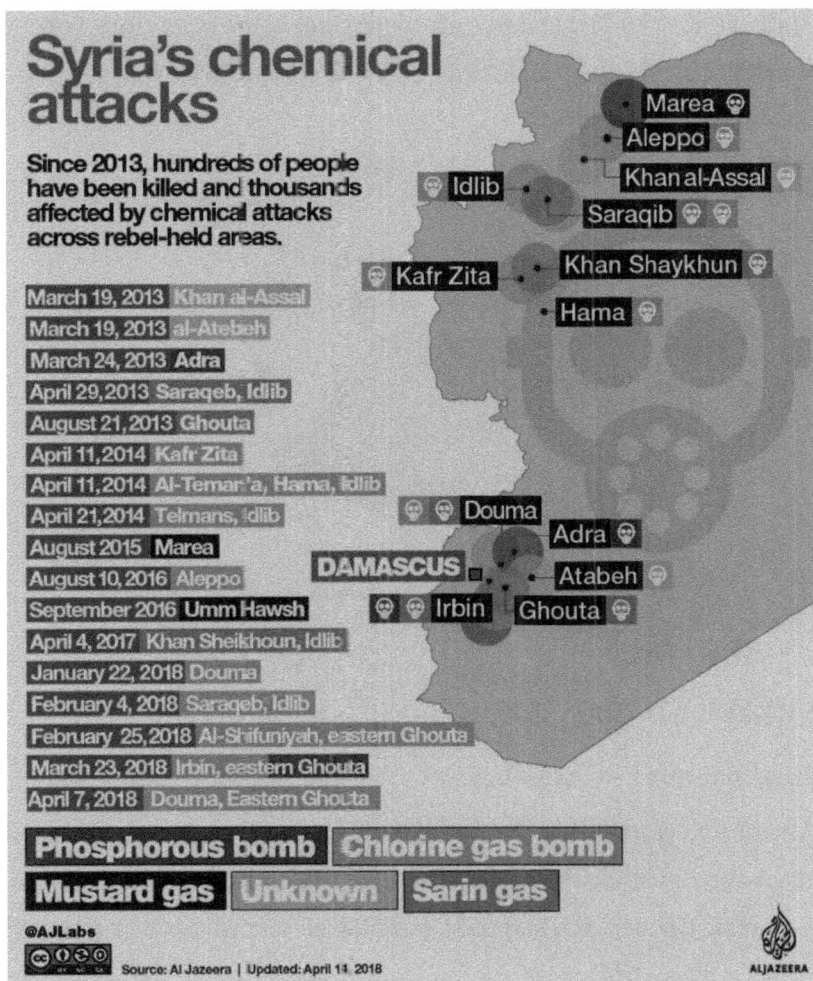

During the first six months of 2018 it was Russia that brokered a string of surrender deals with the rebels, most of whom departed with their families for Idlib, dubbed the 'dumping ground'. Rebel factions in Idlib announced the formation of a new coalition of some 70 000 fighters pledging to fight against Assad's forces. It excludes Hay'et Tahrir al-Sham (HTS), a former al-Qaeda affiliate which currently controls about 60% of the province. The United Nations has warned of a potential 'civilian bloodbath'. However, these opposition groups, particularly the coalition, may be forced into surrendering due to pressure from Turkey, which is eager to avoid an assault. This was seen to be the best scenario.

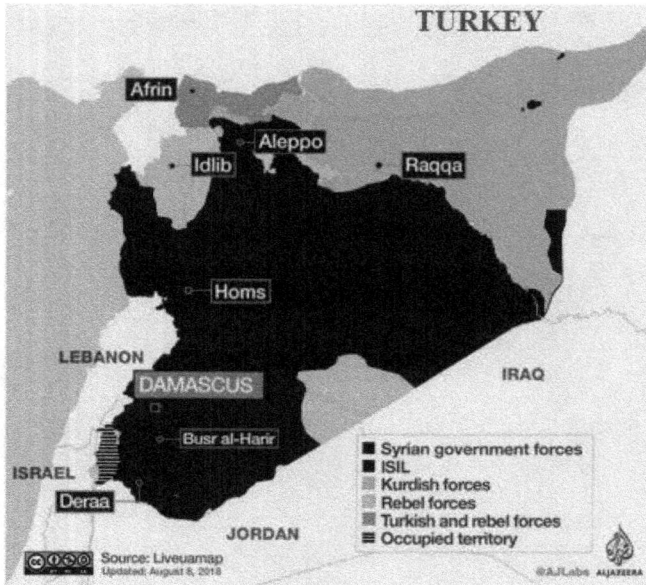

Syria, July 2018   **Aljazeera**

Almost five years earlier, President Obama announced the US would not attack the Assad regime. Instead, he would first seek authorisation from Congress. His decision surprised even his closest advisers. It appeared to have been influenced by an unexpected vote in the House of Commons two days earlier, on 29 August, when David Cameron's plan to order British forces to join allied military action in Syria was blocked. Obama's disregard for his own 'red line' was interpreted in Moscow, Tehran, Damascus and other Arab capitals as confirming a fundamental shift. Unfortunately, it presented Russia with an opportunity: to rebuild Moscow's influence in the Middle East and restore a Soviet-era global reach! Regardless of the outcome of a Western invasion into Syria, one might conclude that it is difficult to see how things could have turned out worse than they are now!

Retrospective analysis might conclude that by hovering passively on the sidelines in Syria, restricting themselves to counter-terrorism operations and vain calls for peace, and by failing to punish war crimes, western democracies effectively undermined the UN charter, the humanitarian agencies, and international law; not to metion severely failing the Syrian people!

At the same time, western timidity, divisions and neglect boosted authoritarian leaders from Moscow and Beijing to Ankara and Riyadh, while arguably encouraging the growth of Islamist terror groups.

When the US and Britain did eventually intervene directly in Iraq and Syria, as part of a multinational coalition in 2015, it was to fight the direct threat to themselves posed by Islamic State, not to uphold the universal values they ostensibly espouse. Taking this perspective, one might justifiably describe the whole Syria debacle as a monumental let down by the West, failing miserably the Syrian people just as we did over Crimea in the Ukraine. History has determined that temporary 'Peace in Our Time' just delays a while something much worse, more tumultuous and hideous with a greater cost in the long term!

However, East Mediterranean offshore gas adventures might soon be confronted by more military skirmishes. Ankara claims that possible offshore reserves are also owned by the Turkish part of the island of Cyprus. Trouble is also brewing from Syria and Lebanon. Lebanon's move to tender offshore gas blocks next to the maritime border with Israel has put the Israelis on edge. In view of Turkey's belligerent attitude towards Israel, the latter has warned international oil and gas companies to keep away from these areas, as it will be seen as a threat to Israeli security.

The author gives thanks to the BBC, The Guardian, CNN, al Jazeera and Wikipedia for much of the material in this chapter. There is also comment by Hizb ut-Tahrir Media (Pakistan) in Appendix F.

Already living in a tent at Atmeh, Idlib for six years!   Where are they now?

Egypt and Turkey

Egypt: Around 3000 BC the Kingdoms of Upper and Lower Egypt unite to form a formidable empire. Successive dynasties witnessed flourishing trade, prosperity and the development of significant cultural traditions carried down to the present day. Writing, including hieroglyphics, was used as an instrument of state with artistry, mathematics, astronomy and some chemical science being developed. Construction of the great pyramids commenced around 2 500 BC drawing on African slaves to create an extraordinary engineering achievement marvelled by tourists today.

Pyramids at Giza

Over the following six hundred years, Egypt is conquered by successive races of people: the Assyrians, Persians, Macedonians and then by the

Romans. In 1517, Egypt becomes absorbed into the Turkish Ottoman Empire.

The Suez Canal was built over the ten years from 1859, bringing Egypt to bankruptcy which led to a gradual takeover by Britain. In 1882 British troops defeated the Egyptian army and absorbed the country into the British Empire as a protectorate. In 1922, Fuad I became King and Egypt regained its independence although British influence remained significant until the mid-1950s.

Temple of Osiris at Abydos

Egypt has gone through much turmoil since the end of the Second World War and more so in the last decade. Tourists favour the capital Cairo, the pyramids and the Valley of the Kings on the Nile.

The Muslim Brotherhood was founded in 1928 by Hassan al-Banna, who was killed in 1949. Campaigns arose to reorient Egypt and the whole of the Muslim Middle East away from Western influence. In

1948 Egypt along with Iraq, Jordan and Syria attacked the new state of Israel. Egypt's army made a poor performance increasing the unpopularity of then King Farouk.

In 1953 coup leader Muhammad Najib became president and Egypt declared a republic. A year later fellow coup leader Gamal Abdel Nasser became prime minister and then in 1956 president, ruling unchallenged until his death in 1970. In July, 1956 President Nasser nationalised the Suez Canal to assist in funding the Aswan High Dam after Britain and the US withdrew finance for the project. In October, Britain, France and Israel invaded the country. However they withdrew at the behest of the US which greatly enhanced President Nasser's standing at home and abroad. Nasser stepped up his campaign to promote pan-Arab unity.

June 1967: occurrence of 'the six day war' - Israeli forces made a pre-emptive attack defeating the armed forces of Egypt, Jordan and Syria, leaving it in control of Sinai up to the Suez Canal plus Egyptian occupied Gaza.

The Suez Canal is closed to shipping.

After the death of Nasser in 1970, Anwar al Sadat takes over the Presidency and steers Egypt back to the West. Egypt and Syria went to war with Israel again in 1973 to reclaim land lost in the previous war. In 1973 the Suez Canal is re-opened for first time since 1967. Egypt is now a major beneficiary of US financial aid. In 1981 Sadat is assassinated by Islamist extremists a month after a clampdown on private press and opposition groups in wake of anti-government riots. He is succeeded by Hosni Mubarak, a high ranking officer of the Egyptian Airforce, who re-imposes a State of Emergency, restricts political activity, freedom of expression and assembly. During the 1990s, Gama'a al-Islamiyya began a campaign of attacks on government and tourist targets, culminating in the killing of 62 people at the Luxor historic site in 1997.

Early 2000s: there are more terror attacks against tourists. In 2006, Egypt is one of at least six Arab countries developing domestic nuclear programmes to diversify their energy sources. In 2008, Military courts sentence 25 leading Muslim Brotherhood members to jail terms in a crackdown targeting the organisation's funding. More than 800 were arrested over a month. In August of the following year, twenty six members of an alleged cell of the Lebanese militant group Hezbollah were put on trial in Cairo on charges of plotting attacks in Egypt and sending weapons to Hamas in Gaza.

February 2011: President Mubarak stepped down, handing power to the

Tahrir Square, Cairo 2013

army council. He was put on trial in August charged with ordering the killing of demonstrators. Protests continued in Cairo's Tahrir Square over the slow pace of political change, with a strong presence of Islamist groups. The army finally dispersed protestors in August.

The court sentenced ex-President Mubarak to life imprisonment. The army toppled Islamist Mohammed Morsi after just a year in power, and crushed his supporters' protests (nothing to do with America!) The

Muslim Brotherhood candidate Mohammed Morsi narrowly won a presidential election serving as the fifth President of Egypt, from 30 June 2012 to 3 July 2013, when General Abdel Fattah el-Sisi removed Morsi from office in the 2013 Egyptian coup d'état after the June 2013 Egyptian protests.

Previously, in December 2012, the Islamist dominated constituent assembly approved a draft constitution boosting the role of Islam and restricting freedom of speech and assembly.

July 2013: Army overthrows President Morsi amid mass demonstrations calling on him to quit. Hundreds killed as security forces storm pro-Morsi protest camps in Cairo. Some 40 Coptic churches were destroyed in a wave of attacks by Muslim extremists. The government declared the Muslim Brotherhood a terrorist group after a bomb blast in Mansoura killed 12.

January 2014: a new constitution bans parties based on religion. In November Sinai-based armed group Ansar Beit al-Maqdis pledges allegiance to the Islamic State movement, which controlled parts of Syria and Iraq. Islamic State carries out attacks at Giza tourist site and is suspected of an attack on tourists in Hurghada. It also beheads 20 Coptic Christians.

May 2015: ex- President Morsi is sentenced to 20 years in prison.

In November 2016 the IMF approved a three year $12 billion loan to Egypt designed to help the country out of its deep economic crisis.

Early 2017: Coptic Christian families flee northern Sinai after a number of killings by suspected Islamist militants. A state of emergency declared after more suicide bombings of churches in the country. Egypt and Saudi Arabia accuse Qatar of promoting terrorism.

March 2018: President Sisi won a second term in elections against a sole minor opposition candidate with other challengers either withdrawing or arrested!

Suicide bombers killed 44 at this Coptic Church in Egypt on Palm Sunday, April 2017. Mar Girgis Coptic Church is in the Nile Delta City of Tanta. Pope Tawadros II, the leader of the Coptic Church was in the Alexandra Cathedral at the time of its simultaneous bombing but was unhurt. ISIS claimed responsibility.

According to Amnesty International, over 40 000 have been detained and prosecuted since July 2014.

A Specific Case: Egyptian teenager has been in jail for over 500 days for wearing an anti-torture T-shirt.

The Detention of Mahmoud Mohamed Hussein

On January 25, 2014, 18 year old Mahmoud Mohamed Ahmed Hussein participated in a protest to commemorate the third anniversary of the January 25 Revolution and to demonstrate opposition to the Muslim Brotherhood and the military in Cairo, Egypt. When heading home in a bus, Mr. Hussein was stopped by police officers at a checkpoint in El-Marg (North-East Cairo); Mr. Hussein had no identifying characteristics about him save for a January 25 scarf and a t-shirt with "a nation without torture" slogan. At the checkpoint, police decided to detain Mr. Hussein. When he asked why he was being detained, Mr. Hussein was beaten by plainclothes police officers for about 30 minutes and then forcibly and violently dragged by his feet to the nearest police station. At El-Marg Police Station, Mr. Hussein was again beaten for about an hour by policemen in what is popularly referred to as a prison 'welcoming party.' The police then accused Mr. Hussein of possessing Molotov cocktails and hand grenades, belonging to a banned group, protesting without authorization, and receiving money to protest.

Mr. Hussein was kept in a small cell that was infested with insects and a total of 50 other detainees despite the fact that it was designed to house only 16 persons. His cellmates beat and threatened him at the instruction of the officers. Afterward he was taken to a National Security investigation. At the investigation an officer told Mr. Hussein that he would be filmed while reading a confession that was written for him by the officers. When Mr. Hussein refused, he was again violently beaten and tortured. Electric shocks were administered to his back, hands, and testicles for over four hours. Desperate to stop the torture, Mr. Hussein agreed under immense duress to 'confess to the crimes' of which the policemen had initially accused him. National Security officers then filmed this confession which was solely and directly a result of duress. Later, Mr. Hussein's family members reported that they observed physical signs that Hussein had been tortured when they visited him in detention. After his recorded confession, Mr. Hussein was then taken to the State Security Prosecutor. There, he denied all accusations and told the Prosecutor that he had been forced to confess. Despite Mr. Hussein's complaint, the Prosecutor did not refer him to forensic examination to investigate his claims of torture. Mr. Hussein was then kept at El-Marg

Police Station for six days. He was later transferred to the Abu Zabaal Prison and remained there until 11 May 2014. In May he was then transferred to the Cairo Appeals Prison and kept there until July 25, 2015. In July he was then transferred to Tora Investigations Prison where he remained. Mr. Hussein has reported being severely beaten by prison guards while in detention on at least two separate occasions in July 2014 and July 2015. During one of the incidents, two prison guards punched him in the stomach and slapped him across the face when he attempted to collect his belongings before a prison transfer. Although his family and attorneys submitted complaints about these abuses, the Prosecutor-General did not inform them of the findings of the investigation or any resolution to the complaints. While in detention, Mr. Hussein celebrated his 19th birthday, was forced to put his academic studies on hold, and missed his brother's wedding.

Mr. Hussein was never formally charged with a single crime and never referred to a trial. Although the presiding judge of the Cairo Criminal Court made determinations regarding the continued pre-trial detention of Mr. Hussein in 15-day or 45-day intervals (as technically allowed by Egypt's Criminal Procedure Code), at least 22 of the instances in which the judge made a detention renewal decision were made while Mr. Hussein was absent from the courtroom! The Ministry of Interior claimed that 'security reasons were behind the inability to transfer prisoners to court.' Additionally, the court delayed at least 24 of Mr. Hussein's detention renewal hearings for five to seven day periods at a time, depriving the process of regularity. At the following renewal session (which was scheduled for November 16, 2015), Mr. Hussein had been in pre-trial detention for 666 days! Prisoner of conscience Mahmoud Mohamed Ahmed Hussein was finally released on 25 March 2016 after spending more than two years in detention without a trial!

Turkey:

There have always been human civilisations in Turkey dating back half a million years.

During the reign of Mehmed II, Constantinople was made the capital city of the Empire following its capture in 1453. The Ottoman Empire continued to expand into the Eastern Anatolia, Central Europe, the Caucasus, North and East Africa, the islands in the Mediterranean, Greater Syria, Mesopotamia, and the Arabian Peninsula in the 15th, 16th and 17th centuries. The empire was frequently at war with the Holy Roman Empire (Europe) and neighbouring Persia. The Ottoman era ranged from 1300 to 1922, after the defeat of Turkey in the First World War.

Mustafa Kemal Atatürk (1881-1938)

Progress and transformation to a modern state was started by Mustafa Kemal, the new republic's first President of Turkey who introduced many radical reforms. Named Atatürk, meaning 'Father', he introduced the Roman alphabet and encouraged education and technological advancement, strengthening ties with Europe and the West. However, he maintained a single party rule over the country. A closer model of multi-party parliamentary democracy did not appear until after the Second World War. In post war years the Truman Doctrine of 1947 spelled out the American intentions to guarantee the security of Turkey and Greece, resulting in large-scale US military and economic support for each. After participating with the United Nations forces in the Korean War, Turkey joined NATO in 1952. Turkish democracy was plagued by military coups in 1960, 1971 and again in 1980. In 1984, the PKK (Kurdish Communist Movement) began an insurgency against the Turkish government- a conflict, which has claimed over 40 000 lives and continues to the present.

2002-2018: But the legacy of Atatürk faces further erosion as the current re-elected president, Recep Tayyip Erdoğan, ushers in a more conservative and religious state. Supporters worship him like a god, as he has shaped Turkish society over the sixteen years of his presidency. Erdogan has pledged to raise a 'pious generation' and has boosted religious teaching in Turkey's education system. In 2014, Erdogan ordered that a vast 1000 room palace be built in the middle of the Atatürk Forest Farm, at a cost of $615 million.

On 15th July 2016, a section of the Turkish military, which the government accused of being controlled by US based cleric Fethullah Gülen, failed in its attempt to overthrow the government. Over the following year since the traumatic coup attempt, 50 000 people were remanded in custody and a further 170 000 suspects investigated for links to the group believed to have masterminded the coup. It is a nation more divided than ever, its newspapers and media silenced, its opposition intimidated, and Erdoğan's power rivalling that of the republic's founder, Mustafa Kemal Atatürk. Erdoğan's win in the 2018 elections paved the road toward a ruling autocracy with the opposition having failed to halt Turkey's descent into a virtual elected dictatorship!

With thousands more arrested and jailed, including judges, teachers, university lecturers and journalists, currently there is no rule of law, no separation of powers, and no independent judiciary in the country!

With the advent of the president and his Justice and Development party

President Erdoğan   2018

consolidating their power over the nation, there are few indications that the rifts between Turkey and Europe and between Turkey and the US will heal in the immediate term.

Conflict with the Kurds: This has been an ongoing armed conflict between the Police and Armed Forces of Turkey and various Kurdish insurgent groups. These have been demanding separation from Turkey to create an independent country or at least to have autonomy with greater political rights for the Kurdish people living inside the Republic of Turkey. The main rebel group is the Kurdistan Workers' Party (PKK), founded in 1978. Since it began more than 40 000 have died and 22 000 imprisoned, many of whom were civilians. The European Court of Human Rights has condemned Turkey for thousands of human rights abuses; these include systematic executions of civilians, torture, forced displacements, destroyed villages and arbitrary arrests. Added to this, there have been murders of journalists, activists and politicians.

Government troops and police have suffered 8 300 killed and 21 000 wounded. The cost to the country is believed to be in the vicinity of $500 billion for military and armaments. The revenue loss from fewer tourists is also extremely high.

Each of the Turkish operations 'Operation Steel' (1995) and 'Operation Hammer' (1997) failed to crush the PKK. After a unilateral cease-fire the PKK forces fully withdrew from the Republic of Turkey and set up new bases in the Qandil Mountains of Iraq declaring in February 2000 a formal end of the war. However the Turkish armed forces continued to raid Kurdish villages and positions across border into Iraq.

After the 2003 US invasion of Iraq, much of the arms of the Iraqi Army fell into the hands of the Iraqi Kurdish Peshmerga militias and Turkey claimed many of these weapons found their way into the hands of other Kurdish groups such as the PKK.

At the start of 2009 Turkey opened its first Kurdish language TV-channel, TRT 6, and on 19 March 2009 local elections were held in Turkey in which pro-Kurdish Democratic Society Party (DTP) won a majority of the vote in the South East. Soon after, on 13 April 2009, the PKK declared its sixth ceasefire! However clashes and deaths continued. In 2011 major Kurdish protests occurred across Turkey as part of a civil disobedience campaign launched by the pro-Kurdish Peace and Democracy Party (BDP). In the election it won 36 seats in the South-East, more than the ruling Justice and Development Party!

In the summer of 2012, the conflict with the PKK altered dramatically as President Bashar al-Assad ceded control of several Kurdish cities in Syria to the PYD, the Syrian affiliate of the PKK.

It is said that at this juncture, Turkey began to arm ISIS and other Islamic groups against the Kurds. Engineered by President Erdogan, again in April 2013, the PKK announced that it would be withdrawing all its forces from within Turkey to Northern Iraq.

In October 2014 riots erupted across Turkey protesting the Siege of Kobane with the Kurds accusing the Turkish government of supporting ISIS and not letting people send support for Kobane Kurds. By

December 2015, Turkish military operations in the Kurdish regions of south-eastern Turkey had killed hundreds of civilians and displaced hundreds of thousands more, causing massive destruction of residential areas.

In January 2018, the Turkish military together with the Free Syrian Army and Sham Legion allies, began a cross-border operation in the Kurdish 'Afrin Canton' in Northern Syria, against the Kurdish led Democratic Union Party in Syria (PYD) and US supported YPG Kurdish militia. In March 2018, Turkey launched military operations to eliminate the Kurdish PKK fighters in northern Iraq.

As predicted by this author, after doing a lot of the heavy work against IS, the Kurds remain a punished minority and their hope of a country of their own is as elusive as ever! Interesting that Turkey continues to deny the Armenian genocide! Will it also deny the mass executions of Kurds in years to come?

Hagia Sofia, Istanbul

Yemen- Averted Eyes of the West

Yemen's war was far more complex than described as a Saudi-Iranian or Sunni-Shia conflict.

Yemen was ruled for a millennium by Zaydi Shia imams until 1962 and the Houthis were founded as a Zaydi Shia revivalist movement. However, the Houthis have not called for restoring the imamate in Yemen and religious grievances have not been a major factor in the war. Rather, the Houthis' demands have been primarily economic and political in nature. In 2013 Yemen's National Dialogue Conference was launched, and was tasked with writing a new constitution and creating a federal political system. But the Houthis withdrew from the process because it left Yemen's transitional government in place. Further inflaming matters was the fact that two Houthi representatives were assassinated during the conference's proceedings.

For three years, Yemen, the Arab world's poorest country, has been wracked by a bloody war between the Houthi rebels and supporters of Yemen's internationally recognised government. The Houthis and the Yemeni government have battled on and off since 2004 but much of the fighting was confined to the Houthis' stronghold, northern Yemen's impoverished Saada province

In September 2014, the Houthis took control of Yemen's capital, Sanaa, and proceeded to push southwards towards the country's second biggest city, Aden. In response to the Houthis' advances a coalition of Arab states launched a military campaign in 2015 to defeat the Houthis and restore Yemen's government.

In 2015, Saudi Arabia formed a coalition of Arab states to defeat the Houthis in Yemen. The coalition included Kuwait, the United Arab Emirates, Bahrain, Egypt, Morocco, Jordan, Sudan and Senegal. Several

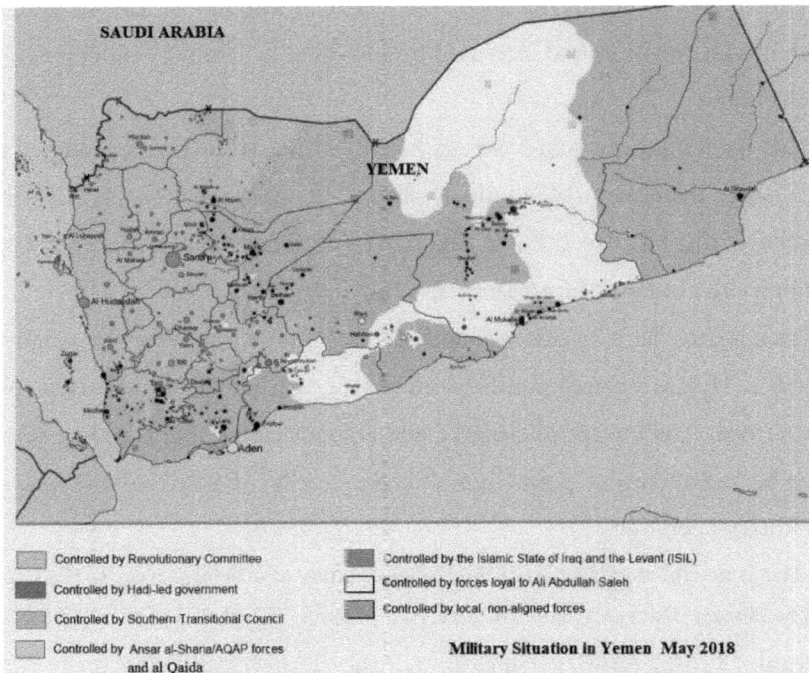

SAUDI ARABIA

YEMEN

Controlled by Revolutionary Committee

Controlled by the Islamic State of Iraq and the Levant (ISIL)

Controlled by Hadi-led government

Controlled by forces loyal to Ali Abdullah Saleh

Controlled by Southern Transitional Council

Controlled by local, non-aligned forces

Controlled by Ansar al-Sharia/AQAP forces and al Qaida

Military Situation in Yemen May 2018

of these countries have sent troops to fight on the ground in Yemen, while others have only carried out air attacks.

The US government regularly launched air attacks on al-Qaeda and ISIS targets in Yemen, and has deployed a small number of troops on the

211

ground. The US along with the UK and France has also supplied the Saudi-led coalition with weapons and intelligence.

But much more than this: 'In the Gulf it was disclosed that British military personnel were **sitting in the control rooms** from which the Saudi Arabian air force was guiding its bombers on to targets across Yemen. The British were helping their Saudi counterparts key in the codes that would help them select and attack their targets. The Saudis were not only flying British built aircraft and dropping British made bombs, they were dropping vast numbers of them with assistance. Over a three month period in 2015, the value of exports of British made bombs and missiles had increased by 11 000%, from £9 million to £1 billion!

This bombing campaign has been heavily criticised by rights groups for causing thousands of civilian deaths. In parliament, the British government has had little to say about this, other than to insist that it **'obeys the norms of humanitarian law'.**

Once again, the government appeared to be quietly pulling the country into a Middle Eastern conflict without any parliamentary oversight or approval. And covert, undeclared and unreported warfare could be seen to be not merely a possibility, but the reality of many of the UK's military operations.'

[This is an edited extract from Ian Cobain's study of official secrecy in the UK, The History Thieves, Portobello 2017]

And, we might ask, which British and American armaments corporations are making such tidy profits?

Iran has denied arming the Houthi rebels but the US military intercepted arms shipments from Iran to Yemen this March (2018), claiming it was the third time in two months that this had occurred. Iranian officials have also suggested they may send military advisers to support the Houthis.

The United Nations Office for the Coordination of Humanitarian Affairs (OCHA), estimates that more than 3 million Yemenis have fled their homes to elsewhere in the country and 280 000 have sought asylum in other countries, including Djibouti and Somalia. Internally displaced

Yemenis often must cope with a lack of food and inadequate shelter. Many Yemenis who have not fled are also suffering, especially those in need of healthcare. As of March 26, 2018 at least 10 000 Yemenis had been killed by the fighting, with more than 40 000 casualties overall. Around 5 500 were civilian deaths. Save The Children estimated at least 50 000 children died in 2017, an average of 130 every day from all causes, but mainly disease and starvation. This figure is said to have jumped to 180 per day!

The United Nations High Commissioner for Human Rights, has estimated that Saudi-led coalition air attacks caused almost two-thirds of reported civilian deaths, while the Houthis have been accused of causing mass civilian casualties due to their siege of Taiz, Yemen's third-largest city.

Thus war crimes have been committed by both the Houthis and the Saudi Arabian Air Force **and by the British Government on behalf of us- the British people!** The international community has sharply condemned both the Saudi Arabian intervention, which has included

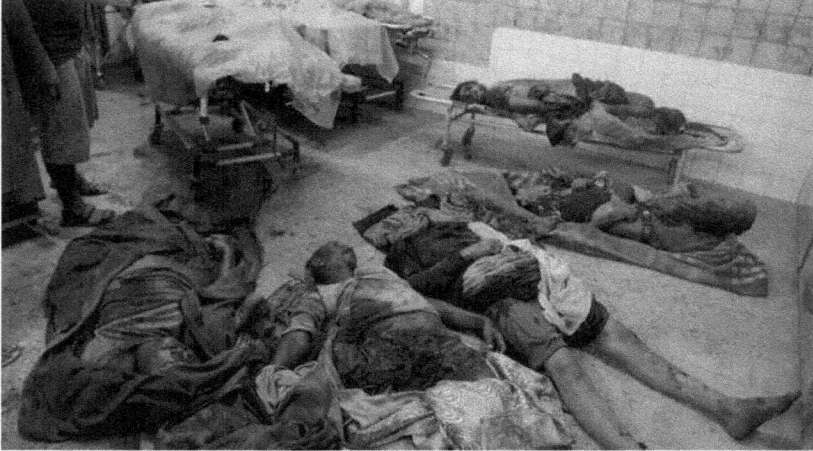

widespread bombing of civilian areas, as well as Iranian support for Houthi militants.

The author condemns ALL those companies and corporations producing military hardware and willing to sell to the Saudis at annual Military Fairs in various capital cities, predominantly in Europe. Whilst the UK (as one example but by no means isolated) approved a £170 million aid package for millions of Yemenis at risk of starvation, Theresa May's government was criticised for allowing arms deals with Saudi Arabia worth billions of pounds. Trump's America is equally culpable! This is flagrant hypocrisy typical of armaments producers in dozens of countries around the globe!

In all these wars in the Middle East we see Muslims murdering Muslims on a grand scale BUT still with the expectation of entering al jannah, firdaus or heaven!

However, leaders and combatants that have killed will see Eternal NOTHING after their death on Earth!

Some of the fiercest fighting occurred in and around Aden in March 2015 where we saw Houthi's in combat with various groups: Yemeni Government troops backed up by Saudi Arabians and their coalition* troops (with logistical support from the US). By September, Sudanese troops had joined.

Mohammad's Jannah

In early 2016 a new conflict began in Aden with IS (Islamic State) and AQAP (al-Qaeda in the Arabian Peninsula) controlling various and adjacent neighbourhoods in the city. The Houthis won battles to the East of Aden but were then in conflict with al-Qaeda and Hadi brigades. Sunni tribesmen were also battling AQAP and Ansar al-Sharia forces.

Since the mid-2000s, the United States carried out targeted killings (using drones) of jihadist militants and ideologues in Yemen particularly known leaders of IS and al-Qaeda, although the US government generally does not confirm involvement in specific attacks conducted by unmanned aerial vehicles as a matter of policy.

Islamic State proclaimed several provinces in Yemen and urged its adherents to wage war against the Houthi movement, as well as against Zaydis in general. ISIS militants conducted bombing attacks in various parts of the country, particularly against mosques in Sana'a!

2017 US involvement: The Yakla raid involving US Navy SEALs (and

[* plus airstrikes from airforces of: Egypt, Morocco, Jordan, Sudan, Kuwait, United Arab Emirates, Qatar, and Bahrain]

approved by President Trump) was executed in January causing several civilian casualties. A 50 minute shootout led to the killing of one SEAL, the wounding of three other SEALs and the deliberate destruction of a $75 million US MV-22 Osprey aircraft. (What could have been done alternatively with such cash?) The US government reported that 14 al-Qaeda in the Arabian Peninsula fighters were killed and acknowledged that some civilian non-combatants were likely to have been killed as well. Human Rights Watch, citing witness statements, reported the death of 14 civilians including nine children. In other words a monumental cock up!

Early March 2017: the US conducted 45 airstrikes against AQAP. The airstrikes were reported to have killed hundreds of AQAP militants.

July 22, 2017: Houthis and forces loyal to Ali Abdullah Saleh launched a missile, a Volcano H-2, on Saudi Arabia targeting the oil refineries in the Yanbu Province followed up by 4 Volcano 1 missiles fired at King Fahad Air Base.

Late 2017: in a gradual escalation of US military action, a group of US Army commandos arrived to seek and destroy Houthi missiles near the Saudi Arabian border. The US government attempted to keep secret the extent of such involvement in Yemen.

In April of 2018 we saw an expanded response by the Saudi Arabian Air

Force. Typically was on April 19, 2018 where a Saudi led coalition conducted airstrikes across Yemen killing civilians and injuring many others. In response to Saudi Arabia's aggression against Yemen, Houthi forces hit a 'mercenary

camp' in Saudi Arabia with artillery and rocket fire killing and wounding several people at the camp, targeted a power plant in the Najran region of Saudi Arabia, and targeted an airport in Jizan. Saudi Arabia later carried out a series of airstrikes in northwestern Sa'ada that destroyed three houses as well as an aerial attack in southwestern Yemen that left 20 people dead. And so it went on! In April alone the Saudis were responsible for over one hundred people killed in air strikes.

CNN reported way earlier in April 2015 that almost 10 160 000 Yemenis were deprived of water, food, and electricity as a result of the conflict. The report also added per sources from UNICEF officials in Yemen that within 15 days, some 100 000 people across the country were dislocated, while Oxfam said that more than 10 million Yemenis did not have enough food to eat, including 850 000 half-starved children. Over 13 million civilians were without access to clean water. Three years on the UN had not been able to end the war in Yemen! But profits from the sale of military hardware were keeping shareholders happy!

War Crimes:

Human Rights Watch wrote that the Saudi-led air campaign that began on 26 March 2015, had 'conducted airstrikes in apparent violation of the laws of war, such as the March 30 attack on a displaced persons camp in Mazraq, northern Yemen, that struck a medical facility and a market'.

Amnesty International said that several Saudi Arabian led airstrikes, documented by it, had hit five densely populated areas namely Sa'dah, Sana'a, Hodeidah, Hajjah and Ibb. It 'raised concerns about compliance with the rules of international humanitarian law'.

In June 2017 a cholera epidemic resurfaced which was reported to be killing a person an hour in Yemen by mid June. News reports in mid

June stated that there had been 124 000 cases and 900 deaths and that 20 of the 22 provinces in Yemen were affected at that time. UNICEF and WHO estimated that, by 24 June 2017, the total cases in the country exceeded 200 000, with 1300 deaths.

The Houthi forces illegally placed anti-personnel mines in many parts of Yemen including Aden which caused hundreds of civilian injuries when they accidentally stepped on a mine. Saudi Arabia shares a long border with Yemen and fears what it sees as 'Iranian expansionism' through its support for Shia armed groups. Commentators in the Arab Gulf States often claim that Iran now controls four Arab capitals: Baghdad, Damascus, Beirut and Sanaa. But it is the author's view that external forces wish to maintain this paranoia between the two main branches of Islam to keep them fighting among themselves for materialistic gain. Oil revenue earned by Middle Eastern nations must somehow be balanced and by selling weapons and armaments is a way of maintaining such a balance at a huge cost to the peoples of the Middle East! It is not difficult to point a finger at the guilty parties!

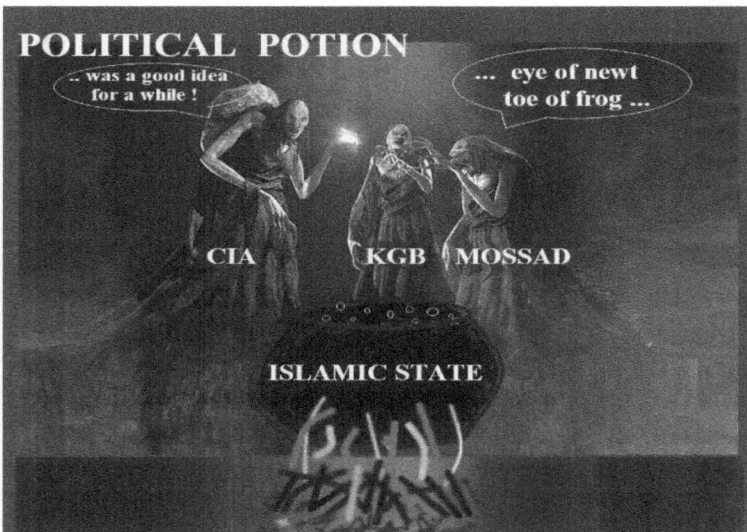

... perhaps should include MI63/4

SAUDI SAYS "LEGITIMATE ATTACK"

WARNING: GRAPHIC VIDEO

WAR IN YEMEN

Dozens of children killed in Saudi-led airstrike on bus

August 9th 2018: More children killed when a bomb dropped from a Saudi Airforce plane hits a school bus in Yemen. The attack sent a flood of victims to overwhelmed hospitals struggling to cope in what the United Nations considers one of the world's worst humanitarian crises. "No excuses anymore!" Geert Cappelaere, UNICEF's regional director in the Middle East and North Africa, said. "Does the world really need more innocent children's lives taken to stop the cruel war on children in Yemen?"

Again the author repeats: Saudi Arabia is supported by the major Western governments and that these also are responsible for approval of the sale of billions of dollars of military hardware to the Arab state. Revenue earned on the suffering of hundreds of thousands of innocents! Something has to be done to halt this madness and evil!

Israel and Palestine

UN COMMITTEE ON THE EXERCISE OF THE INALIENABLE RIGHTS OF THE PALESTINIAN PEOPLE:
The United Nations Committee on the Exercise of the Inalienable Rights of the Palestinian People (CEIRP) was established in 1975 pursuant to General Assembly Resolution 3376, with a mandate to advise the General Assembly on programmes to enable Palestinian people to exercise their inalienable rights, including the right to self-determination without external interference, the right to national independence and sovereignty, and the right to return to their homes and property from which they have been displaced. CEIRP's mandate has been renewed on an annual basis since, most recently pursuant to General Assembly Resolution 72/13.

Israel's occupation of the Palestinian territories is the world's longest military occupation in modern times. Efforts to resolve the Israeli-Palestinian conflict have not resulted in a final peace agreement. In fact at the 70th birthday of the state (15th May 2018) the worst American President in history, one D. Trump, decided to build its embassy in Jerusalem and recognise the ancient city as Israel's capital against the advice of leaders of most of the world's nations! Over several days it caused the death of almost 100 Palestinians (including some children) that protested in anger with around 3 000 being wounded by snipers of the Israeli armed forces! Netanyahu said "they were just doing their job to protect Israel!" Even the US representative in the UN Security Council Nikki Haley said "no country in this chamber would act with more restraint than Israel has" and went on to say that ".. it was the fault of the terrorist group Hamas!" BUT, apart from stones, no weapons were used by the demonstrators! Sheer hypocrisy by the American administration!

The Kingdoms of Israel and Judah emerged during the Iron Age. The Neo-Assyrian Empire destroyed Israel around 720 BCE; Judah was later conquered by the Babylonian, Persian and Hellenistic empires and had existed as Jewish autonomous provinces. The Roman province of Judea was created in 6 CE. Judea lasted as a Roman province until the failed Jewish revolts resulted in widespread destruction and expulsion of the Jewish population.

During the siege of Jerusalem by the First Crusade in 1099, the Jewish inhabitants of the city fought side by side with the Fatimid garrison and the Muslim population who tried in vain to defend the city against the Crusaders.   When the city fell, about 60 000 people were massacred, including 6 000 Jews. In 1187 Sultan Saladin, founder of the Ayyubid dynasty, defeated the Crusaders in the Battle of Hattin and subsequently captured Jerusalem and almost all of Palestine. In time, Saladin issued a proclamation inviting Jews to return and settle in Jerusalem, and according to Judah al-Harizi, they did: "From the day the Arabs took Jerusalem, the Israelites inhabited it." Al-Harizi compared Saladin's decree allowing Jews to re-establish themselves in Jerusalem to the one issued by the Persian king Cyrus the Great over 1600 years earlier.

In 1516 the region was conquered by the Ottoman Empire; it remained under Turkish rule until the end of the First World War, when Britain defeated the Ottoman forces and set up a military administration across the former Ottoman Syria. In 1920 the territory was divided between Britain and France under the mandate system, and the British administered area was named Mandatory Palestine.

During the 19th century, national awakening among Jews led to the establishment of the Zionist movement followed by waves of immigration to Ottoman and later British Palestine.

[Interesting to note here that a significant number of Palestinians supported the British Forces in WWII in what is now Iraq and Syria. British and Australian troops suffered losses due to bombing and strafing by warplanes of the Vichy French Airforce in this war theatre in June 1941!]

After World War II, Britain was in conflict with both the Arab and the Jewish community over Jewish immigration limits. This developed into an armed struggle against British rule. Hundreds of thousands of Jewish Holocaust survivors and refugees were seeking a new life far from their former communities in Europe. Many were turned away or rounded up and placed in detention camps in Cyprus by the British.

On 22 July 1946, Jewish terrorists attacked the British Administrative Headquarters for Palestine housed in the King David Hotel in Jerusalem. A total of 90 people of various nationalities were killed and 50 injured. The attack was conceived as a response to Operation Agatha and was the deadliest against the British during the Mandate period. In 1947, the British government announced it would withdraw from Palestine, as it was unable to arrive at a solution acceptable to both Arabs and Jews. [cf: British withdrawal from India about the same time and subsequent strife between Hindus and Muslims!]

In 1947, the United Nations adopted a partition plan for Palestine recommending the creation of independent Arab and Jewish states and, wait for it, **'an internationalized Jerusalem'**. The plan was accepted by the Jews but rejected by Arab leaders. The following year, the Jews declared the independence of the State of Israel, and the subsequent 1948 Arab-Israeli War saw Israel's establishment over most of the former Mandate territory, while the West Bank and Gaza were held by neighbouring Arab states. The Arabs refer to their failure to regain Palestine as 'Nakba' meaning catastrophe!

Pledge by President Harry S Truman of the United States of America Oct 24th 1948:

So that everyone may be familiar with my position, I set out here the Democratic platform on Israel:

"President Truman, by granting immediate recognition to Israel, led the world in extending friendship and welcome to a people who have long sought and justly deserve freedom and independence.

We pledge full recognition to the State of Israel. We affirm our pride that the United States, under the leadership of President Truman, played a leading role in the adoption of the resolution of November 29, 1947, by the United Nations General Assembly for the creation of a Jewish state.

We approve the claims of the State of Israel to the boundaries set forth in the United Nations' resolution of November 29 and consider that modifications thereof should be made only if fully acceptable to the State of Israel.

We look forward to the admission of the State of Israel to the United Nations and its full participation in the international community of nations. We pledge appropriate aid to the State of Israel in developing its economy and resources.

We favor the revision of the arms embargo to accord to the State of Israel the right of self-defense. We pledge ourselves to work for the modification of any resolution of the United Nations to the extent that it may prevent any such revision.

We continue to support, within the framework of the United Nations, the internationalization of Jerusalem and the protection of the holy places in Palestine."

During the 2000 Camp David Summit with Yasser Arafat and US President Bill Clinton, Prime Minister Ehud Barak offered a plan for the establishment of a Palestinian state. The proposed state included the entirety of the Gaza Strip and over 90% of the West Bank with Jerusalem as a shared capital.

A Small Sample BUT Never to be Forgotten, April 2002:

Civilian Casualties and Unlawful Killings in Jenin.
Shooting of Hani Abu Rumaila, April 3
Shooting of nurse Farwa Jammal, April 3.
The Shooting of Civilian Imad Musharaka, April 3
Shooting of Muhammad Hawashin, April 3
Shooting of Ahmad Hamduni, April 3
The Murder of Palestinian Militant Munthir al-Haj, April 3
Shooting of Atiya Abu Rumaila, April 5
Shooting of Abd al-Nasr Gharaib, April 5
Bombing Death of 'Afaf Disuqi, April 5
Shooting of Abd al-Karim Sa'adi and Wadah Shalabi, April 6
Shooting of Munir Wishahi and Mariam Wishahi, April 6
Bombing of Yusra Abu Khurj, April 6
Shooting of Nizar Mutahin, April 6
The Bulldozing Death of Jamal Fayid, April 6
The Shooting of Jamal al-Sabbagh, April 6
The Shooting of Ali Muqasqas, April 7
Shooting of Muhammad Abu Saba'a, April 9
Killing of Nayif 'Abd al-Jabr and 'Amid Fayid, April 10
Killing of Kamal Zghair, April 10
Killing of Faris Zaiban, April 11

After the 2001 election. Prime Minister Sharon carried out his plan to withdraw from the Gaza Strip and also spearheaded the construction of the Israeli West Bank barrier ending the Intifada. By this time 1100 Israelis had been killed, mostly in suicide bombings. The Palestinian fatalities from 2000 to 2008 reached 4 800.

The inhuman and planned bulldozing and destruction of the Jenin camp in April 2002 was well documented by the International Red Cross and UNRWA [see Human Rights Watch 2002 Vol 14 No 3(E)] where hundreds of dwellings were destroyed and people killed by the Israeli Defence Forces. It was markedly a 'disproportionate and indiscriminate' application of force of little or no military advantage! But then, this has been a pattern over decades.

One is reminded of the indiscriminate murders of Muslims in the Balkans in the 1990s and later the horrific murders of Muslim Rohingya in Burma in 2017. The supply of weapons and covert encouragement of Middle East wars by outsiders and major armaments manufacturers paints a sickening picture of humanity and a sterile United Nations!

Gaza July 2014

After many conflicts firstly by the Palestinian Liberation Organisation then Hezbollah and Hamas, Israel began an operation in Gaza on 14 November 2012, lasting eight days. Israel started another operation in Gaza following an escalation of rocket attacks by Hamas in July 2014. The retaliation was brutal and far far in excess of what is acceptable. After being brutalized by the Nazis in the 1940s, Israel was now behaving like Nazis!

Gaza suffered a 50 day war that left more than 2 200 people dead.

More than 20 000 homes were estimated to have been rendered uninhabitable, reduced to rubble by shelling and air strikes that the Israel Defence Forces (IDF) claimed **targeted only terrorist sites** used by Hamas for military purposes. Around half a million persons were displaced. Israel claimed that more than 3 700 rockets had been fired towards Israel by 20 August. A peace deal was finally struck between Hamas and Israel at a meeting in Cairo, Egypt.

"Thankyou America for all our lovely weapons" cheered the Israeli people!

2014 Gaza war by numbers:

Israeli soldiers killed:	64
Israeli civilians killed:	6
Israeli children killed:	1
Palestinians killed:	2 139
Palestinian children killed:	490
Palestinians wounded:	11 000
Palestinian children wounded:	3 000
Gaza residents displaced:	500 000
Homes destroyed in Gaza:	20 000

How many deaths will it take?

In 2018, Israel's population was an estimated 8 855 400 people, of whom 74.5% were recorded by the government as Jews. Arabs comprised 20.9% of the population, while non-Arab Christians and people who have no religion about 4.6%.

With a $38 billion weapons deal with America, Israel's defence forces will be well prepared for more conflict in the future. The current aid package stands at $3 billion annually, and Israel has asked that the amount for the next 10 year deal be raised to $3.7 billion per year.

In addition to the extra $700 million per year, Israel is also reportedly asking that it include a separate deal for missile defence spending, which could raise the total amount to more than $4 billion annually.

But as Muslims the world over become more angry at Israel and more supportive of Palestine we are likely to see even worse scenarios of war in the future. We have recently seen Mossad taking decisive action in places as far away as Malaysia and Indonesia. This does not bode well for future peace! Will a country of under ten million be able to hold back the wrath of a world population of 1.3 billion Muslims? I think not! A day of reckoning will soon be at hand.

Normal cowardly treatment of Palestinian children by members of the IDF

Whilst Palestine is an observer state at the United Nations General Assembly, it is still NOT recognised as a fully fledged sovereign state despite its recognition by the majority of countries around the world albeit 'those of arrogant and strutting self-importance'.

It isn't a full member state because the US, as Israel's ally, regularly blocks this from happening on the Security Council, the cur!

Further, the pledge by President Harry S Truman back in 1948 never mentioned a 'sovereign state' for the Palestinians!

[cf: The Kurds and the Palestinians are two examples of nations without their own status as states. No doubt there are many others!]

Currently, 136 of the 193 member states of the United Nations and two non-member states have recognized the 'State of Palestine' as a sovereign country providing further evidence that the Security Council should either be scrapped or undergo serious reform!

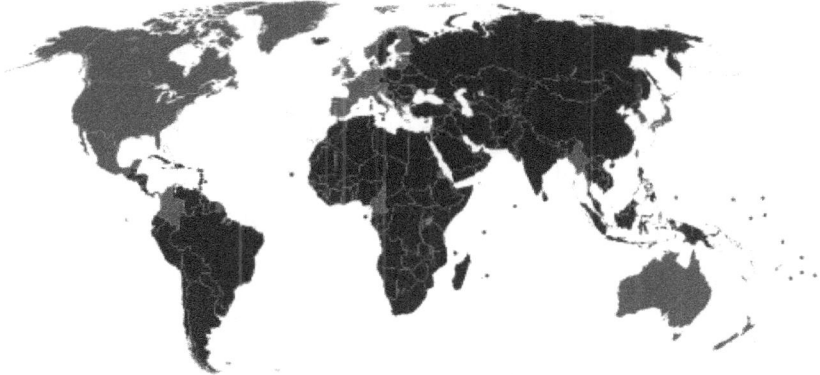

Map depicting countries that recognise the state of Palestine (in dark)

The author finds it disgraceful, sorry no, despicable, that Australia, Canada, New Zealand and the UK all have their bodies wagged by their individual tails sharply bitten by their master- the US! The main issues obstructing an agreement by Israel are borders, security, water rights, the status of Jerusalem and freedom of access to religious sites, ongoing Israeli settlement expansion, and legalities concerning Palestinian refugees including their right of return. This author has stated for years that **'a three state solution'** which falls back on the original declaration in 1948 of Jerusalem being an 'International Enclave' is the best solution. (Probably also the most appropriate place for the United Nations to operate from instead of New York!) But I fear that it might eventually be a 'single state' solution with millions of deaths in its formation! The pariah Israel will be the death of the world!

One might wonder why neither al-Qaeda nor IS have made attacks directly on Israel other than via Hamas and Hezbollah? (During the Second Intifada, Hamas perfected the suicide bomb and used it to kill hundreds of Israeli civilians). IDF strategists suggest that it is due to Israel's stated response culture:

'Israel must be seen as an unpredictable enemy that can react in a very severe and punishing way.'

The dozens of Israeli airstrikes in Syria (2017 and 2018) that Prime Minister Netanyahu acknowledged are calculated components of a strategy that reminds all adversaries of the cost of even minor violations of its rules. It was no accident that Israel reportedly killed a prominent Iranian general on the Syrian Golan Heights as he viewed the Israeli border. Nor was it coincidental that Israel reportedly killed Hezbollah operations officer Samir Kuntar. Prevention of terrorist attacks includes detection i.e deep penetration to identify threats, defence such as the Iron Dome missile-defence system and secure walls or fences on all borders; and decisive defeat. While many states invest heavily in similar efforts, Israel is unique in its placing deterrence at the core of its counterterrorism strategy. But many Jews the world over see this hammer strategy as a gross mistake and misjudgement!

The al-Qaeda terror group urged its followers the world over to target vital interests of the United States, its allies and Israel in response to US President Donald Trump's recognition of Jerusalem as Israel's capital.

April 2018: Palestinian scientist Fadi Mohammad al-Batsh was gunned down in Kuala Lumpur, Malaysia. His family claimed it was an assassination by Israel's Mossad spy agency. Israel described the dead Palestinian, a member of Islamist militant group Hamas, as being no saint and that he had been involved in rocket production. Al-Batsh, was an electrical engineering university lecturer, a devout family man and always held a smile for friends and students in the seven years since he moved to Malaysia from his native Gaza. Israel denies any involvement by Mossad. However the killing is consistent with Israel's policy of 'deep penetration' to deter terrorist attacks and gives a picture of how far-reaching the secret service tentacles pervade.

[Of course, Mossad is the unspoken adjunct to 'five eyes'.]

American and British Jews are not all supportive of the Israeli government's policies and actions. Some are embarrassed by the extreme measures and actions taken by the IDF and do not see a lasting peace from the road taken. At the other extreme, organisations such as Pamela Geller's AFDI churn out extreme hatred against all Muslims! And aggravating author's such as Australia's Peter Townsend that seek a charismatic path to castrate Islam and the Muslim faith! Whilst it is true that some Muslim leaders tacitly supported Hitler in WWII, many Muslims also fought against the Nazis alongside allied troops. Ms Geller should be reminded that the Holocaust was perpetrated by Caucasian Western, Central and Eastern Europeans, NOT by Muslims! In fact some Muslims were exterminated in the Balkans alongside Jews in the 1940s! [see Croation Ustashe horror extermination camps in the 1940s]

It is true that Palestinians supported Hitler. But also true, the Palestine Regiment was an infantry regiment of the British Army that was formed in 1942 with both Arab and Jewish volunteers (and some conscripts) in Mandatory Palestine. During the Second World War the regiment was deployed to Egypt and Cyrenaica. Some were killed in Benghazi where they fought heavy battles against the Germans.

It is this author's view that Muslim-Jew hatred, Jew-Muslim hatred, Jew-Jew hatred and Muslim-Muslim hatred have for decades all been seeded, orchestrated and fostered by Western interests for reasons known only to themselves, but being not too difficult to be guessed at or fathomed!

At the same time, a way forward for Palestine is not by violence from Hamas or Hezbollah but rather the full support of a 'Commonwealth of Islamic Nations'. The Arab League does not include many African or Asian states! Pressure brought to bear by such a world pan-Islamic organisation in the General Assembly of the United Nations and the International Criminal Court would legally assist their cause. Of course as the author has pleaded earlier and is a recurrent theme of this tome, reform of the Security Council is an absolute necessity!

... the black, green and gold !

Interesting that soon after the world abhorrence at the recent Gaza border deaths and injuries, media deflection was brought about by two terror incidents: firstly in Surabaya, Indonesia and secondly in Belgium. The Belgium attack had the hallmark of the 'Monas' attack in Sydney, Australia some years earlier. The gunman who killed at least three people in Liege, Belgium, May 29 2018, was a convicted criminal believed to have been radicalized behind bars but was let out on 'day leave' by the Belgium authorities! The newspapers said "... a prayer mat and Koran were found in his cell" ... why was that worth

reporting? The comparison is that in each circumstance the killer was known to have a criminal record and on the watch list as a potential terrorist. In each case the authorities "**let it all play out**" and also, at the conclusion, conveniently shot the perpetrator dead! In the Belgium event, the man was not of Arab descent but a local convert to Islam. As far as the world is concerned, it was an example of another ongoing brutal act by a Muslim on Western society. The author thinks that these particular events were orchestrated for political purposes by Western 'Secret Service Agencies', without specifically naming them!

And why Iran and Syria so love the murdering Russians is beyond comprehension? Their record against Muslims in Afghanistan and Chechnya is not that of a saint.. but then again, Muslims have been warring against Muslims in the Middle East and Asia for hundreds of years!

Revising those earlier figures regarding the Gaza border demonstrations in April/May 2018, the United Nations Office for the Coordination of

Humanitarian Affairs stated that 104 Palestinians were killed (12 of whom were children) and around 12 500 injured all by the Israeli Defence Force! It was reported that one Israeli soldier was injured. Taken together with years of brutal assaults on Palestinian families in the occupied territories (much now documented from testimonies from former IDF personnel), Israel has reached its bloodied Rubicon. Indeed, Israel has finally crossed 'a red line' and Prime Minister Netanyahu and Defence Minister Lieberman (along with senior Generals in IDF) should be answerable to International Law- no matter how long it takes! Daddy America and Mummy UK cannot continue legitimately or morally in their support for a reckless Child that is creating so much havoc and destruction to another people. As we have seen, no amount of soap and washing with water will clean away the blood stains from off the murderous hands of the King and Queen MacBeth!

... **too late for Israel ! Nurse Razan al Najjar murdered at the Gaza-Israel border fence by IDF June 2018.**

What a sad ending on the Gaza boundary at the end of May! An IDF sniper shot dead 21 year old medic Razan al Najjar while she was treating injured protesters. She would volunteer to treat the injured for many hours before going on to her shift at hospital. In the weeks that followed hundreds of unarmed Palestinians were murdered by IDF snipers along the border fence. Land grabs continue by Israel as it continues to oppress the Palestinians!

July 2018: The Israeli parliament has adopted a contentious new law defining Israel as the national home of the Jewish people, that opposition MPs warn is racist to the country's Arab minority and akin to 'apartheid'. Israel passed the controversial new 'nation-state laws' which sparked both celebration and fierce debate over the very nature of Israel. The laws have three extreme elements, namely:

1. It states that "the right to exercise national self-determination" in Israel is "unique to the Jewish people."

2. It establishes Hebrew as Israel's official language, and downgrades Arabic- a language widely spoken by Arab Israelis- to a "special status."

3. It establishes "Jewish settlement as a national value" and mandates that the state "will labour to encourage and promote its establishment and development."

Each of these statements is highly contentious and racist! Replace the word Israel with Germany and the word Jewish with Aryan and one sees an uncomfortable similarity! **It says everything about the human race!**

      "I was once oppressed by Nazis, but now, I is one!

      Come, let us sing together:

      Israel, Israel, über alles,

      Über alles in der Welt ….. "

If one were an Arab or liberal Jew living in Israel, the thought of leaving soon would be held most strongly in one's mind! After all, Israel has bombed: Iraq (Osirak) in 1981

Syria (Kibar) in 2007

and is threatening to do the same to Iran!

Response to email from US Holocaust Memorial Museum to Tom Law:

Hi USHMM,

In your last email you referred to the rise in hatred and anti-Semitism around the world. As a long time supporter I would like to comment on this. Whilst it is true that there are a lot of wars going on at the moment, particularly in the Middle East and Afghanistan, many Jews are concerned by the behavior of the Government of Israel and the IDF. We have had decades to arrive at a peaceful settlement on the Israel/Palestine issue but the current Government sees that spending immoral amounts of money on weapons and armaments will somehow solve the problem. It won't! Money would be better spent on bringing a feeling of permanence and a reasonable standard of living with opportunities for children and their future on both sides. If Israel continues to take the wrong road things will only continue to get worse for everyone! There needs to be a new and revolutionary paradigm to end the violence and waste of resources!

Tom Law   August 2018

Over the past decade, Israel has spent hundreds of billions of dollars on its total defence budget to include state of the art submarines with nuclear tipped missiles, jet fighters, cyber surveillance and attack systems plus all the usual weapons and war materials… and there is no end in sight to this!

Plight of Myanmar's Muslims

Aung San Suu Kyi winner of the Nobel Peace Prize in 1991 for her tenacious opposition to military rule in Myanmar, has been stigmatized worldwide for her failure to speak out or act against the brutal campaign waged by the Myanmar military and Buddhist religious community against the Muslim Rohingya minority in the poor state of Rakhine. She attempted to do her best with limited power in the fledgling and extremely volatile young democracy. In truth, after home arrest for decades, Aung San accepted a princess position to become merely a figurehead, a puppet on a string, where real power remained in the hands of the generals as it has done for more than fifty years.

Muslims have lived in Myanmar (Burma) since the 11th century AD. Massacres of Muslims occurred periodically by certain rulers over this period to the present day. The history of persecution of Muslims in Myanmar goes back hundreds of years. Myanmar is a Buddhist majority country with a significant Muslim minority. While Muslims served in the government of Prime Minister U Nu (1948–63), the situation changed with the 1962 Burmese coup d'état by the generals. Most Muslims were excluded from positions in the government and the armed forces. In 1982 the government introduced regulations that **denied citizenship** to anyone who could not prove Burmese ancestry from before 1823! This disenfranchised Muslims in Myanmar, even though they had lived in the country for many generations.

The long term plan was to create a 'final solution' of driving the Muslims from the country or face extermination- a classic example of genocide and ethnic cleansing!

Since 1948 successive governments carried out a dozen or more military operations against the Rohingya (in 1975, 1978, 1989, 1991, 1992, 2002). During these, security forces drove the Rohingya off their land, burned down their mosques and committed widespread looting, arson and rape of women and young girls. Frequently, Rohingya were subjected to theft and extortion from the authorities as well as forced labour. Land occupied by Rohingya Muslims was, on occasion, confiscated and reallocated to Buddhists.

Under British rule there were frequent riots and clashes between Burmese Buddhists and Muslims. Panglong, a Chinese Muslim town in British Burma, was entirely destroyed by the Japanese during the Japanese invasion of Burma in 1942. Also, 40 000 Rohingya fled after repeated massacres by both Burmese and Japanese forces at that time.

The anti-Buddhist actions of the Taliban in Afghanistan i.e the destruction of the Buddhas of Bamiyan, was also used as a pretext to commit violence against Muslims in Burma.

In 1997, in Mandalay and other centres, mosques were destroyed and Muslim owned businesses and property vandalized. Copies of the Qur'an were burnt. The military junta turned a blind eye to the disturbances; hundreds of monks were not stopped from participating in the terror attacks. On 15 May 2001 anti-Muslim riots broke out in Taungoo resulting in the deaths of about 200 Muslims. A dozen mosques were destroyed and more than 400 houses burnt to the ground. Some Muslims were beaten to death by the pro-junta forces.

Murders of Muslims in Rakhine state commenced in 2012. Since March 2013, riots flared up in various cities in central and eastern Myanmar which coincided with the rise of the 969 Movement- a Buddhist nationalist movement.

Enters the internet, July 2014: a Facebook post emerged of a Buddhist woman being raped by a Muslim man. In retaliation an angry mob of 300 people started a rampage against Muslims and Muslim property. In July 2016, Buddhist villagers of Hpakant in Kachin state set a mosque ablaze. Shortly after, a group of men destroyed a mosque in central Myanmar in a dispute over its construction (a not uncommon practice against Christian Churches in Indonesia- author).

Rohingya coming ashore at Bangladesh after fleeing Myanmar   **2017**

2016-2017: In retaliation to continuing violence against their communities, Rohingya militants attacked 31 police posts in the eastern part of the country, Rakhine state. A military response commenced with the burning of whole villages some 350 in all, with murder by shooting or cutting of the throat of men and boys, rape of women and girls, even the burning alive of some women and children by soldiers of the Myanmar military. This was a well planned response defined as 'clearance operations' by senior generals and politicians in the government. It was a sickening genocide by a dysfunctional and fake democratic government.

Deaths of Rohingya are estimated between 10 000 and 15000 persons, with some 900 000 persons fleeing to neighbouring Bangaladesh as refugees by the end of 2017. Close to 7 000 were murdered over the period August/September 2017 alone! Around 800 of these were children UNDER THE AGE OF FIVE!

The government and Aung San Suu Kyi continued to be in total denial of these horrific events, refusing entry of UN observers and journalists, with some journalists jailed for possessing anti-national sentiments! (i.e for photographing, telling and reporting the truth).

Stateless Persons: The Government of Myanmar claims that the Rohingya are illegal immigrants who arrived during the British colonial era, and were originally Bengalis (only a small number came from India during British rule). Those Rohingya that are allowed to stay in Myanmar are considered 'resident foreigners' and not citizens. Their movements are severely restricted and consequently they are forced to live in squatter camps and slums. The government of Myanmar has broken just about every civilised law and ruling created by the United Nations regarding Human Rights. Charged with the crime of genocide, several of the most powerful people in the country should reasonably be the subject of an international investigation and eventually brought to trial, HOWEVER LONG THIS TAKES! This includes military leaders as well as politicians. The United Nations has yet to declare whether the actions of the Myanmar military are specifically defined as an act of genocide!

The refugee camp in Bangladesh is the largest in the world as of April 2018. Due to the large population of Rohingya inhabiting such a small area, disease spread easily. In November 2017 diphtheria had killed nine Rohingya and infected about 700 others.

In November 2017 Myanmar and Bangladesh signed a memorandum of understanding for the return home of Rohingya refugees. In April 2018 the first group of Rohingya refugees returned to Myanmar from Bangladesh.

Small section of Bangladesh refugee camp for Rohingya people,   **2018**

The strain on Bangladesh is considerable as it is a high density country already and bearing a lot of poverty. Some Bangladeshis would prefer to see the Rohingya return to Myanmar. How the Buddhist country can overcome its prejudices and learn to live peacefully alongside Muslims is yet to be seen. But a general tolerance and exemplary behaviour from political, military and religious leaders is the key to the problem. Civil strife always leads to a waste of resources and economic downturn wherever it occurs!

ARSA: A recent report by Amnesty International points to war crimes committed also by the Arakan Rohingya Salvation Army fighters against Hindus and other ethnic communities with brutal attacks in 2017. A Rohingya armed group brandishing guns and swords was responsible for at least one and possibly a second massacre of up to 99 Hindu women, men, and children as well as additional unlawful killings and abductions of Hindu villagers in August 2017, Amnesty International revealed after carrying out a detailed investigation inside Myanmar's Rakhine State.

Rebuilding Program: It appears from satellite imagery that many of the cleared sites of previous Muslim villages have started to be rebuilt upon by Buddhist communities. Also, land previously farmed by the Rohingya has also been taken and used to rebuild or extend Buddhist villages. This trend is likely to greatly hinder any resettlement program promised by the central government in Nay Pyi Taw.

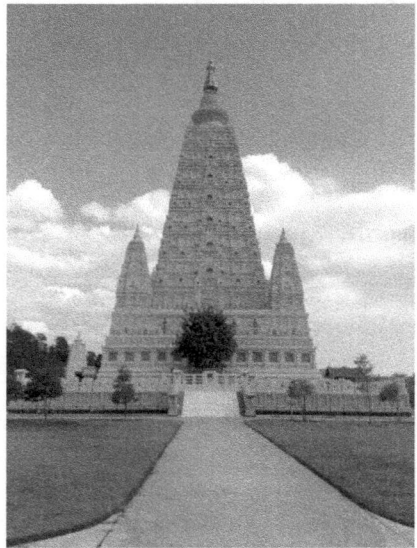

Buddha Gaya

Unwarranted Influence

Plight of the Kachin People, North Myanmar: Civil war and rapid development in the north has left many internally displaced people in this part of Myanmar, fearing they will never be able to return home.

In Kachin state, the military and rebels have been fighting for decades with accusations of land being confiscated and exploited by the government. In many cases villagers have been driven from their land which has been handed over to local and Chinese companies for development of resources.

Thousands of civilians have fled, but thousands more are trapped without supplies. An officer with the Kachin Independence Army said they would keep fighting as long as the Burmese keep coming at us.

This particular civil conflict goes back a long time, to the 1960s in fact, and while it has ebbed and flowed for years, recently it has intensified.

You take our resources and repay us with bombs!

When Myanmar gained its independence in 1948, its many ethnic groups were promised that they would later be able to break away and form their own lands. But that has not happened and ever since, several ethnic armies have fought against the Myanmar forces. Recently in Kachin state, the pressure has escalated with government forces using air strikes, artillery and small arms fire against villages. There has been little progress regarding peace talks, with some of the biggest ethnic groups, including the Kachin Independence Army, refusing to take part. It appears that, as with the similar plight of the Rohingya people, a revised constitution needs to be drawn up and a 'confederation of Burmese states' formed with some degree of autonomy in each state. Again, assistance from the UN is the only way forward. It is imperative

Kachin girls with guns made of wood!

that independence armies lay down their arms but with the central government recognizing land rights of these various ethnic groups. It is probable that the Chinese are there to exasperate these problems for self interest, offering no sensible solution… but happy to sell weapons and guns to all sides!

Two Reuters journalists were jailed for seven years after being tried by judges fearful of the army and consequential recriminations if they came up with anything less! The journalists had reported on murders of Rohingya by the Burmese army. A sad day for Aung San Suu Kyi !

Indonesia, Malaysia and the Philippines

Indonesia: After WWII the Dutch, assisted by the British, attempted a colonial come back to regain their power and influence over the country after the defeat and exit of the Japanese. But all was in vain as Indonesia saw its chance for freedom from its former master and commenced a guerrilla war. Tired from the world war the Dutch eventually capitulated and signed an agreement to hand power back to a new domestic government.

President Soekarno

The Republic of Indonesia first saw light on August 17, 1945 when its independence was proclaimed just days after the Japanese surrender to the Allies. Pancasila became the ideological and philosophical basis of the Republic, and on August 18, 1945 the Constitution was adopted as the basic law of the country. Soekarno became the first President and Chief Executive, and Mohammad Hatta the first Vice-President of the Republic. On September 5, 1945 the first cabinet was formed. On November 14 of the same year, the newly appointed Prime Minister, Sutan Syahrir, introduced a parliamentary system with party representation.

On December 22, Sutan Syahrir announced Indonesia's acceptance of the British proposal to disarm and confine to internment camps 25 000 Japanese troops throughout the country. This task was successfully carried out by TNI, the Indonesian National Army. Repatriation of the Japanese troops began on April 28, 1946.

Because fighting with Dutch troops continued, the seat of the Republican Government was moved from Jakarta to Yogyakarta on January 4, 1946.

Lieutenant Colonel Suharto led an all-out attack on the Dutch troops in Yogyakarta on March 1, 1949 and occupied the city for several hours. This offensive is recorded in Indonesia's history as 'the first of March all-out attack' to show to the world at the time that the Republic and its military were not dead.

Consequently, on May 7, 1949 an agreement was signed by Mohammad Roem of Indonesia and Van Rooyen of the Netherlands to end hostilities, restore the Republican Government in Yogyakarta and to hold further negotiations at a round table conference under the auspices of the United Nations.

The Round Table conference was opened in The Hague on August 23, 1949 under the auspices of the UN. It was concluded on November 2 with an agreement that Holland was to recognize the sovereignty of the Republic of Indonesia.

On December 27, 1949 the Dutch East Indies ceased to exist. It now became the sovereign Federal Republic of Indonesia with a federal constitution.

Despite constant troubles with both Dutch and Islamic Indonesians in the early years of the Republic, the country settled down.

A War Crime: during the rule by President Soekarno the communist party of Indonesia, PKI, had grown and certain politicians and army heads were becoming nervous of the situation (along with the CIA and Western nations). In October 1965 a group of Indonesian

Unwarranted Influence

Army officers kidnapped and brutally murdered six army generals as part of a planned coup. The murdered generals were labelled to be pro PKI, but this was grossly untrue. Under the direction of General Suharto, what followed was a purge and massacre of close to one million people, presumably with connections to the communist party. Many Chinese business people were murdered on this pretext with their property either destroyed or confiscated. In later years it was stated that the CIA supplied lists of names for Suharto's assassination squads. The pro-communist attempted coup was also CIA inspired (see later chapter: 'Seeding Wars'). At the time, Western media, particularly in Britain and America, participated in a whitewash of the massacre. Soekarno was removed from power in 1967 and replaced by Suharto whom was immediately offered economic aid from the West.

Suharto was lauded as the saviour of Indonesia having done what was best for the country. But this included the granting of lucrative concessions to western mining and oil companies. For 32 year he held an iron grip on the country and described by some as one of the most corrupt dictators of the 20th century. However, he will remain in history as an enigmatic figure in the sculpturing of modern Indonesia.

President Suharto

Malaysia: The Japanese Imperial Forces occupied Malaya and Borneo from 1941 until the surrender in 1945. The Malayan Emergency (*Darurat Malaya*) was a guerrilla war fought in the pre- and post-independent Federation of Malaya, from 1948 until 1960. The belligerents were the British Commonwealth armed forces against the Malayan National Liberation Army (MNLA), the military arm of the Malayan Communist Party. Despite the ending of violence in 1960, communist leader Chin Peng renewed the insurgency against the Malaysian government in 1967. This second phase of the insurgency lasted until 1989, after which he fled to Thailand where he lived until his death in 2013.

The first shots of the Malayan Emergency were fired at 8.30 am on 16 June 1948, in the office of the Elphil Estate twenty miles east of the Sungai Siput town, Perak. Three European plantation managers were killed by three young Chinese men. The Malayan Communist Party (MCP) was outlawed and the police were given the power to detain communists and those suspected of assisting them. The MCP, led by Chin Peng retreated to

Chin Peng

rural areas and formed the MNLA in January, 1949. The communists employed guerrilla tactics, sabotaging installations, attacking rubber plantations and destroying transportation. The MNLA gained the support of the Chinese because they were denied equal rights to vote, had no land rights and were usually very poor.

In April 1950, General Sir Harold Briggs, the British Army's Director of Operations was appointed to Malaya. Briggs' plan was multifaceted, which included the forced relocation of some 500 000 rural Malayans, including 400 000 Chinese from squatter communities on the fringes of the forests into guarded camps called 'new villages'. The villages were newly constructed and surrounded by barbed wire, police posts and floodlit areas. Sir Robert Grainger Ker Thompson applying his vast experience in civil-military relations, was one of the chief architects of the counter-insurgency plan. After the assassination of High Commissioner Sir Henry Gurney in October 1951, General Gerald Templer was appointed as his replacement. Templer changed the situation in the Emergency and his actions and policies were a major part of British success under his command. Finally, the conflict involved a maximum of 40 000 British and Commonwealth troops (Australian, New Zealand, Fijian, Nyasaland and Rhodesians) against a peak of about 8 000 communist guerrillas.

With the independence of Malaya under Prime Minister Tunku Abdul Rahman in August 1957, the communists lost their stance as a war against colonialism. MRLA guerrillas surrendered in the Telok Anson marsh area in 1958, with some fleeing to the Thai border and further east. On 31 July 1960 the Malayan government declared the state of emergency over. [The new name Malaysia was adopted in 1963]

Lincoln Bomber Crew

War Crimes: In the 'Batang Kali massacre', 24 villagers were killed by 7th Platoon, G Company, 2nd Scots Guards, after they surrounded a rubber plantation at Sungai Rimoh near Batang Kali in Selangor in

December 1948. Many of the victims' bodies were found to have been mutilated and their village of Batang Kali was burned to the ground.

Dozens of other villages were burned around this time.

British troops cut off the heads of deceased communist guerrillas; the reason given that it was easier to transport them out from the jungle for identification.

Some civilians and detainees were executed by shooting.

Tens of thousands of homes were destroyed and many people were interned in guarded camps called 'new villages' but were characteristic of concentration camps.

During the Malayan Emergency, Britain was the first nation to employ the use of herbicides and defoliants to destroy bushes, food crops, and trees with chemical agents such as 2,4,5-T; 2,4-D and trioxone.

Widespread saturation bombardment was used by the Royal Air Force throughout the conflict in Malaya. Britain conducted 4 500 air strikes in the first five years of the Malayan war. During the twelve year conflict it was estimated that close to 1 000 non-combatants were killed by bombing.

Sir Henry Wells inspects Australian troops in Malaya   **1956**

Unwarranted Influence

No charges have ever been brought against a member of the British forces that participated in the war.

Communist Intimidation: The Communist guerrillas lived in close proximity to villagers and were not afraid to threaten violence or torture and even murdered village leaders as an example to others, forcing them to assist with food and information.

The communists were reluctant to take and keep prisoners. Thus many soldiers and civilians just disappeared.

Casualties of the Malay War:

British Commonwealth	Communist	
Killed: 1 346 Malayan troops and police 519 British and Commonwealth military personnel Wounded: 2 406 Malayan and British troops/police	Killed: 6 710 Wounded: 1 289 Captured: 1 287 Surrendered: 2 702	
Civilian casualties: 2 478 killed, 810 missing		

The Philippines: With the arrival in 1521 of explorer Ferdinand Magellan sailing from Spain, marked the beginning of the Philippines

as a colony of the Spanish Empire and ending with the outbreak of the Spanish-American War of 1898. This was the start of the American colonial era of the Philippines. The initial contact saw the death of Magellan and many local tribes' people.

Las Islas Filipinas was name after Philip II of

Spain. A Spanish expedition of 500 men led by Miguel López de Legazpi arrived off Cebu on February 1565, conquering it despite some Cebuano opposition. Over succeeding years, more settlements followed. The archipelago was Spain's outpost in the orient and Manila became the capital of the entire Spanish East Indies. The colony was administered through the Viceroyalty of New Spain (Mexico) until 1821 when Mexico achieved independence, after which the colony was governed directly from Spain.

During Spain's 333 year rule over the Philippines, the colonists fought off Chinese pirates, Dutch forces, Portuguese forces, Japanese and the British plus putting down various indigenous revolts. Muslims from western Mindanao and the Sulu Archipelago also raided the coastal Christian areas of Luzon and the Visayas, capturing men and women for slaves. Roman Catholicism was imposed on the natives and many cathedrals and churches were built.

In the nineteenth century there were uprisings as Philippine nationalism took grip. The response brought about the mass deportation of nationalists to the Marianas and Europe in 1872. By 1893 there were 35 Masonic lodges in the Philippines, of which nine were in Manila. The first Filipina freemason was Rosario Villaruel. Freemasonry was important during the time of the Philippine Revolution; it aided the reform movement and carried out propaganda work. The 'Cry of Balintawak' or 'Cry of Pugad Lawin' were terms meaning revolution. Leaders were executed by the colonial authority for treason. Andrés Bonifacio, the father of the revolution,

Andrés Bonifacio

called for a general offensive on Manila and was defeated in battle at the town of San Juan del Monte. He regrouped his forces and was able briefly to capture the towns of Marikina, San Mateo and Montalban. Spanish counter-attacks drove him back and he retreated to the mountains of Balara and Morong from which he engaged in guerrilla warfare. By August 30, 1896 the revolt had spread to eight provinces. Governor General Ramon Blanco declared a state of war in these provinces and placed them under martial law. These were Manila, Bulacan, Cavite, Pampanga, Tarlac, Laguna, Batangas, and Nueva Ecija. They would later be represented in the eight rays of the sun in the Filipino flag.

After defeat and capture, Bonifacio was tried and executed for treason in May 1897.

In April 1898, the Spanish-American War began. On May 1 in the Battle of Manila Bay, a naval force led by Commodore George Dewey aboard the *USS Olympia* decisively defeated the Spanish naval forces in the Philippines. With the loss of control of Manila Bay, Spain lost the ability to defend Manila and the Philippines as a whole. At the Treaty of Paris in 1898, the United States purchased the Philippines from Spain for $20 million.

The following year in February, the Philippine-American War began with the Battle of Manila between American forces and the newly born Philippine Republic. The Philippines did not achieve independence from the United States until after the end of WWII on July 4, 1946. Manuel Roxas became the first president of the new republic.

Japanese War Crimes in the Philippines during the Occupation: The landing of the main Japanese forces on December 22, 1941, at Lingayen Bay, west of central Luzon, coordinated with the landings of three detachments at north and south eastern approaches to Luzon Island. From there, the Japanese made a swift advance notwithstanding stiff resistance from US and Philippine forces, reaching the outskirts of Manila by January 1, 1942.

The Battle of Bataan began January 7, 1942 and continued until April 9, when the US commander, Major General Edward King, Jr., surrendered to Col. Mootoo Nakayama of the 14th Japanese Army. The Battle of Bataan proved to be arduous and long with total Japanese casualties of the first Bataan campaign amounting to 2 700 deaths, 4 050 injured, and 15 500 sick cases suffering mainly from dysentery and malaria.

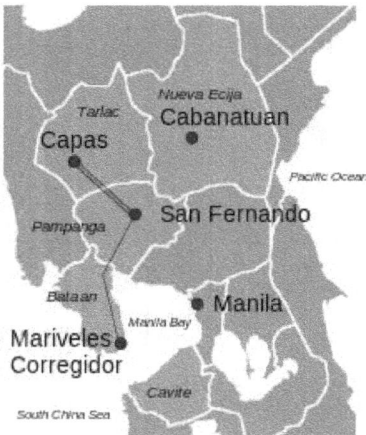

The Bataan Death March in April 1942 was the forcible transfer by the Imperial Japanese Army of about 60 000 Filipino and American prisoners of war together with another 40 000 civilian refugees from Mariveles, Bataam to Camp O'Donnell, Capas in Tarlac. The transfer began after the three month Battle of Bataan. The total distance marched was just over 100 km. During the forced march estimates include up to 18 000 Filipino deaths and around 600 American deaths due to severe physical abuse and wanton killings.

The Manila massacre involved atrocities committed against civilians in Manila, the capital of the Philippines, by Japanese troops at the Battle of Manila February 3 to March 3, 1945. The combined death toll of civilians for the battle of Manila was about 100 000. The Japanese commanding general, Tomoyuki Yamashita, and his chief of staff Akira Mutō, were held responsible for the massacre.

The United States Army advanced into the city of Manila in order to drive the Japanese out. Japanese troops took their anger and frustration out on the civilians in the city. Violent mutilations, rapes, and massacres occurred in schools, hospitals and convents, including San Juan de Dios Hospital, Santa Rosa College, Santo Domingo Church, Manila Cathedral, Paco Church, St. Paul's Convent, and St. Vincent de Paul Church. In one scenario, only 50 out of more than 3 000 men that were herded into Fort Santiago survived a massacre. At a hotel, women and girls, many of them 12 to 14 years old, were raped by Japanese enlisted men and officers.

In Tokyo, January 1946, the International Military Tribunal for the Far East (IMTFE) began prosecuting major Japanese war criminals. The US military commission tried, convicted and sentenced to death Honma and Yamashita on charges of war crimes (1945-1946), while Kuroda was tried, convicted and sentence to life in prison similarly on charges of war crimes by the Philippine military commission (1948-1949). General Tanaka Shizuichi, who commanded the 14th Army committed suicide at the end of the war thus avoiding any trial.

Contemporary Conflicts in the Philippines:

The Philippine Drug War: refers to the drug policy of the Philippine government under President Rodrigo Duterte. It has been criticized locally and internationally for the number of deaths resulting from police operations and summary executions but supported by the majority of the local population as well as leaders of China, Japan and the United States. In January 2018, estimates of the death toll reached up to 20 000, mostly urban slum dwellers. In February 2018 the International

Rodrigo Duterte

Criminal Court in The Hague announced a 'preliminary examination' into killings linked to the Philippine government since July 1, 2016. Participants of the killings are said to have included: The Communist Party of the Philippines, the Moro National Liberation Front (an Islamic group), vigilantes and hired hitmen. **However, the National Police and the Philippine Armed Forces played a significant role.** Those leaders responsible include President Rodrigo Duterte, Oscar Albayalde, Aaron Aquino and Chiefs of Staff of the Armed Forces: General Ricardo Visaya, General Eduardo Ano, General Rey Leonardo Guerrero and General Carlito Galvez Jnr.

After winning the 2016 Philippine presidential elections Duterte promised to kill tens of thousands of criminals and urged people to kill them along with drug addicts. Earlier, when Mayor of Davao City, Duterte was criticized by groups like Human Rights Watch for the extrajudicial killings of hundreds of street children, petty criminals and drug users carried out by the 'Davao Death Squad', a vigilante group.

At the 2016 ASEAN Summit, US President Barack Obama cancelled a meeting with Duterte after Duterte referred to Obama

Ukraine murders of Jews by the SS, 1945

as a 'son of a whore'. Late in 2016 Duterte compared himself to Adolf

256

Hitler and the killing of the Jews! Not a bad description seeing that a dozen or more special police squads had been authorized to continue with unlawful killings similar to that committed by the notorious SS Einsatzgruppen death squads of Nazi Germany!

Soco investigate a 'Death Squad' murder of drug suspects, Manilla 2016

Duterte had named dozens of persons suspected of being part of the drug trade, including local politicians, police, judges and military personnel. He even went so far as to say that 'human rights defenders' should also be targeted! In February 2017 a retired police officer told reporters at a press conference that as a leader of a Davao Death Squad, he had carried out extrajudicial killings on the orders of Duterte. He said death squad members were paid between 20 000 and 100 000 pesos per hit. He also confessed to his involvement in the bombing of a mosque on Duterte's orders.

In March 2017, former police officer Arturo Lascanas gave evidence to a Senate committee testifying that he had killed approximately 200 criminal suspects, media figures and political opponents on Duterte's orders. Further evidence that a proportion of the killings were part of

Duterte's plan to consolidate 'absolute power' in the country through fear, intimidation and murder of perceived opponents!

Duterte rebuffed criticism from Europe with the response that European nations had murdered thousands during their colonial past. Thus he was giving himself a pardon. Also in 2017, Duterte 'pledged to kill another 20 000 to 30 000 of his own people, many simply because they suffer from a drug use disorder.'

In February 2018, the ICC announced a preliminary examination into killings linked to the Philippine government's war on drugs. Prosecutor Fatou Bensouda said the court will analyze crimes allegedly committed since at least 1 July 2016! There is no doubt that the Philippines had, and still has, an extreme societal problem with drugs. However the measures taken by the Duterte government have brought about the murder of thousands of innocents, not just the drug lords and gangsters alone. Without the due process of law, a society soon falls into the abyss of uncivilised chaos. This author advises Mr Duterte to have his toothbrush and overnight bag packed and ready for an imminent trip to the Netherlands!

Islamic Extremism 2017: in Marawi the nightmare is over. The city lies in the South of the Philippines, the capital of the province of Lanao del Sur, on the island of Mindanao. It was occupied by Islamic Jihadists from May 2017 and finally liberated by the regular army. It took 148 days of siege carried out with aerial bombardments, to finally drive out more than 800 militants. The urban guerrilla warfare was fought with the aid of more than seven thousand military personnel.

Filipino President Rodrigo Duterte confirmed the liberation and thanked soldiers for their strenuous effort against Jihadist terrorism. The conflict left over one thousand dead: 163 soldiers, 822 militants plus 47 civilians.

Muslims have lived in the Philippines for hundreds of years. In fact, before the coming of the Spanish bringing Christianity, it was divided into sets of Kingdoms, Rajahnates and Sultanates. Some were part of a larger Empire outside of modern day boundaries of the Philippines. For example, Manila was once part of the Bruneian Empire. Another example is that Mindanao was thought to have been part of the Majapahit Empire with its capital located in East Java. Unfortunately most written records no longer exist as zealous Spanish Christian missionaries burnt whole libraries of documents as they considered them to be pagan.

In 1380, Makhdum Karim, the first Islamic missionary to the Philippines brought Islam to the Archipelago. Subsequent visits of Arab, Malay and Javanese missionaries helped strengthen the Islamic faith of the Filipinos. The Sultanate of Sulu, the largest Islamic kingdom in the islands, encompassed parts of Indonesia, Malaysia and the Philippines. The royal house of the Sultanate claim descent from Muhammad.

Around 1405, the year that the war over succession ended in the Majapahit Empire, Muslim traders introduced Islam into the Hindu-Malayan empires and for about the next century the southern half of Luzon and the islands south of it were subject to the various Muslim sultanates of Borneo.

Around the year 1500, the Sultanate of Brunei under Sultan Bolkiah attacked the Kingdom of Tondo and established a city with the Malay name of Selurong, later to become the city of Maynila. The traditional Rajahs of Tondo, the Lakandula, retained their titles and property but the real political power came to reside in the House of Soliman, the Rajahs of Manila.

MILF: The Moro Islamic Liberation Front is a group based in Mindanao seeking an autonomous region for the Moro people from the central government. The group has a presence in the Bangsamoro region of Mindanao, the Sulu Archipelago, Palawan, Basilan, and other neighbouring islands. Tensions between Moros and Christians were caused by disputes about land ownership and disenfranchisement of Muslims following the Government's 'Homestead Program' where Christians took up land in Bangsamoro

map of Southern Philippines showing close proximity to Indonesia

region. The MILF took part in terrorist attacks and assassinations to achieve their goals. The government in Manila sent troops into the southern Philippines to control the insurgency. In 1976, Libyan leader Muammar Gaddafi brokered a negotiation between the Philippine government and MILF Leader Nur Misuari which led to the signing of the MNLF-GRPH Tripoli Agreement of 1976 wherein the MILF accepted the Philippine government's offer of semi-autonomy of the regions in dispute. It wasn't until November 1990 that an agreement was offered on the establishment of the Autonomous Region of Muslim Mindanao. But it was rejected by MILF. Violence and killings continued on and off for many years with no permanent agreement. On October 7, 2012, President Benigno Aquino announced a peace deal with the MILF for a final and enduring peace in Mindanao, calling for the creation of the new Muslim autonomous entity called 'Bangsamoro'. Then in 2013, the Nur Misuari faction declared independence for the Bangsamoro Republik and attacked Zamboanga City. Other factions with more extreme demands emerged with the advent of foreign fighters coming to the Southern Philippines to fight against the Philippine Armed Forces ending with the Battle of Marawi in June 2017. Whether Muslims and Christians can live together peacefully in Mindanao remains to be seen.

Drake Equation

$$N = R^* \cdot f_p \cdot n_e \cdot f_l \cdot f_i \cdot f_c \cdot L$$

N = The number of civilizations in the Milky Way galaxy whose electromagnetic emissions are detectable.

R^* = The rate of formation of stars suitable for the development of intelligent life.

f_p = The fraction of those stars with planetary systems.

n_e = The number of planets, per solar system, with an environment suitable for life.

f_l = The fraction of suitable planets on which life actually appears.

f_i = The fraction of life bearing planets on which intelligent life emerges.

f_c = The fraction of civilizations that develop a technology that releases detectable signs of their existence into space.

L = The length of time such civilizations release detectable signals into space.

Astronomers now believe that most stars have at least one planet!

Seeding Wars

WWII: Whilst it is not the case that American government policy during the 1930s was to promote a war in Europe, it is however sadly true that many American registered companies provided materials and technology by which the Nazis benefited and thus contributed to Germany's war effort. Coca Cola continued to sell its product and even collected its war time earnings after the war. Banks including Chase Manhattan, JP Morgan and CitiBank were involved in the freezing of Jewish accounts in Paris. Alcoa and Dow supplied chemicals and materials which Germany made use of to build its various war machines. Henry Ford had written an anti-semitic book which took as authentic the fake 'Protocols of Zion' and warned against Jews. Woolworths were said to have fired all its Jewish employees. The private bank Brown Brothers Harriman during the 1930s acted as a US base for the German industrialist Fritz Thyssen, who helped finance Adolf Hitler. General Motors retained its plant in Berlin, supplied rubber and manufactured trucks for the German Army. Lastly, International Business Machines provided its punch card machines in Holland which were used in 1941 to store data on Dutch Jews to be exterminated.

Many of these companies retrieved profits made at the end of WWII! At that time in the US, complicity in crimes against humanity were subject to a 'statute of limitation' which permitted companies that profited from 'both sides' of the war from escaping prosecution!

The Falklands: From the mid 1970s to April 1982, Argentina was experiencing a crackdown on unions and the left wing among its peoples with thousands imprisoned and thousands more having disappeared, presumed murdered under the Peron dictatorships and later by the military regime under General Galtieri. Galtieri had reason to believe the super powers would support or at worst remain neutral if Argentina seized the Falkland Islands. He had assumed the presidency under extremely good relations with the United States. The Reagan administration was particularly pleased with Galtieri's strong anti-communist stand. Galtieri also enjoyed favourable relations with Moscow. The Soviets had reason to be grateful for Argentine grain shipments during the American grain embargo imposed during the Carter administration. The Junta decided to begin, 'prioritizing the Islas Malvinas issue' (in reference to the Falkland Islands)

General Galtieri

firstly to create unity and solidarity among the Junta and secondly to divert attention of the public away from the contracting economy and towards, 'a national symbol shared by nearly all segments of society.' The ruling party thought the use of an external 'scapegoat' was the perfect antidote to the growing dissatisfaction of the people i.e actions undertaken for the purpose of enhancing internal political support. Just a week after massive labour demonstrations against the regime, people took to the streets this time in enthusiastic support for the invasion.

With the withdrawal of the icebreaker HMS Endurance, British Foreign Secretary Lord Carrington said the vessel "plays a vital role in both political and defence terms in the Falkland Islands and dependencies. Such action would be interpreted by the Argentines as a reduction in our commitment to the islands and in our willingness to defend them."

At the time, Britain appeared to lack any commitment to the region; it was even muted an effort to promote a negotiated settlement with Argentina might be possible. This is baffling in view of the fact that when Argentina invaded, the British government's response was quick and decisive with Prime Minister Margaret Thatcher declaring: 'the Falkland Islands and their dependencies remain British territory'. The cost of backing away was now untenable to the Argentine government; Galtieri said, "he would not last a week if he withdrew from the Malvinas". The United Kingdom and Argentina were the only major participants in the conflict; however some satellite intelligence was relayed from America.

Casualties and losses:

Britain	Argentina
	649 killed
255 killed	1,657 wounded
775 wounded	11,313 POWs
115 POW	
	1 cruiser
2 destroyers	1 submarine
2 frigates	4 cargo vessels
1 LSL ship	2 patrol boats
1 LCU craft	1 spy trawler
1 container ship	
	25 helicopters
24 helicopters	35 fighters
10 fighters	2 bombers
1 bomber	4 cargo aircraft
	25 COIN aircraft
	9 armed trainers

Questions the author asks here are these:

1. Were their secret communiqués between Washington and Buenos Aires just prior to the invasion?

2. Was Galtiere either (i) misled by the Americans or (ii) even encouraged by providing the knowledge that they would 'do nothing' in the event of an invasion?

3. Was the British Government and leaders of the British Armed Forces 'in the know' of an imminent invasion and 'just let it happen'?

4. Were their secret communiqués between Washington and London just prior to the invasion?

5. Were there definite political advantages for Mrs Thatcher and the Tory Party for the war to go ahead in the confidence that it would be easily won with minimal cost?

6. Did both Argentina and Britain speculate on potential oil and gas reserves in the South Atlantic as the true prize of the war?

Certainly there were circumstances in Britain making the early Thatcher years uncomfortable. At the end of 1981, union membership was at an all time high: in excess of 13 million workers. Unemployment was above 10% (not seen since the Great Depression) and rising, inflation was still above

Margaret Thatcher

10% with interest rates around 13.5%. After the war, things only got worse for the British people with mean house prices rising from £23 500 in Jan 1981 to £184 000 by end 2007! Poverty increased dramatically: in 1979, 13.4% of the population lived below 60% of median incomes before housing costs. By 1990, this had risen to 22.2%.

Despite these, the war definitely gave Ms Thatcher's Conservative government a huge boost at the June 1983 general election, providing a 144 seat majority in the House of Commons:

1979 (MPs) 3 May 1979   Margaret Thatcher   Conservative   43 majority

1983 (MPs) 9 June 1983   Margaret Thatcher Conservative 144 majority

1987 (MPs) 11 June 1987 Margaret   Thatcher Conservative 102 majority

Iran-Iraq War: The causes and beginnings of this war in 1980 have been thinly described earlier. The peripheral details of the rewards to the 'spectator West' and other countries has not been mentioned. At the time, Iraq was producing squillions of barrels of oil and billions of dollars in revenue were rolling into the country. Did the government spend this wisely on schools, hospitals, infrastructure and glittering megacities for the benefit of its people? NO! Instead it went on a huge spending spree on weapons, armaments, missiles, jet fighters, tanks etc. which many countries East and West were glad to provide to balance their books from the cost of oil imports. Iran was still going through its religious revolution but never the less still earned billions from its healthy oil sales. But the worst aspect of this war was that it was permitted to go on for nearly eight years with countries selling more armaments to fuel it and of course make huge profits. Many countries sold their vile wares TO BOTH SIDES! This paints a most despicable picture of the international conglomerates and players in the arms industries around the world. THEY HAVE NO MORALS WITH PROFIT COMING AHEAD OF HUMANITARIAN PRINCIPLES. They need to be dismantled. They ought to be severely punished. The author points to some of the bigger corporations in the next chapter. You might like to go back and review the appalling human cost of this war to both sides in an earlier chapter!

Iraq Invasion of Kuwait: The Iraqi arguments for the invasion have already been stated earlier. One significant piece of information was the suggestion that Washington had given Baghdad the 'green light' with the inference that it would turn a blind eye to the invasion. This cannot be proven without access to relevant documents and communiqués from that time. However, despite Iraq's massive army and stockpile of weapons, there is no doubt that the coalition force assembled to oust Saddam Hussein from Kuwait had every confidence that it could do so without great loss to its combat forces. It provided an opportunity to demonstrate American (plus NATO allies) prowess in war as well as test both armaments and stratagems with such a combined force. In the build-up to the invasion, Iraq and Kuwait had been producing a combined 4.3 million barrels of oil a day. The potential loss of these supplies, coupled with threats to Saudi Arabian oil production, led to a rise in price from $21 per barrel at the end of July 1990 to $28 per barrel by August 6. On the heels of the invasion, 2nd August 1990, prices rose to a peak of $46 per barrel by mid October. It took some years before the two countries' oil production rose to pre-war levels, giving advantage to other oil producers and the OPEC countries with both supply and the higher price! The author again asks questions:

1. Did Western intelligence know of an impending invasion by Iraq into Kuwait?
2. If yes, then could this invasion easily have been prevented?
3. Which countries benefited from the invasion and consequent drastic reduction in both Iraqi and Kuwait oil production?
4. Despite its debts, did not Iraq again build up its armaments and weapons through further purchases of such from eager suppliers from EVERYWHERE!
5. Was the true reason for the later US led invasion of Iraq to continue to benefit these other oil producing countries (as well as international arms corporations)?
6. Was Islamic State a further invention of the West for the same reason: to benefit other oil producing countries?
7. Has there been a vicious and continual ploy by the state of Israel to maintain infighting and chaos amongst neighbouring Arab nations as part of its own guaranteed survival?

The author sees parallels between both the Falklands invasion and the Kuwait invasion where there were domestic benefits to be had by the conquering participants!

Whilst focusing on oil, making matters worse for Venezuela, the US (the Latin American country's biggest oil customer) threatened to impose an embargo on its crude exports in April 2018. However, for other oil exporters around the world, including fellow members of OPEC, the crisis in Venezuela's oil sector was seen as good news as they could produce more without leading to a drop in the market price! But when a recalcitrant nation (read as socialist state) fails to play ball with the US, it activates its various branches to rein them in: the intelligence agencies, the NGOs, the assassins and, if all else fails, the US military. The opposition party has one goal: privatize state assets, especially petroleum and gas, then hand them over to international (mainly US) corporations to be exploited at no benefit for the Venezuelan people! The CIA eventually admitted its deep involvement in Chile in the 1970s to replace socialist President Allende with Augusto Pinochet. Slush money was used to encourage the fascists (Contras) to destabilise the country through propaganda, terror and even murder. By August 2018, thousands of Venezualian citizens have left their native home due to economic collapse. Has it been fostered and engineered?

In her book 'A Problem from Hell' America and the Age of Genocide, Samantha Power describes the intransigency of the government with regard to a whole gamut of horrific events during the latter half of the twentieth century. This indifference did not extend to the evil moguls in the weapons industries of America, China, Russia Great Britain or many other European nations who made tidy profits from the misery of millions! Whilst brave and notable persons exposed 'ethnic cleansing' in various hot spots, the majority of American politicians chose to do nothing! The court at The Hague was seen to be a nuisance and in fact in 1995 the US at first opposed the formation of the International Criminal Court!

War Crimes not dealt with in this book include:

Burundi
Rhawanda
Congo
Nigeria
Kurds in Turkey.

Unwarranted Influence

One Slip of Logic

Like many, the author was intrigued by the mystery over the disappearance of Malaysian flight MH 370 on 8th March 2014 on a flight from Kuala Lumpur in Malaysia to Beijing in China. Many theories were put forward for this disappearance including fire, suicide, terrorist hijacking, loss of oxygen and missile strike either deliberately or by accident due to mistaken identity. The one thing that nags at the mind is the following sequence of events:

8th March 2014:	disappearance of Malaysian flight MH 370 on a flight from Kuala Lumpur to Beijing
17th July 2014:	shooting down of Malaysian flight M 17 by a Russian made Buk missile over Eastern Ukraine on a flight from Amsterdam to Kuala Lumpur
15th Oct 2015:	Russian plane crash: Kogalymavia flight 7K9268 crashed in Egypt on a flight from Sharm El-Sheikh to St. Petersburg.
4th March 2018:	Sergei Skripal, a former Russian military officer and double agent for UK intelligence services, and his daughter Yulia Skripal were poisoned in Salisbury, England, with a Novichok nerve agent.
30th June 2018:	A similar poisoning of two British nationals in Amesbury, seven miles from Salisbury, involved the same nerve agent. A man found the nerve agent in a perfume bottle and gave it to a woman who sprayed it on her wrist.The woman, Dawn Sturgess, fell ill within 15 minutes and died on 8 July.

There were no survivors of disasters two and three, and as far as we know, no one survived the disappearance! Now, one does not wish to be a scare monger or drift off into wild fantasies of conspiracies without any evidence. However, it is a definite uncomfortable feeling that somehow these three air disasters may have been related and fell like predictable dominoes after an initial push! The Russians have always denied any involvement in the Ukraine crash.

Islamic State group's affiliate in Egypt claimed it was responsible for the crash of the Russian plane. Charlie Winter, a London-based extremism researcher said that any militants operating in the region where the plane went down would not have had a weapon capable of hitting the plane at its projected altitude of 31 000 ft (10 000 metre). The author, to avoid legal or physical threats to his person, will continue and expand in hypotheticals:

It was discovered by intelligence gathering of the secret service of Nation I (with some assistance from Nations A and U) that Nation M was harbouring extremists from its close enemy, Nation P. Further, that the extremists were to hijack a commercial aircraft on which a large bomb had been installed with the intention of releasing such or crashing into the prime city of Nation I. Having a submarine in the Indian Ocean at the time, a missile was launched to bring down the commercial plane. Later, by the same intelligence sources, a repeat attempt was to be made by another commercial plane belonging to the same Nation M. This attempt was also thwarted again by a missile from a submarine either in the Red Sea or in the Eastern Mediterranean. Not being totally aware of the true nature of these events, Nations U and H organized a bomb on commercial flight of Nation R as a retaliatory measure but, due to false intelligence, not against the true culprit! To further assist in a deteriorating relationship between Nation R and Nations U and B, a poison was used inside Nation B by Nation I but with a trail indicating Nation R as the culprit!

Of course this is all supposition but illustrates the possibility of a major conflict between superpowers e.g Russia and NATO being ignited on the premise of perhaps an accident coupled with misinformation or incorrect analysis of some event. Thus it is possible that some random event, possibly innocent, due to human error or a system failure, might spark a major conflict threatening the survival of the whole of humanity!

Soldiers of Conscience: Edward Snowden and Julian Assange

Matthew 24:21-24   King James

For then shall be great tribulation, such as was not since the beginning of the world to this time, no, nor ever shall be.

And except those days should be shortened, there should no flesh be saved: but for the elect's sake those days shall be shortened.

Then if any man shall say unto you, Lo, here is Christ, or there; believe it not.

For there shall arise false Christs, and false prophets, and shall shew great signs and wonders; in so much that, if it were possible, they shall deceive the very elect.

War Industries East and West

"In the councils of government, we must guard against the acquisition of unwarranted influence, whether sought or unsought, by the military-industrial complex. The potential for the disastrous rise of misplaced power exists and will persist. We must never let the weight of this combination endanger our liberties or democratic processes. We should take nothing for granted. Only an alert and knowledgeable citizenry can compel the proper meshing of the huge industrial and military machinery of defense with our peaceful methods and goals, so that security and liberty may prosper together."

President Dwight Eisenhower, 'Farewell Address to the Nation', January 17, 1961.

In an ever more dangerous world, revenue from arms and military services at the world's 100 largest defence contractors totalled $374.8 billion in 2016, a 1.9% increase from the previous year according to the Stockholm International Peace Research Institute (SIPRI).

Unwarranted Influence

The author thinks it a false premise that maintaining state-of-the-art arsenals can act as a deterrent against aggressors.. history has not shown this! Feeling that superior weapons can change the outcome of a conflict, governments across the globe invest accordingly, wasting their citizens' resources and collective cash! Sales of defence contractor Lockheed Martin to the US government alone totalled $35.2 billion in 2017, more than the annual budgets of many federal agencies, including the Department of the Interior and the Environmental Protection Agency (and obscenely greater than the economies of a handful of small poor nations!)

President Eisenhower

Let me repeat that in the majority of countries, **the wrong people float to the top and get into government!**

As far back as 1961, Eisenhower, a retired five-star Army general, the man who led the allies on D-Day, made potent and pertinent remarks in his farewell speech from the White House: he gave the nation a dire warning about what he described as **a threat to democratic government from what he called 'the military-industrial complex'**, a formidable union of defence contractors and the armed forces (he did not label the CIA as co-conspirators at that time!)

Much has been said about the assassination of JFK in November of 1963. It was claimed by some that the critical shots were the result of an accident by a CIA member suffering a hangover and with no weapons experience.

Ngo Dinh Diem

More importantly, was the CIA and US military involvement in the assassination of President Ngo Dinh Diem and his brother in Vietnam

just a few weeks earlier coupled with the fact that Kennedy wished to start pulling out of Vietnam? The relationships between the CIA, the US military and BIG BUSINESS in the armaments industries of America were not going to let the

President John F Kennedy

chance of making ginormous profits slip away. "In God We Trust, but everything else is to be in CASH thankyou!"

Of course the other contender for the murder of JFK was MOSSAD due to the fact that the President wished to prevent Israel from developing a nuclear bomb. It had already had its first Nuclear Power Station built in the desert and refused the IEAE to inspect the facility. The then Prime minister of Israel, David Ben-Gurion was determined to get the bomb to protect Israel from the Arabs. Were the rich and powerful Jews in America going to let this Irish Catholic President stand in their way?

David Ben-Gurion

In the end, the Commission pointed the finger at the deranged Lee Harvey Oswald for the killing even though he only managed a single shot through the President's neck which would not have killed him!

The following is a review of the 20 companies with the highest revenue from arms sales in 2016, based on the 'Top 100 Arms-Producing and Military Services Companies' report from SIPRI and provided to the media by 24/7 Wall St. in March 2018. While the companies on this list

275

span Russia and Western Europe, the United States is home to the vast majority of the largest defence contractors with the UK not too far behind.

20: Booz Allen Hamilton

Based in Virginia, consulting firm Booz Allen Hamilton has clients in both the private and public sectors. Once called the world's most profitable spy organization, the company is working for several US intelligence agencies, including the National Security Agency and the Department of Homeland Security, and branches of the US military. While much of the company's business is confidential, it provides intelligence and data analysis, engineering, and cyber security services in many aspects of defence. Defence and intelligence contracts alone accounted for over two thirds of the company's revenue in 2017.

The company's partnership with the US government goes back to 1940, when it began advising the Secretary of the Navy in preparation for US involvement in World War II. Booz Allen Hamilton's relationship with the US government has been close ever since. Some 30% of the company's workforces are veterans and 70% have security clearance.

Country: United States

Arms sales: $4.0 billion

Total sales: $5.8 billion

Profit: $252.0 million

Employees: 23 300

19: United Shipbuilding

United Shipbuilding Corp. is one of two Russian companies to rank among the top 20 arms producing and military services companies in the world. While the company manufactures a range of commercial shipping vessels, its military vessels account for the majority of its business. The company is currently developing 11 different models of military submarine and 16 different warships, in addition to a variety of vehicles used as minesweepers, landing ships and patrol vessels.

United Shipbuilding was established in 2007 by decree of Russian President Vladimir Putin and is now the largest shipbuilding company in Russia as well as the geographic region between the Baltic Sea and the Pacific Ocean. United Shipbuilding vessels comprise nearly the entire Russian Naval fleet.

Country: Russia

Arms sales: $4.0 billion

Total sales: $4.5 billion

Profit: $90.0 million

Employees: 89 650

18: Harris

Florida based government contractor Harris Corp. reported $5.9 billion in revenue in 2016, the vast majority of which came from arms sales and military service. The company's divisions include electronic systems, which provide products and services related to electronic warfare, avionics, undersea systems, and air traffic control as well as communication systems, manufacturing night vision and tactile communication products. The company has clients in over 100 countries. Standing contracts include lucrative deals with the US Army, US Air Force, and Special Operations Forces.

The company's history with the US government stretches as far back as WWII when US bombers began using Harris Corp.'s newly developed bombsight that enabled more precise bombings at high altitude.

Country: United States

Arms sales: $4.2 billion

Total sales: $5.9 billion

Profit: $553.0 million

Employees: 17 000

17: Leidos

Leidos is a defence contractor based in Reston, Virginia. The company, which was known as SAIC until it shed part of its operations in 2013, was awarded its first long term government contract in 1970 by the former Defense Nuclear Agency. Soon after, the company also provided support to weapons development projects of the US Air Force and cruise missile development projects of the Department of Defense. Today the company is heavily involved in the global underwater arms race, developing unmanned submarines to shadow otherwise virtually undetectable Russian, Iranian, and Venezuelan submarines that might pose a threat to US interests. Leidos revenue from military services and arms sales in the 2016 calendar year totalled $4.3 billion, a 29.1% increase from the previous year.

Country: United States

Arms sales: $4.3 billion

Total sales: $7.0 billion

Profit: $246 million

Employees: 32 000

16: Rolls Royce

Rolls Royce is one of only two defence contractors based in the United Kingdom to rank among the world's 20 largest arms and military services companies by arms sales. Primarily known as a luxury automaker, the company's arms sales and military services accounted for just 24% of its revenue in 2016.

Rolls Royce is currently the only company in the world manufacturing engines that allow fighter jets to take off vertically. The company's vertical lift jet technology is currently used by the US Marine Corps. Other military grade products Rolls Royce develops include rotary engines for medium and heavy lift air transport vehicles, engines for long range patrol aircraft and an engine for unmanned aerial vehicles (drones).

Country: United Kingdom

Arms sales: $4.5 billion

Total sales: $18.6 billion

Profit: N/A (but enormous, probably close to $1.0 billion)

Employees: 49 900

15: Textron

Textron is a Rhode Island based aerospace and defence company. Bell Helicopter, a subsidiary of Textron, manufactures a range of military aircraft, including the Osprey, Valor, and Zulu helicopters. In addition, Textron develops and manufactures unmanned air and surface vehicles, armoured combat vehicles as well as missiles and missile defence systems. Textron has either designed or built the re-entry vehicle for the entirety of the US Air Force's current arsenal of intercontinental ballistic missiles.

Despite the substantial size and scope of the company's defence division, the majority of Textron's business is unrelated to arms sales and military services. The company has a lucrative financial services division as well as a commercial and industrial fuel systems segment. Military products and services accounted for just 34.5% of Textron's revenue in 2016.

Country: United States

Arms sales: $4.8 billion

Total sales: $13.8 billion

Profit: $843.0 million

Employees: 36 000

14: Bechtel

Based in San Francisco, construction and civil engineering company Bechtel operates in multiple businesses including infrastructure, mining, oil and gas, and defence. Bechtel has been a defence contractor for over 50 years, providing missile defence services, and developing and maintaining bases and other infrastructure critical to military operations. The company's current projects include a missile defence and space surveillance program at the Ronald Reagan Ballistic Missile Test Site in the Marshall Islands. Additionally, Bechtel was recently awarded a project management contract with the UK Ministry of Defence to improve efficacy and efficiency.

Bechtel is one of the largest private companies in the United States. Arms sales and defence services revenue alone totalled $4.9 billion in the 2016 calendar year.

Country: United States

Arms sales: $4.9 billion

Total sales: N/A

Profit: N/A (but unimaginable! Again close to $1.0 billion)

Employees: 53 000

13: United Aircraft

Established by decree in 2006, United Aircraft Corp. is the largest defence contractor in Russia by arms sales revenue and the 13th largest in the world. The company is the result of the merger of several aircraft manufacturers and other related companies. Though the company also manufactures commercial aircraft, the bulk of its revenue comes from military aircraft sales. While the company has several international clients along with joint ventures in India and Italy, the Russian Foreign Ministry of Defence has accounted for the majority of the company's military aircraft business since 2013. Among the many aircraft the company manufactures is the iconic Mikoyan MiG fighter jet.

Despite billions in revenue, United Aircraft is the only company on this list to report a negative gross profit margin in 2016. That year, the company's costs exceeded revenue by $67 million. The company expects to reach a minimum of 10% profitability by 2025.

Country: Russia

Arms sales: $5.2 billion

Total sales: $6.2 billion

Loss: of $67.0 million

Employees: N/A but probably between 30 000 and 50 000

12: Huntington Ingalls Industries

Splitting from Northrop Grumman in 2011, Huntington Ingalls Industries is a far younger company than most major defence contractors. However, the Virginia-based contractor is the largest military shipbuilding company in the United States. The company's plant in Newport News (a city on the James River in coastal Virginia) is the sole manufacturer of US Navy aircraft carriers (the largest warships in the world) and one of only two nuclear submarine manufacturers. The company also has a shipbuilding facility in Pascagoula, Mississippi which is responsible for the construction of about 70% of all US Navy warships.

The private and commercial sector accounts for a considerable share of revenue for the majority of companies on this list. **Huntington Ingalls is an exception, however, as weapons sales account for about 95% of its annual revenue.**

Country: United States

Arms sales: $6.7 billion

Total sales: $7.1 billion

Profit: $573.0 million

Employees: 37 000

11: United Technologies

A multinational conglomerate, United Technologies Corp. is the third largest company on this list with over $57 billion in total revenue in 2016. Arms sales and military services accounted for a relatively small 12% share of the company's revenue that year. However, the $6.9 billion the company made on defence contracts in 2016 was more than all but 10 other companies worldwide.

A considerable share of arms sales came through subsidiary Pratt & Whitney, a military aircraft engine manufacturer. Sales from defence contracts at Pratt & Whitney, which works with 34 militaries worldwide and manufactures the engines that power the F-22, F-15 and F-16 fighter jets, totalled $4.5 billion in 2016. United Technologies' non-military subsidiaries include the Otis elevator company and the Carrier climate control company.

Country: United States

Arms sales: $6.9 billion

Total sales: $57.2 billion

Profit: $5.4 billion

Employees: N/A but likely to be 50 000+

10: Thales

French defence contractor Thales develops and manufactures electrical and weapons systems for ground, sea and air operations. The company's products include field optics, armoured vehicles, missile defence systems and helicopter navigation equipment. The company also produces naval anti-aircraft systems, sonar, unmanned aerial vehicles and military avionics.

One of the largest defence contractors in Europe, Thales' arms sales and services accounted for about half of its 2016 revenue. The company's other segments include space exploration, mass transportation and security services.

Country: France

Arms sales: $8.2 billion

Total sales: $16.5 billion

Profit: $1.1 billion

Employees: 64 100

9: Leonardo

Leonardo, formerly known as Finmeccanica, is the larger of only two Italian defence contractors to rank among the 100 largest weapons and military services companies in the world. Like many companies on this list, Leonardo's operations span multiple fields of defence, including aircraft, electronics, information and artillery. The company's aircraft division produces a range of military vehicles, including fighter jets, helicopters and unmanned aerial vehicles. The company also manufactures a range of naval, aerial and surface ammunition, including missiles and torpedoes.

Although Leonardo also manufactures equipment for non-military space programs, defence contracts accounted for 64% of the company's revenue in 2016.

Country: Italy

Arms sales: $8.5 billion

Total sales: $13.3 billion

Profit: $561.0 million

Employees: 45 630

8: L-3 Communications

Defence contractor L-3 Communications is based in New York City. Each of the company's four business segment: electronic, aerospace, communication, and sensor systems has contracts with the federal government for defence purposes. L-3's products and services include unmanned aerial vehicle controls, submarine propulsion systems and pilot training programs. L-3's market is not limited to the United States. The company has locations in 29 countries and lucrative contracts with multiple foreign governments including Australia, Canada, Japan, and Saudi Arabia.

Outside of defence contracting, L-3 also manufactures sensor systems commonly found at airport security checkpoints. Military sales and services accounted for nearly 85% of the company's $10.5 billion in revenue in 2016.

Country: United States

Arms sales: $8.9 billion

Total sales: $10.5 billion

Profit: $647.0 million

Employees: 38 000

7: Airbus Group

Airbus is the second largest defence contractor in Europe and the seventh largest worldwide by total weapons sales. Defence contracts accounted for $12.5 billion of the company's $73.7 billion 2016 revenue. The company's military products and services range from cyber security to fighter jets, attack helicopters, and unmanned aerial vehicles. Currently, 526 of the company's Eurofighter Typhoon fighter jets are in operation in eight countries; four of which are outside of the aircraft's intended market of Europe.

Apart from weapons systems and military services, the company derives the bulk of its revenue from commercial aircraft and spacecraft.

Country: Trans-European

Arms sales: $12.5 billion

Total sales: $73.7 billion

Profit: $1.1 billion

Employees: 133 780

6: General Dynamics

Headquartered in Falls Church, Virginia, defence contractor General Dynamic has operations in 46 countries. From its beginnings in the 1950s through the early 1990s, the company manufactured tanks, missiles, rockets, warships and submarines to all branches of the US armed services. Due to the defence industry downturn in the early 1990s, General Dynamics sold all of its branches with the exception of its electric boat and land systems operations.

Today, the company manufactures armoured vehicles and tanks in addition to nuclear-powered submarines and surface vessels. The company has also made several considerable acquisitions in recent decades, including Bath Iron Works in 1995 and Gulfstream Aerospace in 1999. Bath Iron Works (shipyard located on the Kennebec River in Bath, Maine) is where the company is building the state of the art Zumwalt-class destroyer for the US Navy.

Country: United States

Arms sales: $19.2 billion

Total sales: $31.4 billion

Profit: $3.0 billion

Employees: 98 800

5: Northrop Grumman

Falls Church, Virginia-based defence contractor Northrop Grumman employs some 67 000 people in over 25 countries and in all 50 states.

… always money for war and armaments industries !   **Fonsi**

One of the world's largest defence contractors by revenue, the company is behind one of the most advanced aircraft of the US military arsenal. The B-2 Spirit Stealth Bomber can fly 6 000 nautical miles without needing to refuel and carry up to 20 tons of ordnance, either nuclear or conventional. The US military relied on the bomber in both Iraq, Afghanistan and most recently in Libya. Adjusted for inflation, a single B-2 bomber costs over $2 billion and the US Air Force currently has 20 in operation. (Tell that to all the impoverished people of the world! Sorry, tell that to all the impoverished people living in America!)

The company's other business segments include unmanned aerial vehicle manufacturing, cyber security, and logistics. Arms sales and military services accounted for 87.3% of the company's $24.5 billion in revenue in 2016.

Country: United States

Arms sales: $21.4 billion

Total sales: $24.5 billion

Profit: $2.2 billion

Employees: 67 000

4: BAE Systems

BAE Systems is the largest defence contractor in the United Kingdom and the fourth largest in the world. Though headquartered in England, the company employs some 83 000 people worldwide with a heavy presence in the United States, Saudi Arabia, and Australia. The company designs and builds fighter jets, surface combat vehicles, artillery systems, military electronics, and provides cyber security services.

While many companies on this list also have substantial commercial operations, BAE Systems is not one of them. Of the company's $24.0 billion in revenue in 2016, nearly **95% came from arms sales and military services.**

Country: United Kingdom

Arms sales: $22.8 billion

Total sales: $24.0 billion

Profit: $2.4 billion

Employees: 83 000

3: Raytheon

Raytheon was established in the early 1920s as a consumer electronics company. With the onset of WWII Raytheon began producing critical components for British and American radars in addition to proximity fuses for anti-aircraft shells. Today the Massachusetts based contractor specializes in defence and cyber security and ranks as the third largest arms company in the world.

The company also designs and manufactures a range of laser and satellite guided missiles, torpedoes and munitions as well as missile defence systems. Over a dozen countries, including the United States, Germany, Japan, and Saudi Arabia, rely on the Raytheon's Global Patriot Solutions missile defence system. The US also uses the company's more advanced 'Terminal High-Altitude Area Defense' which is capable of intercepting warheads as they re-enter the earth's atmosphere. Earlier this year, the US Department of Defense inked a $650 million contract with Raytheon to sell 280 SM-2 missiles (which are typically used to defend naval vessels from aerial attack) to the Netherlands, South Korea, Japan, and Australia.

Country: United States

Arms sales: $22.9 billion

Total sales: $24.1 billion

Profit: $2.2 billion

Employees: 63 000

2: Boeing

Chicago based aeronautics company Boeing reported $29.5 billion in arms sales in 2016, the most of any company in the world after Lockheed Martin. The US Navy, US Air Force and Marines in addition to allies abroad, rely on long range munitions from Boeing's 'Harpoon Weapon System'. Boeing also manufactures and sells such fixtures in the US arsenal as the Apache attack helicopter, the Chinook transport helicopter, the B-52 bomber, the F-15 Eagle and F/A-18 Super Hornet fighter jets.

Although Boeing ranks as the second largest defence contractor in the world, arms sales comprise a relatively small share of the company's overall revenue; just 31.2% of the company's 2016 sales came from defence contracts. Boeing-built commercial airliners total more than 10 000 and comprise nearly half of all in service aircraft worldwide.

Country: United States

Arms sales: $29.5 billion

Total sales: $94.6 billion

Profit: $4.9 billion

Employees: 150 500

1: Lockheed Martin

With over $40 billion in arms sales in 2016, Lockheed Martin is the largest defence contractor in the world by a wide margin. The vast majority of the company's revenue comes directly from the US government. Lockheed's F-35 Joint Strike Fighter in particular has been a boon. A 60 year deal for the stealth fighter jet is valued at an estimated $1 trillion- the most expensive weapons deal in the Defense

Department's history. Lockheed sold 66 F-35 jets to the United States and its allies in 2017 and is projected to sell another 90 this year. The F-35 is one of the newer additions to the company's products which includes the F-22 Raptor and F-16 fighter jets, the C-130 Hercules airlifter and, following Lockheed's 2015 acquisition of Sikorsky, the Black Hawk helicopter.

Lockheed Martin's other business segments include missile defence, radar, naval warfare technology and intercontinental ballistic missiles.

Country: United States

Arms sales: $40.8 billion

Total sales: $47.2 billion

Profit: $5.3 billion

Employees: 97 000

But sadly as well as the above, there exist literally thousands of smaller companies manufacturing armaments and military hardware in dozens of countries the world over. These industries in some cases are so woven into a countries economy that there is little prospect for their demise in the near future. Only by International Law through the United Nations will there be any chance of curbing the evil industries of death and destruction. But citizens of every country can question their government and demand that certain armaments industries be curtailed with money going to alternative projects such as housing, schools, universities, hospitals and other more worthwhile social infrastructure for the nation's benefit.

So if you are an African, Arab, Asian or European and your wife and children have recently been blown to pieces by a bomb or missile, you can be certain that one of the above companies was responsible for the weapon being manufactured and that it was sold for profit to maintain a high standard of living for the citizens of its home country!

Military Expos and Fairs:

Companies such as Clarion Defence run regular exhibitions around the globe each year attracting high government officials and defence personnel to view all the latest technology and gismos for killing people and destroying human civilisation. Visiting dignitories are continuously fed all the propaganda via the media on the need to be secure, prepared and well equipped in a dangerous world. "KEEPING CITIZENS SAFE" Of course all this hype is about money. Sale of armaments and peripheral technology is exceedingly BIG Business and helps to 'make America Great Again' and 'Keep Britain Prosperous' etc. etc. etc.

MEDICAL INNOVATION
PROLONGED CARE
2-3 October 2018
Edgbaston, Birmingham
www.medical-innovation.c...

Asia MilSim
29-30 JANUARY 2019
Marina Bay Sands, Singapore

SCTX
SECURITY & COUNTER
TERROR EXPO

SeaAirSpace
The Navy League's
Global Maritime Exposition

UDT
Undersea Defence Technology
26-28 June 2018
SEC, Glasgow

UDT ASIA
29-30 JANUARY 2019
Marina Bay Sands, Singapore

US CANADA BORDER CONFERENCE
SEPT 20-21, 2018 DETROIT, MI

WORLD COUNTER TERROR CONGRESS
5-6 March 2019
Olympia, London

FOR MORE INFORMATION PLEASE VISIT OUR WEBSITE - WWW.CLARION-DEFENCE.COM
OR CALL US ON - +44 (0)20 7384 7770

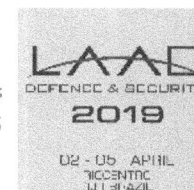

ADECS
ASIA DEFENCE EXPO &
CONFERENCE SERIES 2019

Ambition
THE EPRR EXPO
5-6 March 2019
Olympia, London

BIDEC
Bahrain International Defence
Exhibition and Conference
28-30 October 2019 | Bahrain International
Exhibition & Convention Centre

BORDER SECURITY EXPO.
JAN 31-FEB 2, 2018 SAN ANTONIO, TX

BORDERPOL
FACTIS FAMAM EXTENDERE

DSEI
10-13 September 2019
The World Leading
Defence & Security Event
ExCeL, London www-DSEI.co.uk

DSEI JAPAN
18-20 November 2019
Makhari Messe

EGYPT DEFENCE EXPO
3-5 DECEMBER 2018
EGYPT INTERNATIONAL EXHIBITION CENTRE

Electronic Warfare Europe
5-7 June 2018
Congrès Beaulieu, Lausanne

Electronic Warfare Asia
29-30 JANUARY 2019
Marina Bay Sands, Singapore

FORENSICS EUROPE EXPO

GCC FORENSICS EXHIBITION & CONFERENCE
16-17 OCTOBER 2018 | DUSIT THANI, ABU DHABI

ITEC
15-17 May 2018
Stuttgart, Germany

INTERNATIONAL SUMMIT ON BORDERS

LAAD DEFENCE & SECURITY 2019
02 - 05 APRIL
RIOCENTRO
RJ | BRAZIL

MARITIME DEFENCE ASIA
29-30 JANUARY 2019
Marina Bay Sands, Singapore

You are thinking 'this is an unbalanced and cynical view!' Well if you look to the immediate past, especially the devastation of whole cities in the Middle East and Afghanistan, you get a picture of what all these contemporary weapons can do. Taking into account words written in previous chapters such as the 'seeding of wars' one is suspicious that these corporations among us are so powerful and pervasive in our society that even governments with the best of intentions are sterile if there is any move to dampen down these industries.

They are so integrated and provide not only hundreds of thousands of jobs but make a significant contribution to our economy (in the UK > 10%). The concern of the author is that eventually 'the worm will turn' and many smaller nations having suffered the most hideous of destructive wars will strike back at our 'safe democracy' and inflict the same in a boomerang effect. This is the helter skelter scenario that we may be creating for future generations.

I give here Clarion's statement on its evangelical cause from its website:

> **"The Clarion Events' portfolio of defence and security events is acknowledged as the world's leading forums where high level government officials and senior military personnel converge. Leading global equipment and services providers meet to share ideas, discuss industry developments, conduct business, develop partnerships and network for future growth. Whilst military systems and technology are at the core of the industry and the events, the sector is also diversifying and adapting to meet the changing needs of the world. In addition to the threat of war, national security can be threatened by humanitarian disasters resulting in mass displacement of people or food and water shortages, from terrorism or other pandemic events.**

The UK defence industry represents ten per cent of UK high technology manufacturing and is the number one exporter in Europe, second only to the US globally. DSEI, which is based at ExCeL London, is a crucial part of that industry. The industry employs over 300 000 people and generates over £35 billion per year to the UK economy. The industry also works hand-in-hand with the UK Armed Forces from factory to frontline.

The economic benefits are not just about the defence industry. The 35 000 exhibitors, visitors and contractors attending DSEI occupy over 100 000 room-nights at London hotels during the week of the event, generating an estimated £23 million direct benefit to the London economy in the process, even before taking into account all of their associated expenditure on travel, restaurants and the like across the capital during their stay.

All defence and security exhibitions in the UK including DSEI can serve only the legitimate defence and security industry which is the most tightly regulated industry in the world. This means exhibitors and visitors must adhere to the highest regulatory scrutiny, complying with UK and international laws, treaties and conventions. DSEI itself works closely with government departments including MOD, Department of International Trade, Foreign and Commonwealth Office, BIS and Home Office to ensure this strict compliance with all rules, regulations and laws. Furthermore, the UK Government itself is responsible for inviting international delegations."

Many have scoffed and jeered at Mr Trump's building of an even greater defence force to be ready to confront China, Russia, Islam and other perceived enemies of America (which includes little green and blue aliens from other worlds!) But in truth, Britain has precisely the same values and ideology as our friends across the water. What both nations fail to realise is that the world has shrank. Nowhere is safe from the mountainous brutality of modern weapons and no matter how much we spend or place in reserve at the ready, NOTHING CAN OR WILL SAVE US! The world needs a new rhetoric, new leaders, new symbols of decency and civilisation, new goals to combat degradation, a new morality of humanism, new and innovative ideas to sustain a lasting peace for future generations and above all a respect for all spheres and enclaves of humanity spread across this diminishing area of land and sea with the ideal of lifting them up out of poverty and hopelessness! But instead, we continue down a road where money and resources are channelled into massive amounts of armaments sold to even the poorest and most needy of nations. Such squandering can only end in total global disaster!

Our very enemy are those gargantuan international conglomerates that are too powerful and heed not governments or the wishes of the General Assembly of the United Nations. In my book Helter Skelter I point to the five permanent members of the Security Council and describe them as the 'BIG UGLY GIANTS' that each have a will of their own and eternally protect themselves in the Security Council by the power of veto on anything that does not suit their own interests. This has to be challenged!

No amount of eloquent language in Clarion's bullshit, poetically contrived by some Etonian nancy boy, can hide the true facts that the nation maintains its wealth by the production and sale of armaments that are tearing the social fabric of poorer nations completely to shreds. Women, children and the elderly blown apart and cruelly disfigured by weaponry that a civilised world should have made illegal by now. Cities reduced to rubble by bombs and missiles as in the distant Second World War! CEOs of companies, political leaders and military leaders all need to be held accountable for these heineous deeds and punished through the channels and application of international humanitarian law!

Education and awareness of these sins by the elect as well as the people of all nations is our only chance of a turn around. The small nations in the General Assembly are akin to the populace of individual nations. If the UN is to be a true reflection of a democratic and wise human structure, then ALL the voices of the nations of the world must be heard and act to stand up against the insanity of the all too powerful. The big five need to be humbled. The world must no longer be pummelled and bullied by the Giants. The smaller nations must no longer succumb to threats and vial economic measures to silence their voice. Such devices as fiscal strangulation by the controllers of world finance and money need to be exposed. Incursions by secret agencies of the powerful nations to bend the smaller nations to their will must also be exposed. More individuals such as the brave and noble Julian Assange and Edward Snowden are needed in every country 'to keep the bastards honest'. Power corrupts but absolute power corrupts absolutely!

Unwarranted Influence

[Note: July 2018: Bank of America, Paypal, Mastercard and other notable financial institutions have blocked donations to Wikileaks at the behest of the American Government. The author appeals to the world community to continue to support Mr Assange and Wikileaks for its most noble work in exposing the underhand dirt of Governments and secret services doing wrong!]

Food For Thought:

A journalist for a mainstream UK media outlet has methodically tracked weapons shipment serial numbers and English-language paperwork recovered from al-Qaeda groups in Syria. He showed up at arms factories and questioned arms dealers, including officials at the Saudi Embassy in London, and asked *"why are your weapons in the hands of terrorists?"*

Veteran Middle East war correspondent Robert Fisk recently published a bombshell report entitled *"I traced missile casings in Syria back to their original sellers, so it's time for the West to reveal who they sell arms to."* In it, Fisk recalls a bit of detective sleuthing he was engaged in after stumbling upon a batch of missile casings and shipment paperwork last year (2017) hidden in what he describes as 'the basement of a bombed-out Islamist base in eastern Aleppo' with the words *"Hughes Aircraft Co/Guided Missile Surface Attack"* emblazoned on the side of the spent tubes. Hughes Aircraft Co was founded in California back in the 1930s by the infamous Howard Hughes and later sold in 1997 to Raytheon, the massive US defence contractor whose profits last year came to $23.35bn!

Fisk wrote that even if he doesn't ultimately come up with the American base from which the missiles originated, as well as the specific factory where they were made, he knows one thing for sure, that both Hughes/Raytheon and the US government have created a paper trail

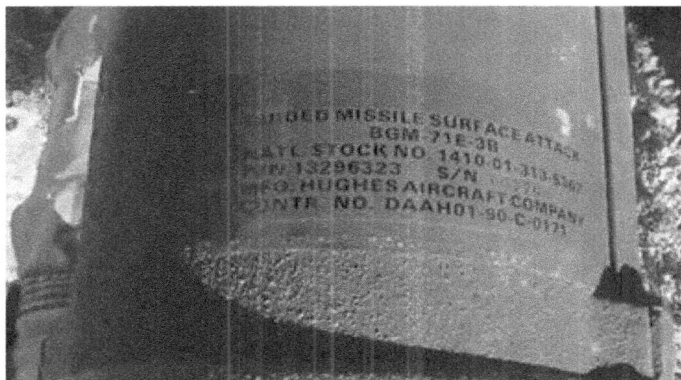

Example of a spent 'Hughes' missile tube

system designed to shield them from violating anti-terror laws!

Theoretically, there exists an 'End User Certificate' (EUC), a document of impeccable provenance which will be signed by the buyers- in this case by whoever purchased these missiles in very large numbers- stating that they are the final recipients of the weapons.

However, there is no actual way of knowing that the official 'recipients' identified as the 'end user' are in fact the true end users, as Fisk's investigation proves, evidenced by the fact that he found the missile batch in a former Nusra/ISIS/al-Qaeda stronghold!

He presented shipping and manufacturer's paperwork proving that various medium weaponry went straight from European factories to terrorist groups in Syria via the Saudis! The question to be asked and answered is: *"Why does NATO not track all these weapons as they leave Europe and America? Why do they not expose the real end-users of these deadly shipments? Why can the details of end user certificates not be made public for scrutiny?"*

One simple answer was in the fact that billions of dollars were made available to al-Qaeda, Taliban and Mujahidin during the Russian occupation of Afghanistan during the 1980s! ISIS also gleaned large amounts of weaponry from the Iraqi army in central Iraq in 2015!

Children dig graves for children in Yemen killed by Saudi bombs made in UK

Remnant of missile casing that killed a bus load of Yemenis children in August 2018. Manufacturer identified as Lockheed Martin! They must pay!

Money, money, money money! Turi Defense Group

Turi Defense Group describes itself on LinkedIn as:

'a global risk management consulting firm involved with defense procurement. We support US national security and foreign policy objectives for defense, diplomacy and international development'

Asked who served as his arms-brokering mentor, Turi responded cryptically: "The USG!"

In 2005 Marc Turi (born Marc Chapman) became involved with government contracts, munitions and other ordnance, and began doing business under Turi Defense Group LLC. By 2010, Turi Defense Group had hit pay dirt, supplying $14 million in arms to the National Directorate of Security, Afghanistan's CIA-supported intelligence agency.

About this time, federal agents in a Phoenix sting operation let smugglers move thousands of weapons to Mexican drug criminals. With Libya's Gaddafi under threat from rebels and opportunity ripe, Turi Defense Group applied to the State Department for a permit to ship "$195 million worth of Eastern European light and heavy armaments and ammunition" to Libya. The list included mortars, machine guns, anti-tank rockets, combat rifles and millions of rounds of ammo. Chris Stevens, then special US representative to Libya, met with Mustafa Jibril, leader of the rebels' National Transitional Council. President Obama simultaneously authorized air attacks on Gaddafi's military. The application from Turi Defense Group was denied on March 22, 2011.

Turi came up with a Plan B: Seek a permit for the arms deal, but don't show Libya as the ultimate destination. He submitted a new State Department application with an identical weapons list, this time listing Qatar as the recipient.

301

Hillary Clinton (then US Secretary of State), was still weighing US support for the insurgents. According to Politico, she said in an email to a State Department colleague "FYI, the idea of using private security experts to arm the opposition should be considered." Turi's guns-to-Qatar application was approved. The price tag was now elevated to $276 million.

On July 14, 2011, Clinton family confidante Sidney Blumenthal sent a note to Clinton about an upcoming visit to Turkey, where she could meet with retired Army Maj. Gen. David Grange, another arms broker. Blumenthal wanted the US to sign a $114 million contract for Grange's company, Osprey Global Solutions, to deliver equipment to anti-Gaddafi forces via a hospital ship. A day after Blumenthal's email to Clinton, the Obama administration recognized the National Transitional Council as Libya's government, giving it access to $30 billion held in US accounts previously controlled by Gaddafi. Both Turi's and Grange's deals were shut down.

In December 2012, based on unnamed sources, the *New York Times* reported that Obama's administration "secretly gave its blessing to arms shipments to Libyan rebels from Qatar. But American officials later grew alarmed as evidence grew that Qatar was turning some of the weapons over to Islamic militants."

In September 2012, Islamic militants from Ansar al-Sharia attacked the US Embassy in Benghazi, killing Ambassador Chris Stevens and three other Americans.

Ambassador Stevens

A criminal probe launched by the FBI produced criticism of Clinton, but no charges were laid.

Turi came under investigation because millions of CIA dollars vanished during the Afghanistan arms deal and some weapons were never delivered as promised. On this he said:

"The administration had good reason to cover their facilitation of massive amounts of weapons and ammunition into the region ... by coming after me the USG could claim it was a rogue contractor!"

He also said that he was targeted because his proposed arms-to-Libya deal was interfering with an Obama administration operation that "would be in direct violation of United Nations sanctions."

"I was a contractor for the Central Intelligence Agency; all of my colleagues were former CIA officers and active members of the CIA who were engaged with numerous members of Congress."

In the end, prosecutors dropped their five-year, multimillion dollar case just weeks before the November 2016 election.

Turi added: "It would have disclosed a covert weapons operation during a presidential election!"

Private defence companies are here to stay

Investors are betting that an increase in defence spending will provide a windfall for these firms. For instance, General Dynamics, a large contractor that develops combat vehicles and weapons systems for the US military, saw its stock price jump by more than 30 percent in the months after the Trump election victory. Likewise, Kratos Defense and Security Services, a smaller firm that builds drones for the US Air Force, saw its shares soar more than 75 percent between November 2016 and May 2017. What is certain is that *for-profit* military and intelligence firms will remain an integral part of US national defence. These companies are primarily responsible to shareholders rather than the American people. How can they be held accountable to the nation's interests?

During the wars in Iraq and Afghanistan, the US military relied heavily on contractors to support counterinsurgency operations. However, high-profile incidents of alleged human rights abuses by the company CACI at Abu Ghraib Prison in Iraq and Blackwater at Nisour Square, Iraq brought to light the difficulty the American military faces monitoring private defence companies. With their emphasis shifting from ground troops, they are increasingly assisting military and intelligence agencies with counterterrorism and cyber security; traditionally these were duties of public employees! It logically follows that in future, Government agencies and courts must be able to hold defence firms accountable if they break the law overseas.

Merchants of Death- International Arms Dealers

Where do all the weapons come from that make all the various wars possible? With the United States now approaching $100 billion in overseas weapons sales, the question becomes more vexing.

In April 2012, Viktor Bout, perhaps the single biggest private arms trader in the world, was convicted in a New York court and sentenced to twenty-five years in prison. Bout, a Russian citizen, began his private business as a military transporter and weapons supplier in the early 1990s following the collapse of the Soviet Union.

He had flown weapons to anti-Taliban forces in Afghanistan during the 1990s and aided the French government in transporting goods and UN peacekeepers to Rwanda after the genocide there. According to UN documents, in exchange for illicit diamonds Bout had supplied former Liberian President Charles Taylor with weapons to help destabilize Sierra Leone. In court, Bout was found guilty of conspiracy to kill Americans and US officials by delivering anti-aircraft missiles and aiding a terrorist organization. The case against Bout was built upon a sting operation with DEA agents posing as would-be buyers from FARC, the Revolutionary Armed Forces of Colombia. Bout was prepared to supply anti-aircraft missiles so that FARC could shoot down American pilots working with Colombian government officials.

Bout exemplified the re-emergence of the leading role of private suppliers in the global arms business as opposed to the country-to-country transactions that dominated the Cold War era. Although the second hand arms trade proved vast, with the illegal trade in weapons very hard to control, the big money was found in the manufacturing and selling of the new weapons to governments. In that arena the major military industrial producers included Krupp (Germany), Schneider-Creusot (France), and Vickers (Britain).

Sir Basil Zaharoff, the infamous sales agent for Vickers and the world's best known arms dealer throughout World War I, once boasted to a newspaper: "I made wars so that I could sell arms to both sides. I must have sold more arms than anyone else in the world!"

Arms to the Free Syrian Army

In January 2013, a British blogger began to notice weapons made in the former Yugoslavia appearing in videos and images posted online by rebels fighting in southern Syria. The recoilless guns, assault rifles, grenade launchers and shoulder-fired rockets appeared to be from an undeclared surplus from the 1990s Balkan wars, stockpiled by Croatia.

The weaponry had apparently been sold to Saudi Arabia and that planeloads had left Croatia since December 2012, bound for Turkey and Jordan. They were then passed on to to several Western-aligned FSA groups. Croatia's foreign ministry and arms-export agency denied any such shipments occurred.

War Games for the Kids

When I was a kid a thousand years back (actually in the 1950s) we had cap guns and bows and arrows to play 'Cowboys an' Indians'. Our heroes were John Wayne, the Cisco Kid, Roy Rogers and Hopalong Cassidy to name a few. War movies at the cinema and the new invention of TV were a permanent diet as we fought the dastardly Germans again and again. It never entered our heads that this was all propaganda and conditioning to accept war, weapons and killing. In my mid twenties I was a half committed hippy… with long golden locks and beard but was not into drugs and serious alternatives. I did build my own home but my family never went without the luxuries of mains electricity, satellite TV and all the white home appliances to make life easy!

With the advent of home computers, I tried hard to steer my kids away from mind destroying games that depended on the speed and agility of one's wrist to 'blast' an enemy or monster. Now however with ipads, ipods, laptops and x-boxes, the sophistication of war games has made a quantum leap where reality of war scenarios is frightening and one can play out the role of a hero or baddy, whatever turns one on! Our kids are becoming even more conditioned to war and killing to an extent where many believe that soldiering is the best career to follow as an adult. Alas, those that have been to Afghanistan, Iraq and African states and dumped into the real thing have hardened their opinions on both war and our governments that sent them there for King and Country! They often come home disillusioned and asking themselves the same old questions: "Why were we there? … what was it all about?"

Mostly it was about resources, western bullying and, of course, money!

Coming back to computer aps for war games and role play. On visiting a friend and staying overnight, after dinner I looked forward for some idle chat and banter with mine host... but it was not to be. He went straight to his special room or den and, in front of a very large wall screen commenced with playing a war game. Firing a machine gun, hurling grenades and even hand to hand combat with deadly Taliban terrorists kept our friend enthralled for hours before he finally retired to bed in the wee small hours. On enquiring of his spouse whether we had offended our host in some way she replied: "oh no, don't think that, John spends nearly all of his free time at home on his computer playing games!"

One wonders what sort of a marriage and family life they shared with this obsession?

The other concern with children, especially once they reach ten or so, is the interactive games on the internet where there are other characters running around being controlled by strangers i.e multiplayer games. These entail violent confrontations and sometimes accompanied by verbal abuse. But the absolute downside is that one is not aware of the profile of the strangers that are sometimes quite possibly adults of various ages just wishing to interact with children.

There are many constructive alternatives for children such as SimCity and Minecraft where one can build one's own world and learn creative skills. Parents need to be mindful of the amount of time their children spend in front of screens (collectively) as well as what they are involved in to avoid time wasting or unwanted soliciting by weirdoes online, of which there are many!

But then TV and movies bring considerable violence into the home with war epics, cop shows, border security, secret service, SAS etc and the public everywhere seem to lap it up. What is all this violence depicted each day on our screens doing for the human psyche?

Battlefield 1 .. realistic WWI role play by DICE

The challenge for parents is for them to instruct their children that:

- War is the most horrific thing in this world.
- Generally there are no real winners of war, everyone loses!
- You don't get another chance with your life, when you're dead, you're dead permanently!
- These games are fantasy no matter how real they look.
- They are NOT teaching good social values, more often they teach hatred and a desire to kill.
- An uncontrolled and habitual obsession with these games can lead to psychosis and unstable personality traits that destroys

the ability to function as a normal human. (a bit similar to the effects of dope and drugs!)

- Multiplayer games have downsides for children! Anonymous players are sometimes adults of which children are unaware. This may lead to unwanted consequences!

Fast Radio Bursts

There are said to be 3 x 10^{11} stars in our galaxy and 3 x 10^{11} galaxies in the universe, giving approximately 10^{23} stars in all. An interesting comparison is that there are six times more than this number of water molecules in just 18 gram of water!

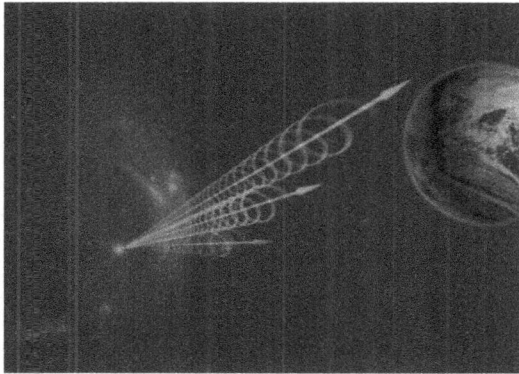

FRBs were discovered in 2007 by Duncan Lorimer and David Narkevic. They are huge bursts of energy whose source we are uncertain of but probably due to interactions of neutron stars and black holes. The burst is usually of durance of between one and five milliseconds. They reach the Earth from somewhere in the universe about one every second. Astronomers wish to eventually find intelligent life in other parts of the galaxy. The author suggests this to NOT be a good idea given our own record of violence and destruction. Indeed, it may be that FRBs are evidence of the complete annihilation of star systems containing intelligent but belligerent and unwanted societies of aliens!

Russia, China, India and Pakistan

Russia: March 2018. Relations between Britain and Russia plunged to a chilly level not seen since the Cold War as Prime Minister Theresa May expelled 23 diplomats, severed high-level contacts and vowed both open and covert action against Kremlin meddling after the poisoning of a former spy. Undeclared intelligence officers were given one week to leave Britain.

"This will be the single biggest expulsion for over 30 years," May said, adding that it would 'fundamentally degrade Russian intelligence capability in the U.K. for years to come.' May spoke after Moscow ignored a midnight deadline to explain how the nerve agent Novichok, developed by the Soviet Union, was used against Sergei Skripal, an ex-Russian agent convicted of spying for Britain, and his daughter Yulia. But this event was not the first Russian attack in Britain. Alexander Litvinenko was a former officer of the Russian Federal Security Service FSB (and earlier KGB), who fled from court prosecution in Russia and received political asylum in the United Kingdom. On 1 November, 2006 Litvinenko suddenly fell ill and was hospitalized. He died three weeks later, becoming the first confirmed victim of induced acute radiation syndrome, having received a lethal dose of polonium-210.

In each case, Russia vehemently denied responsibility.

Downing of Malaysian Flight MH17 in Ukraine: Investigators probing the 2014 downing of flight MH17 stated that the missile which brought down the plane over eastern Ukraine came from a Russian military brigade. The Joint Investigation Team came to the conclusion that the BUK-TELAR that shot down MH17 came from the 53rd Anti-aircraft Missile Brigade based in Kursk in Russia. As reported by Dutch investigator Wilbert Paulissen: "the 53rd Brigade forms part of the Russian armed forces". All 298 passengers and crew, most of them

Dutch, were killed in the disaster. But the toll included members from sixteen other nations on board among them Australians, Britons, Malaysians and Indonesians.

The Crimean peninsula was annexed from Ukraine by the Russian Federation in March 2014. The annexation was accompanied by a military intervention by Russia in Crimea that took place in the aftermath of the 2014 Ukrainian revolution and was part of wider unrest across southern and eastern Ukraine. Following pro-Russian demonstrations in the Crimean city of Sevastopol, masked Russian troops without insignia took over the parliament of Crimea leading to the installation of the pro-Russian Aksyonov government. The conducting of a Crimean status referendum and declaration of Crimea's independence occurred on 16 March 2014. According to the United Nations and multiple NGOs, the Russian Federation was responsible for multiple human rights abuses and instances of discrimination in Crimea since the illegal annexation, particularly against the Tartar community and human rights activists.

Donbas Civil War begins: In 2014, Ukraine was divided between those who wanted to affiliate with Russia and those who leaned toward Europe. In Kiev the pro Europe faction overthrew the President, Viktor Yanukovych. By February 2018, it was four years on since Vladimir Putin annexed Crimea and helped foment a rebellion in Ukraine's industrial east. Since then about 10 000 people* have died, including 3 000 civilians, with more than

[*Some estimates put the total death toll as high as 50 000]

311

1.7 million persons being displaced. Aid agencies say that 4.4 million people have been directly affected by the continuing hostilities, while 3.8 million need urgent assistance. But the world has turned its gaze elsewhere.

When we describe this war as a civil war that description is not quite true! At the outset, the Russian military shelled Eastern Ukraine from across the Russian border mid 2014 and Russian military personnel aided the rebels in their fight against the Ukraine forces **on Ukraine soil!** A convoy of military vehicles, including armoured personnel carriers with official Russian military plates crossed into Ukraine near the militant-controlled Izvaryne border crossing on 14 August. The Ukrainian government later announced that they had destroyed most

of the armoured column with artillery.

Map of Luansk Donetsk region marking destruction of hospitals, schools etc.

Secretary General of NATO Anders Fogh Rasmussen said this incident was a 'clear demonstration of continued Russian involvement   in the destabilisation of eastern Ukraine'. In 2015, Kiev and Moscow signed the 'Minsk Agreement' which stipulated a ceasefire and a special constitutional status for the rebel held territories of the Donbass region, which would re-integrate into Ukraine and hold elections. None of this has come to fruition with ceasefire violations running into the thousands. A low intensity conflict, squalid and deadly, has continued to grind in a region that no longer sees a way out of its misery. Mortar shells still fly sporadically between government controlled territory and the self-declared 'Peoples Republic of Donetsk'. Hospitals, schools and public buildings are continuing to be bombed and destroyed! Russian convoys and the International Red Cross provide a minimum of humanitarian aid to rebel-held areas, where the conventional economy has more or less broken down. EU humanitarian aid agencies contribute to the other side of the line. But as the conflict sinks into stalemate there is now a grim fatalism in the towns and villages close to the contact line born from the sense that the wider world has become indifferent to their fate. Ukraine has written this region off as a home to separatists, fifth columnists, thugs and murderers.

Unwarranted Influence

Entry into the Syrian Conflict: Russia has supported the internationally recognised government of Syria* since the beginning of the Syrian conflict in 2011. Firstly on a political level, then with military aid, and finally since October 2015, through direct military involvement. In fact, early 2012 Russian contracts with Syria for arms were estimated to be worth 1.5 billion US dollars, comprising 10% of Russia's global arms sales! Entry to the conflict marked the first time since the end of the Cold War that Russia became involved in an armed conflict outside the borders of the former Soviet Union. Russia rejected the demands of Western powers and Arab allies that Bashar al Assad not be allowed to play a role in any Syria settlement. Russian military strikes targeted not only ISIL, but also rebel groups including the Free Syria Army, al Nusra Front and al-Qaeda. In March 2013 the Arab League gave its members the right to arm the Syrian rebels and further, at a summit in Doha, the League recognised the National Coalition for Syrian Revolutionary and Opposition Forces as being the legitimate representatives of the Syrian people. From 2014, Western countries, most notably the US, Britain and France, began to participate in direct military action against ISIL in the territory of Syria. Israel used this opportunity to target Hezbollah and Iranian forces in Syria.

In October 2015 about 26 '3M14T cruise missiles' were launched from Russian naval vessels in the Caspian Sea against 11 targets in Syria, some 1500 Km away! These missiles are designed to penetrate air defences of stationary ground targets such as administrative and economic centers, weapon and petrochemical storage areas, command posts, seaports and airports. This event represents the first recorded operational use of the 3M14T missile. Some reports suggested that four missiles crashed in Iran en route.

[* many Western governments have called for the resignation of al Assad]

RUSSIAN CRUISE MISSILE ATTACK ROUTES INTO SYRIA

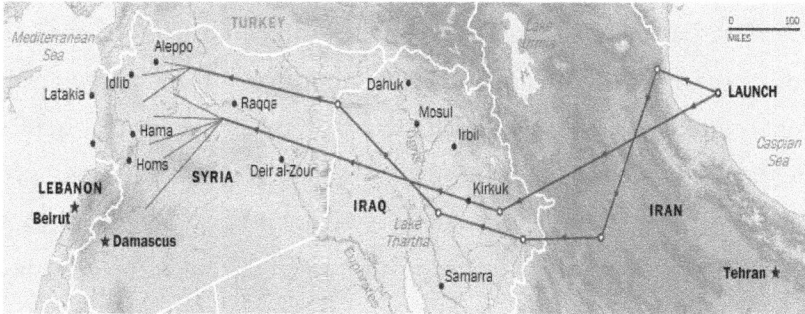

As of September 2015, an estimated 2 500 Russian nationals were fighting alongside ISIL and President Putin declared that their return to Russia would be a threat. With the increase in civilian casualties due to Russian air strikes from bombs and missiles, President Vladimir Putin dismissed such media reports of alleged casualties as 'information warfare' against Russia. As well as Russian Airforce participation, around 2000 Russian contract fighters had been taking part in combat in Syria before the formal Russian intervention began in September 2015!

On 14 April 2018, the United States, France, and the United Kingdom carried out a series of military strikes involving aircraft and ship based missiles against multiple government sites in Syria. It was in response to the Douma chemical attack against civilians on 7 April, which they attributed to the Syrian government; however the Syrian government denied involvement in the Douma attacks and called the airstrikes a violation of international law. France and the United States cited positive urine and blood samples collected as proof of chlorine being used in Douma and reminded al Assad that this was not the first time such weapons had been used by his military.

Monitoring groups in Syria accused Russia as having killed thousands of civilians through airstrikes, violating international law. For Russia, keeping Assad in power protects Russia's naval base leases in

Tartus, its only Mediterranean port. It also underlines the point that Russia remains a powerful military force and that any road to reconciliation in Syria must run through Moscow. In the long term, Moscow wants a reliable client state in the Middle East. Russia's defence minister admits that nearly 50 000 Russian soldiers have at some point been deployed to Syria and it is estimated that Russian airstrikes were costing Moscow some $4 million a day back in 2015. Estimating the real cost of a military conflict is always difficult because so many factors need to be considered, but a Moscow economist was quoted that even if one ignores direct human and property losses, Vladimir Putin's wars (in Ukraine and Syria) had cost Russia approximately 94 billion US dollars per year! With poverty in Russia now soaring (government estimates around 20 million but a true figure is considerably more) one wonders why the Russian people allow such waste on sophisticated armaments and participation in wars. But it is a worldwide phenomenon not restricted to Russia alone!

Universal equation of truth:

PRIVATE ARMAMENTS MANUFACTURES	+	WARS →	PROFITS FOR COMPANIES	+	DEATH AND DESTRUCTION	+	POVERTY AT HOME

Only a World Movement of 'People Demand' will ever change this!

Hypersonic Weapons: Putin indicated that his country's military was building a new hypersonic missile and a nuclear powered cruise missile with 'unlimited range' that could evade detection by Russia's enemies. (I assume he means us, people living in the West!) Another threat from Russia is a hypersonic glide vehicle which could fly 20 times faster than the speed of sound and make sharp turns to avoid being detected or struck by missile defence systems. It has also developed an underwater drone and laser weaponry. China announced in early 2018 that its defence budget will rise to 1.1 trillion Yuan (US $200 billion) this year with an emphasis on building hypersonic weapons.

The threats have left some senior US military officers and politicians looking to **space** for a new type of deterrent! The American President has also hinted that **space** is no longer off limits for US weaponry!

In a recent TV interview Mr Putin again described Russia's new advanced technologies regarding nuclear tipped missiles. He accused the United States of violating the nuclear balance and warned against a 'Third World War' during the broadcast. Mr Putin called for new arms control negotiations and quoted Albert Einstein's aphorism that "World War IV will be fought with sticks and stones". But he also said Russia had developed weapons to overcome US missile defences after Washington left the anti-ballistic missile treaty in 2002.

"Why is there money for tanks, bombs, planes and machine guns in this country, but not for people?" was one question put to the Russian leader, but the show presenters ignored it!

Many of these **'new weapons'** should be banned by the UN. Massive bombs, high power laser and maser weapons (now installed on superpower naval ships), ICBMs, very high db sonar devices and others.

Incidentally, the RDS-220 hydrogen bomb, or **Tsar Bomba**, was the biggest and most powerful thermo nuclear bomb ever to be exploded. By the Soviet Union on 30 October 1961 over Novaya Zemlya Island in the Russian Arctic Sea, it was rated at 50 Megaton TNT.

China: During its long history China has been involved in many military conflicts both from outside invaders and between feudal Lords domestically. In the modern era it suffered two wars with the Empire of Japan and two minor skirmishes with Russia.

The First Sino-Japanese War was from July 1894 until April 1895 and was fought between the Qing Empire and the Empire of Japan primarily over Korea. After more than six months of success by Japanese land and naval forces and the loss of the port of Weihaiwei, the Qing government sued for peace in February 1895.

The war demonstrated the failure of the Qing Empire's attempts at modernisation of its military when compared with Japan's successful Meiji Restoration. For the first time, regional dominance in East Asia

 shifted from China to Japan and this humiliating loss of Korea fomented a public outcry eventually leading to revolution.

Japanese soldiers beheading Chinese captives

The Treaty of Shimonoseki was signed in April 1895. The Qing Empire recognized the total independence of Korea and ceded the Liaodong Peninsula, Taiwan and Penghu Islands to Japan 'in perpetuity'.

Casualties:	China	Japan
Killed or wounded:	35 000	5 000
		+ 12 000 from disease

The Second Sino-Japanese War commenced with the Japanese invasion of Manchuria which began in September 1931. The Kwantung Army of the Empire of Japan invaded Manchuria establishing the puppet state of

Manchukuo. The occupation lasted until the Soviet Union and Mongolia launched the Manchurian Strategic Offensive Operation in 1945. Japanese forces occupied Chinchow in January 1932 after the Chinese retreated without giving combat. The Japanese immediately occupied Shanhaiguan completing their military takeover of southern Manchuria. The Japanese then turned north to occupy the whole of Manchuria.

It was not until 1937 that conflict again broke out when China began a full-scale resistance to the expansion of Japanese influence in its territory. The war may be seen as being in three phases: a period of rapid Japanese advance until the end of 1938; a period of virtual stalemate until 1944; the final period when Allied counterattacks, principally in the Pacific and on Japan's home islands, brought about Japanese surrender.

In the spring of 1934 a pronouncement from Tokyo in effect declared all China to be a Japanese preserve in which no power could take important action without its consent. Nationalist leader Chiang Kai-shek did not initially oppose the Japanese forces, preferring instead to pursue his campaign against the Chinese communists.

Chiang Kai-shek   But in December 1936 he was seized by his own generals and compelled to ally with the communists in a United Front against the Japanese.

Infamous was the Nanking (Nanjing) Massacre after its fall in December 1937. As many as 300 000 Chinese civilians and surrendered troops were murdered with tens of thousands of women raped on the orders of Commander Matsui Iwane.

The strength of the Communists, under Mao Zedong, had grown. As Japan withdrew divisions to fight in the Pacific islands, the communist armies were able to move in and organize more liberated areas. Civil war between the Communists and the Nationalists was inevitable.

Mao Zedung 1944

It is believed that the total Chinese deaths as a result of WWII and civil war amounted to no less than 14 million. After 1949 when the civil war was over, the Nationalists were exiled to Taiwan, and Mao was

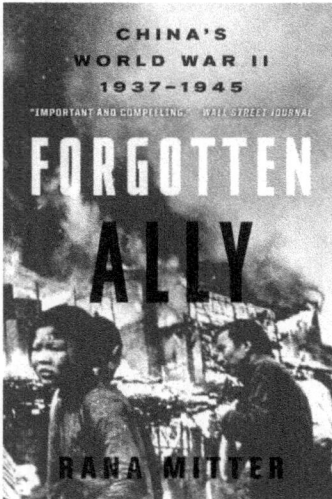

victorious on the mainland. At that time, one saw essentially a virgin history in the mainland of China: that the only people who had made a contribution to fighting and defeating the Japanese were the Chinese communists! The contribution that had actually been made by the much larger Nationalist army was essentially either dismissed or wiped out of the official history taught in China- a sort of historical black hole!

In 1841, China ceded the island of Hong Kong to Britain and in 1842 the Treaty of Nanking was signed, formally ending the First Opium War. On July 1, 1997, Hong Kong was peaceably handed over to China in a ceremony attended by numerous Chinese and British dignitaries. In 1898, Britain was granted an additional 99 years of rule over Hong Kong under the Second Convention of Peking. In September 1984, after years of negotiations, the British and the Chinese signed a formal agreement approving the 1997 turnover of the island in exchange for a Chinese pledge to preserve Hong Kong's capitalist system. To some extent, China has maintained the 'one country two systems' policy and Hong Kong continues to prosper. There have been attempts to infiltrate the local government by Beijing and maintain control by selection processes of permitted parliamentarians and intimidation of opposition candidates.

Nationalist China, now called Taiwan, has born psychological threats and intimidating rhetoric from the mainland since its inception. The view of Beijing is that it will eventually be enveloped back as part of the Peoples Republic. However, it is a thriving country with a strong economy and would serve China no purpose if it were to take it over by military force other than to boost nationalistic ego. More recently China has made overtures that the whole of the South China Sea belongs to China and has increased a military presence there to the chagrin of immediate neighbours Vietnam, the Philippines, Malaysia and Indonesia. As an international waterway such action can only serve to interrupt the movement of commercial shipping so again is, in the long run, of no value to China other than temporary nationalistic trumpeting.

China itself has become a leading economic force in the world producing everything from plastic toys to military aircraft carriers. Its rise in industrial prowess will assist in dragging millions of extremely poor to a more healthy and acceptable standard of living. Will it engender arrogance leading to military adventurism as with other powers in the past? Hopefully not as such behaviour by leaders always leads to eventual destruction and misery. Xi Jin Ping is now leader for life if he so wishes... a huge responsibility. With China turning to space it will be interesting to see if they can reach the moon or even Mars in the next decade or two.

There is continuing unrest in the most Western province of Xingjian which, historically, belonged to the Kazak and Uyghur peoples and who are predominantly of the Muslim faith. In 1948 they had hoped for their own country, namely East Turkestan, but the Chinese communists were never going to let it happen!

Sky blue flag East Turkestan

"When the Chinese government invaded East Turkestan in 1949 and turned us into the Xinjiang province of China, they promised us autonomy- that we would be masters of our land, have control over our natural resources, like oil, protect our social ways and develop our own economy- basically run everything in our region as we wanted. But the reality is the Chinese government has denied us basic rights and freedoms. Our oil and resources have become a curse for us because the Chinese government just wants to rob us of them.

In 1949 only five percent of our population was Chinese; the rest were all from the Turkic ethnic family, with Uyghur as the clear majority. Since then, the Chinese government has transferred so many Han

Chinese into our land that they are now the majority and have made the Uyghur a minority in our own land. If you count the number of migrant Chinese workers in Xinjiang now, they outnumber us." Rebiya Kadeer, Uyghur human rights activist.

Thousands of Uyghur have been detained under the new 'Anti-Terrorism' laws and political prisoners have been executed after unfair trials. Chinese authorities have arrested numerous Muslim preachers and religious leaders, destroyed several Mosques, and closed down many Muslim religious schools. The unrest continues.

Violent Uprising in Urumqi: On Sunday 5th July 2009 some two thousand Uyghur commenced what appeared to be a peaceful march, demonstrating against the repressive rule of Beijing and more importantly on this day, in remembrance of the murder of several of their people at a factory some weeks before in another province of China. At 3 p.m about 300 Uyghur, many of them students, held a sit-in at the People's Square. Video from Uyghur sources that circulated on the internet for a few hours before being removed by Chinese censors showed a crowd that appeared to be about 3000 strong, marching through the city. In another scene, people subdued with hand-cuffs and ropes were lying on the pavement.

By midnight, it was reported by the authorities that some 148 persons were dead and another 900 seriously injured. The Special Forces were flown into the province (army and police) and rioting continued between the two ethnic groups (Chinese Han and Uyghur) over the following three days.

The callous brutality of Beijing was clearly seen on our TV screens in June 1989 when the army was instructed to crack down on the freedom and democracy demonstration in Tiananmen Square. Most of the shootings and murders took place in side streets away from the cameras where it is said that some two thousand five hundred persons died, mainly students, which included those that just disappeared, never to be heard from again.

Tibet: this former country has also been swallowed by the Peoples Republic and the Dalai Lama continues to protest for his country and his people to be free of Chinese suppression and colonialism!

With the collapse of Japanese Imperialism at the end of 1945 the Chinese People's Liberation Army quickly moved into East Turkestan and Tibet, putting down any resistance. In the case of East Turkestan, their leaders were murdered. The Dalai Lama of Tibet was forced to retreat into exile after the uprising in 1956.

During the 1956-1959 revolt, Khampa warriors and freedom fighters in eastern Tibet rebelled against Communist Chinese rule. Up to 20 000 Tibetan guerrillas battled the Chinese army. By March 1959, the situation in the capital Lhasa had deteriorated as tens of thousands of Chinese troops occupied the city and made preparations for an attack on the Dalai Lama's palace and its guard. On March 17, 1959 after two Chinese mortar shells landed near the palace, the 14th Dalai Lama escaped from Lhasa with his bodyguards and headed into exile in

Tibetan National Flag

neighbouring India. In Lhasa, the brave Chinese troops attacked the Dalai Lama's palace, killing thousands of Tibetan civilians who had encircled the palace to prevent the Chinese from seizing their spiritual leader. Over the next days, several urban warfare struggles continued in the Tibetan capital, as the Chinese consolidated their control over the city. Many Tibetan monks and civil leaders were publicly executed. Over the following thirty years the Chinese exercised a deliberate policy of ethnic and cultural cleansing in Tibet, levelling as many as five thousand Temples and places of worship. Tibetans resisting the will of their new oppressors were summarily executed. It is uncanny and ironic that a people who so recently suffered extremes of atrocities under the Japanese could turn around so quickly to mete out the very same to another people. This fact must be recognised and taken aboard the Chinese national psyche if, as a people, they are ever to move forward with dignity and a knowledge of the past. To 'red-wash' these facts from the country's collective awareness and consciousness is to deny history and to deny justice. An old adage and repeated here: "if a nation does not recognise and learn from past errors, it is almost certain to repeat them".

China Newspaper Xinhua 2009-03-13, Beijing: "Stability and development of Tibet has demonstrated the Chinese central government has carried out the right policies in the region" said Premier Wen Jiabao. "The situation in Tibet on the whole is stable. The Tibetan people hope to live and work in peace and stability" Wen told a press conference after the conclusion of the annual session of the National People's Congress.

"Both China's Constitution and the Law on Ethnic Regional Autonomy safeguard the freedom and rights of people in Tibet, particularly in religious belief" the premier said. He added that the central government has increased fiscal input to Tibet to accelerate the region's economic development and to improve the well-being of farmers and herders.

"The Tibet Autonomous Region will continue to follow the opening-up policy for the sake of its own development" Wen concluded.

This author has no doubt that the Tibetan people wish to live in peace and with a stable society. But in their heart of hearts do they see themselves as Chinese? Do they wish, have they ever wished, to be part of China? But, alack, the Chinese people and the authorities never ask themselves these questions. Nor do they see themselves as conquering colonialists providing the 'correct' path for the Tibetan people. "Even now, seventy years later, how is it that elements of resistance still exist after all we have done for them?" some Chinese ask. We find the same feelings and mentality when referring to Xinjiang. "We have done so much to enrich their lives... building roads, schools, providing work... they are so ungrateful!"

[Extract from "All On That Day" by Tom Law, Longership 2010]

We are now seeing the imprisonment of tens of thousands of Uyghurs in Xinjian for "re-education" by the Chinese totalitarian state!

Weapons Manufacture and Export: China is one of the more prolific manufacturers of weapons and military hardware with annual international sales running into billions of dollars. It has fighter jet factories in Pakistan and is not particular to whom it sells its Kalashnikov copies and other heavy machine guns, with many falling into the hands of terror groups. In the decades immediately following WWII, China (along with Russia) supplied both weaponry and troops to various communist insurgencies around the world. This has consequently brought about the deaths of millions.

China became a nuclear weapons state with its successful atomic tests in 1964 (codenamed '596') followed by hydrogen bomb tests in 1967 (codenamed 'Test No. 6') all carried out at Lop Nur, located between the Taklamakan and Kumtag deserts in the south-eastern portion of the

Xinjiang Uygur Autonomous Region. The number of nuclear warheads in China's arsenal is a state secret, with varying estimates of around 300 total warheads. This is thought likely to more than double by the mid-2020s, with dozens of warheads fitted to ICBMs.

[Details: https://en.wikipedia.org/wiki/List_of_nuclear_weapons_tests_of_China]

Its naval capacity is currently under rapid expansion with significant production of carriers, warships and submarines fresh into the water, many of which are nuclear armed posing a new threat to world peace!

India: India's first successful atomic bomb test occurred in May 1984. Its first hydrogen bomb was successfully tested in May 1998. India has not made any official statements about the size of its nuclear arsenal but estimates suggest it has anywhere between 100 and 200 nuclear weapons. R Chidambaram who headed India's Pokhran-II nuclear tests said in an interview that India is capable of producing a neutron bomb.

The Strategic Nuclear Command was formally established in 2003, with an Air Force officer, Air Marshal Asthana, as the Commander-in-Chief. The joint service SNC is the custodian of all of India's nuclear weapons, missiles and assets. However, the Cabinet Committee on Security is the only body authorised to order a nuclear strike. In April 2013 Shyam Saran, convener of the National Security Advisory Board, affirmed that regardless of the size of a nuclear attack against India the country will retaliate massively to inflict excessive damage!

Having had short and intermediate range missiles for some years, India has also recently developed ICBMs :

Agni-VI   **Intercontinental ballistic missile, MIRV**   **8000-12000 Km**

Surya   **Intercontinental ballistic missile, MIRV**   **12000-16000 Km**

The Mirage 2000 of the Indian Air Force is believed to be assigned the nuclear strike role and the Dassault Mirage 2000s and SEPECAT Jaguars are able to provide a secondary nuclear-strike role.

A submarine-launched system consisting of at least four 6 000 tonne nuclear powered ballistic missile submarines of the Arihant class is being produced. The first vessel, INS *Arihant*, has been commissioned and declared operational. She is the first nuclear-powered submarine to be built by India. It has been claimed that Russia provided the technological aid to the naval nuclear propulsion program. The submarines will initially be armed with up to 12 Sagarika (K-15) missiles armed with nuclear warheads.

It is to be noted that India is the only country with nuclear weapons which is **not a party to the NPT** (nuclear non-proliferation treaty) but permitted to carry out nuclear commerce with the rest of the world! A prime example is the sale of Uranium ore to India by the mining whore, Australia 'FOR MONEY' and to hell with any moral viewpoint!

India objected to the lack of provision in the NPT for universal nuclear disarmament within a time-bound framework. India also demanded that the treaty ban laboratory simulations. India's nuclear program dates back to 1948, just one year after independence. The Nehru government looked to nuclear power as an inexpensive energy source for the young country. An Indian Atomic Energy Commission was created that year to oversee the country's nuclear efforts. Due to a lack of uranium on Indian territory, the country naturally gravitated towards using plutonium instead. India's first nuclear reactor, Apsara, was built with help from the United Kingdom and went critical in August 1956. Currently (2018) she boasts seven operational nuclear power plants with four more planned or under construction.

In recent years India has spent more money on buying arms than any other country. Since 2010 the country has doubled the amount of its expenditure (around $ US 60 billion) compared to the previous decade, making it a lucrative market for international arms exporters. But India's

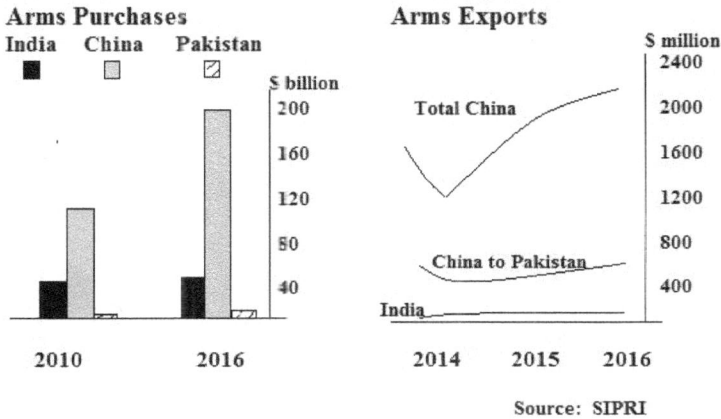

Arms Purchases

India   China   Pakistan

■   ▢   ◨

$ billion
200
160
120
80
40

2010   2016

Arms Exports

$ million
2400
2000
1600
1200
800
400

Total China

China to Pakistan

India

2014   2015   2016

Source: SIPRI

aim is to become a leading arms exporting nation. The Brahmos is the most advanced among the defence ministry-endorsed list of its military hardware. Other items for export include armoured vehicles, warships, tanks, electronic warfare devices, software, bombs and torpedoes aside from typical items such as ammunition, rifles, small arms and military training equipment. The government aspires to make India a manufacturing giant. However, compared to China and other big players, it still has a long way to go. Apart from duties serving with the UN, minor clashes at the Chinese border and the ongoing squabble with Pakistan over Kashmir, Indian military forces have kept a fairly low profile on the world stage.

India suffers from internal political strife as well as periodic violence between its religious groupings. The Mumbai terror attack was perpetrated by Muslim extremists from Pakistan. It is a challenge for the government to maintain peace and democracy for a country containing the largest population in the world, some 1.4 billion in 2018.

Brahmos missile launchers

Partition: "Human beings had instituted rules against murder and mayhem in order to distinguish themselves from beasts of prey. None was observed in the murderous orgy that shook India to the core at the dawn of independence." The Pity of Partition by Saadat Hasan Manto

On the 15th August 1947, the Union flag was lowered in India and the new flag rose to indicate India's day of independence from the Empire. Lord Mountbatten, Viceroy of India attended the ceremony with

Vicereine Lady Edwina Mountbatten, Jawaharlal Nehru and dignitaries. Naturally, Britain was severely criticised for the way independence and partition proceeded and the aftermath of the transfer of millions of people across the new boundaries. Even the boundaries themselves were unsatisfactory to both parties, with the squabbling over Kashmir going on to the present day with no resolution! But the essence of partition and consequent catastrophe in clashes and deaths may be laid at the feet of religious leaders, Muslim and Hindu. Under the Raj, these people shared villages and provinces with a relative amount of peace. After partition and the two way exodus, it is said that up to two million people (including women and children) were murdered. The bottom line is that these two religions fail to live side by side in harmony. But many historians, particularly from India, still place the blame on Lord Louis Mountbatten, the last Viceroy. Witnesses to the bloodshed described the most terrible atrocities and brutalities: "pregnant women having their breasts cut off and babies hacked out of their bellies, infants were found literally roasted on spits."

Mountbatten and the British Government were being pressured by US Presidents Franklin D. Roosevelt and Harry S. Truman who fully understood that it was time for Britain to leave India and that it needed to be done soon. True that Mountbatten's partition plan left the fate of Kashmir undecided. But what difference would it have made? Kashmir was thought to progress to a third independent region with

Viceroy and Vicereine of India, Lord and Lady Mountbatten   **1947**

complete autonomy. It was the Indian political leaders themselves (i.e Indian and future Pakistani) that contributed to the chaos that was 1947! Mountbatten did NOT bestow a legacy of acrimony on India and Pakistan; that is a gross and treacherous lie. The Indians by virtue of their various religions and piety manifestly brought down hell upon themselves without need of any external assistance.

Would ANY more attention and more weeks of effort in 1947 have spared the world a nuclear-tipped time bomb that keeps ticking on both sides today? THIS AUTHOR DOUBTS IT! After all: **it was the 'Muslim League' that would not accept Indian independence if it were to be governed by the Hindu dominated Congress party. It was agreed between British Prime Minister Clement Attlee and the Indian leaders (Muslim, Hindu and Sikh) that 'two nations should be created', one for Muslims and another for Hindus and Sikhs.**

Further, the British had put forward the Cabinet Mission Plan. According to this plan India would be kept united but would be heavily decentralised with separate groupings of autonomous Hindu and Muslim majority provinces. The Muslim League accepted this plan as it contained the 'essence' of Pakistan **but the Congress rejected it!**

Pakistan: Today's Pakistan has a population of around 200 million. It is a troubled nation with infiltrators from Afghanistan and Muslim extremist groups abiding in the North West of the country. It has suffered hundreds of terrorist strikes as well as drone strikes by the American military against Taliban, al-Qaeda and Islamic State sympathisers. Tensions with India flare up periodically, particularly over Kashmir, a region that both India and Pakistan lay claim to (though it would be better if it were a third independent country). Since its formation in 1947 it has experienced democratic governments as well as intermittent military juntas. The military still plays an important role in how the country is run, maintaining it as an Islamic Republic. In the late 1950s, the western contingent's lawmakers determinately followed the

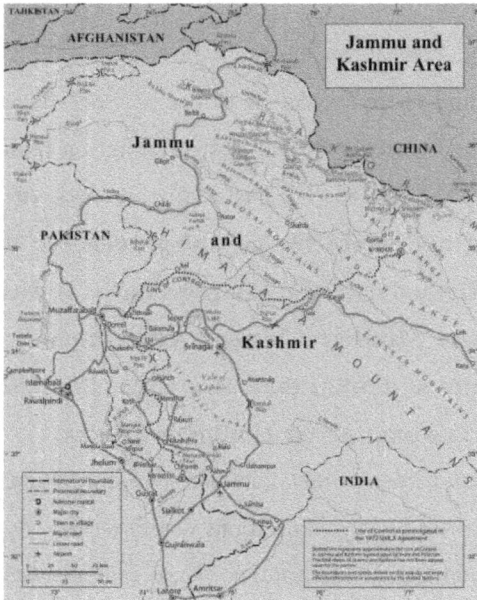

idea of a westernised Parliamentary form of democracy, while East Pakistan opted for becoming a socialist state. In October 1958 President Iskandar Mirza issued orders for a massive mobilisation of the Pakistan Armed Forces and appointed Chief of Army Staff General Ayub Khan as Commander-in-chief. President Mirza declared a state of emergency, imposed martial law, suspended the constitution, and dissolved both the socialist government in East Pakistan and the parliamentary government in West Pakistan. In 1965, after Pakistan 'Operation Gibraltar', India declared full-scale war against Pakistan which ended in a stalemate. At this time, nuclear power expansion was accelerated with the signing of a commercial nuclear power plant agreement with General Electric Canada, and several other agreements with the United Kingdom and France.

1971: Indian Prime Minister Indira Gandhi announced support for the Bangladesh liberation war and provided direct military assistance to the Bengalis. In March 1971 regional commander Major General Ziaur Rahman declared the independence of East Pakistan as the new nation of Bangladesh. As many as 500 000 civilians died during this brief war.

With India working to attain a nuclear weapon, Pakistan also continued its research to obtain a similar weapon. Relations with the United States deteriorated as Pakistan normalised relations with the Soviet Union, North Korea, China, and the Arab world.

1977 to 1988: After the takeover by General Muhammad Zia-ul-Haq in a bloodless coup and execution of President Bhutto in 1979, Zia-ul-Haq committed himself to establishing an Islamic state and enforcing *sharia* law. Zia's Islamization sowed the seeds of sectarian divisions in Pakistan between Sunnis and Shias due to his anti-Shia policies. Hindus and Christians also experienced a decline in political power.

After the Soviet Union's intervention in Afghanistan (1979), US President Reagan immediately moved to help Zia supply and finance an anti-Soviet insurgency. Zia's military administration managed multibillion dollars in aid from the United States. Millions of Afghan refugees poured into the country, fleeing the Soviet occupation and atrocities. Some estimate that the Soviet troops killed up to 2 million Afghans and raped many Afghan women.

Democracy returned again in 1988 with general elections which were held after President Zia-ul-Haq's death. The elections marked the return of the Peoples Party to power. Their leader, Benazir Bhutto, became the first female prime minister of Pakistan as well as the first female head of government in a Muslim-majority country. This period, lasted until 1999.

Benazir Bhutto

Pakistan's intelligence agency, the Inter-Services Intelligence (ISI), became involved in supporting Muslims around the world in a variety of war conflicts and oppression. Pakistan was one of only three countries which recognised the Taliban government and Mullah Mohammed Omar as the legitimate ruler of Afghanistan!

1998: After the revelation that India now had the bomb, Pakistan's new prime minister Nawaz Sharif ordered the Pakistan Atomic Energy Commission to perform a series of nuclear tests in the remote area of the Chagai Hills. Pakistan had become the seventh declared nuclear-weapon state and the first in the Muslim world.

1999–2007: Third military era heralded by the deposition and exile of Sharif and accession of General Musharraf as President. Ties with the United States were renewed by Musharraf who endorsed the American invasion of Afghanistan in 2001. Fighting against al-Qaeda operatives in the North West forced Musharraf to recognize the Taliban once more. Stepping down from the military, he was sworn in for a second presidential term on 28 November 2007.

After a period in exile in the UK, whilst departing an election rally in Rawalpindi on 27 December 2007, Benazir Bhutto was assassinated by a gunman who shot her in the neck and set off a suicide bomb. With the ascent of Yousaf Raza Gillani to Prime Minister, Musharraf announced his resignation ending his nine year reign on 18 August 2008.

Tomb of Founding Father
Muhammad Ali Jinnah

2011: Pakistani-American relations worsened after a CIA contractor killed two civilians in Lahore and the US military killed Osama bin Laden at his home less than a mile from the Pakistan Military Academy.

336

Unwarranted Influence

Strong US criticism was made against Pakistan for allegedly supporting bin Laden (which went back 30 years to the anti-Russian period). Nawaz Shareef returned to become prime minister on May 28 2012 after a lengthy exile in Saudi Arabia.

The One Stop Nuclear Bazaar of Dr Khan:

Dr Abdul Qadeer Khan, is described as the 'father' of Pakistan's nuclear program and chief proliferator of nuclear knowledge and technology to Iran, North Korea, and Libya But let us not forget that nuclear weapon states have long turned a blind eye or actively supported proliferation, in violation of their Nuclear Non-Proliferation Treaty commitments. China is a classic example, where its nuclear physicists provided Khan with all the blueprints and knowhow needed to produce Pakistan's first nuclear device. Beijing also provided materials and played a central role in the nuclearization of the world's most volatile regions. The doctor made many visits to China's nuclear installations since the early 1980s providing assistance to China's weapons program including design of Dutch centrifuge technology stolen by Khan in the mid-1970s! To the disappointment of the world community, Beijing fully supported General Musharraf's decision to pardon Dr. Khan for all his 'nuclear sins.'

It was Libya's Colonel Gaddafi that 'spilled the beans' so to speak with his revelations regarding the China-Pakistan-Libya relationship! 55 000 tonnes of nuclear material plus documents that Libya turned over to the United States were flown to the Oak Ridge National Laboratory in Tennessee in early 2004. This crucial evidence provided clinching proof of Beijing's involvement in Pakistan's nuclear weapons program and provided insight into both Chinese and North Korean nuclear weapons capabilities. It must be deemed inconceivable that Chinese security agencies were unaware of Pakistan's nuclear dealings with North Korea, Iran and Libya.

[At one point, the IAEA uncovered 1300 cases of illicit trafficking through Dr Khan's nuclear bazaar, netting him in excess of $400 million.]

Of course China has long been a provider of military hardware to Pakistan, building factories and providing engineers. Its latest deals include state of the art jet fighters and diesel powered submarines.

The **JF-17 Thunder** is a low-cost combat aircraft designed in China and assembled in Pakistan. It is set to replace Pakistan's ageing fleet of Dassault Mirage III/5 fighter jets by 2020. Also, Beijing has agreed to sell Pakistan eight modified diesel-electric attack submarines by 2028 in a deal valued at between US$ 4 billion and US$ 5 billion. The vessels will be supplied by China Shipbuilding Trading Company.

Type 039 and Type 041 Yuan-class conventional submarine.

China will not stay as a mute spectator to any gradual denuclearization of Pakistan. On the contrary, it is likely that Islamabad's dependence on

Beijing for both missiles and nuclear technology will increase, not decrease, if it is to keep up with India.

Do Drone On!

Since 2004, the United States government has attacked thousands of targets in Northwest Pakistan using unmanned aerial vehicles or drones operated by the United States Air Force under the operational control of the CIA's Special Activities Division. Most of these attacks have been on targets in the Tribal areas along the Afghan border in Northwest Pakistan. Estimates for civilian deaths range from 150 to 1000. Amnesty International found that a number of victims were unarmed and that some strikes could amount to war crimes. These strikes began during the administration of President George W. Bush, and increased substantially under Barack Obama.

Pakistan's former Prime Minister, Nawaz Sharif, had repeatedly demanded an end to these strikes, stating: "The use of drones is not only a continual violation of our territorial integrity but also detrimental to our resolve and efforts at eliminating terrorism from our country"

The Peshawar High Court ruled that the attacks were illegal, inhumane, violate the Universal Declaration of Human Rights and constitute a war crime. The Obama administration disagreed, contending that the attacks did not violate international law and that the method of attack 'was precise and effective' ... a matter of extreme conjecture!

The New America Foundation estimated that 80% of those killed in the attacks were militants. However some experts have stated that in reality, far fewer militants and many more civilians have been killed.

Casualties:

Year	Number of Attacks	Militants	Civilians	Unknown	Total
2010	122	788	16	45	849
2011	70	415	62	35	512
2012	48	268	5	33	306
2013	26	145	4	4	153
2014	22	145	0	0	145
2015	10	57	0	0	57
2016	3	9	0	0	9
2017	8	36	2	1	39

According to the Long War Journal, the Bureau of Investigative Journalism, and the New America Foundation, 2006, 2007, 2008, and 2009 had some of the highest civilian casualty ratios of any years. According to Pakistani Government sources, in this period 176 of the 746 reported dead were civilians.

Some US politicians and academics have condemned the drone strikes, asserting that their use is a violation of international law i.e carrying out strikes against a country that never attacked the United States. Further, that since the drone operators of the CIA were civilians directly engaged in armed conflict, this makes them 'unlawful combatants' and subject to prosecution (i.e boys and girls in front of their computers playing war games!)

The Obama administration offered its first extensive explanation on drone-strike policy in April 2012, concluding that it was 'legal, ethical and wise'. The CIA's general counsel, Stephen Preston, in a speech entitled 'CIA and the Rule of Law' at Harvard Law School on 10 April

2012, claimed **'the agency was not bound by the laws of war'**; in response, Human Rights Watch called for the strike program to be brought under the control of the US military.

With such attitudes and behaviour, one shouldn't be surprised in a contemporary world that some people's reaction is to 'cross the line' towards 'direct action' and become what we term a rebel or a terrorist!

July 2018: Now another Khan has taken Pakistan into his sporting hands to do his best for the country. The ex-cricketer Imran Kahn was sworn in as Prime Minister on a popular wave of discontent of the previous regime in July. A firebrand nationalist, he has promised to create millions of jobs and build world-class hospital and school systems in the mainly Muslim country. To accomplish this he must bring in a period of austerity first to avoid an economic melt-down. His hands will be tied somewhat by the shadow of the military that still holds sway in how the country is run. To reduce military spending will be an almost impossible task, but that would be a most sensible direction to meet the cost of his new 'for the people' program! The generals will not like him for that! If he can make amends with India and avoid further incursions into Kashmir, seeking a final peace for that contentious region, then he will have achieved a great work! Let us hope he makes all the right choices for his country and is not hindered extensively by the generals!

Germany and Japan

The author had intended in adding a detailed chapter on these very important countries that are economic leaders and industrial giants. However we will restrict comments to recent events relating to wars and political tensions.

Germany, under Angela Merkel, took in around one million refugees from Syria, Iraq, Turkey and Afghanistan between 2014 and 2018. This was both a most generous and also a confusing action given that it has brought stress and strain to the German people! As an industrial giant of considerable wealth Germany

Angela Merkel

is able to assimilate more people into its industrial machine. Even before the wall came down, however, we saw ugly scenes in East Germany with Turkish migrants being harassed and even murdered by extreme right thugs. There have been isolated incidents of Islamic terror in the country but not overwhelming when compared to national statistics of heinous crime. As part of NATO and being susceptible to pressure by America, Germany has participated (albeit reluctantly at times) in wars in Afghanistan, Iraq and elsewhere with loss of life of some of its armed forces. With the unfortunate decision (and a bad one at that) of Britain leaving the European Union, Germany and France together now form the stronger contributors. The Union will go on as a key player in the world of production and trade and as a fierce competitor to China, the US and other trading blocs! It is hoped that Europe remains stable and prosperous despite a sharp movement to the extreme right of one or two of its member states, primarily as a reaction to immigrants arriving from Africa and the Middle East.

Germany has not been 'faint-hearted' when it comes to producing armaments and military hardware for the world market. Its contracts for submarines include Greece and Israel, manufactured by Howaldtswerken (HDW), part of the ThyssenKrupp Marine Systems. In fact many have wondered if they are to carry nuclear tipped missiles. Experts in Germany and Israel have finally confirmed that nuclear-tipped missiles have been deployed on the vessels, and the German government has long known about it! So, with the help of German maritime technology, Israel has managed to create for itself a floating nuclear weapon arsenal: submarines equipped with nuclear capability. [The US Navy recorded an Israeli submarine-launched cruise missile test in the Indian Ocean ranging 1500 km] Israeli Defence Minister Ehud Barak stated "Germany can be proud of the fact that it has secured the existence of the State of Israel for many years to come." The German government however sticks to its hypocritical position that **"it does not know anything about an Israeli nuclear weapons program!"**

Dolphin II class Submarine:

INS *Tanin*	Howaldtswerke-Deutsche Werft	2012	2014 Active
INS *Rahav*	Howaldtswerke-Deutsche Werft	2013	2016 Active
INS *Dakar*	Howaldtswerke-Deutsche Werft	Soon to be delivered	2018

Such a nuclear arsenal causes countries like Iran, Syria and Saudi Arabia to regard Israel's nuclear capacity with fear, envy and anger, with considerations of building their own nuclear weapons. This makes the question of its global political responsibility all the more relevant for Germany. Should Germany, the country be allowed to assist Israel in the development of a nuclear weapons arsenal capable of extinguishing hundreds of thousands of human lives? Answer: "it is too late to consider... the deed is done!" As far back 2002, Chancellor Gerhard Schröder summarized his position when he said: "I want to be very clear: Israel receives what it needs to maintain its security."

A whole range of other military equipment is exported by Germany. Machine guns made in Germany are particularly popular, with Heckler & Koch having exported its MP5 to more than 50 countries, including South Korea.

Chemnitz September 2018: Again Germany has witnessed violent protest by extreme right wing thugs against immigrants living in the country. The region of Saxony, where Chemnitz is located, is a stronghold for the anti-Islam far-right party, Alternative for Germany, and has long struggled with neo-Nazi aggression.

Extremists and hooligans took to the streets, harassing those who looked foreign and shouting xenophobic slurs. The next day, violence reached a pinnacle as 6 000 protestors mobilized in the streets, facing off against 1 500 counter-demonstrators and overpowering the police force. The 2015 immigration policy has brought newly emboldened Nazi sympathizers out of the shadows. However, they remain a small minority in the country as seen by a 'peace and anti-racist' concert that was attended by tens of thousands soon after.

Japan: Japan has for centuries been a monolithic high culture that in the post WWII period has prospered due to its innovative and highly skilled technical work force. In the nineteenth century it tried hard to resist the influences of the outside world, but due to the rise in imperial powers and their superior weaponry and armed forces, Japan reluctantly was forced to modernise if it were to remain as an independent sovereign nation.

It has flooded the world with its canny products such as automobiles, cameras and electronic goods. Although trade between Japan and China has been strong, an emerging China has presented differences and monologue over disputed territory i.e islands in the seas between the two nations. Despite this, millions of Chinese tourists float into Japanese ports each year on cruise ships eager to spend big on Japanese goods, hotels and cuisine! Japan's constitution forbids it to participate in overseas aggression by its military forces. Unfortunately, again due to pressure from America, it has relaxed this position a little with its joining of UN expeditions into countries experiencing minor conflicts. Much discussion is currently under way in Japan on its constitutional position especially following recent threats from both China and North Korea. **Japan is among the top ten spenders on military hardware which it states is solely for defensive purposes.**

December 2017: Japanese Prime Minister Shinzo Abe's Cabinet approved the biggest 5.19 trillion yen (US $45.82 bn) defence budget to bolster ballistic missile defence capability amid escalating threats from North Korea.

Being the only country ever having suffered a nuclear attack, it has a non-nuclear weapons policy. However it has several nuclear power stations of which Fukushima suffered an horrific accident in 2014 rendering a large swathe of surrounding countryside uninhabitable due to high counts of radiation.

Fukushima Nuclear Accident Clean Up

Many Westerners now live and work in Japan and many more attend Japanese Universities which have a high standing in the world. With the neighbouring emerging economies such as China and South Korea it will feel some pressure with this new competition for sales of high tech products, particularly where they can be manufactured and sold more cheaply on world markets. Hopefully such tensions will not spill over into greater military posturing by all the local players in Asia!

Austria: Austria, December 2017:   This month Austria became the only western European country with a far-right presence in government after Sebastian Kurz, of the conservative Austrian People's Party (ÖVP), struck a deal with the Freedom Party (FPÖ), a nationalist group founded after the Second World War by former members of the Nazi party. Kurz's ÖVP won 32% of the vote in the October elections, securing 62 seats in the 183-seat national council. The FPÖ came third with 26% of the vote and 51 seats giving a total of 113 seats between them.

Ingrid Haunold, a freelance writer from Vienna said:

"Austria took in many refugees, as we should have, but the government did not do enough to ease people's fears in regard to cultural and religious differences between mostly Catholic Austrians and the newly arrived, mostly Muslim."

Anti-fascist demonstration Vienna, Austria 2018

Following the election results, students, feminists and anti-fascist groups took to the streets in protest. People held placards reading "Refugees welcome- Nazis out!"

The new government plans to shut down several mosques and expel dozens of imams in what politicians have described as a crackdown on "political Islam". Chancellor Sebastian Kurz said authorities would shut what was described as "hard-line mosques". Austria, a country of close to nine million people, is home to a 600 000-strong Muslim community, most of whom were either born in Turkey or are of Turkish descent. These actions are in violation of universal legal principles, social integration policies, minority rights and the ethics of co-existence! The term 'political Islam' is now bantered around by politicians as a catchcry in an attempt to obscure their true inner value of contempt and prejudice!

Didn't my Bierhalle freund Herr Schicklgruber hail from Austria? ... and he caused the world a lot of trouble! Austria does not have a particularly good record concerning relations with ethnic minorities!

Glock G29

Glock G29   This striker-fired semi-auto has a 10mm cartridge that delivers power levels approaching those of the .41 Magnum. It's a handy trail gun for those wandering through bear, wild boar, or mountain lion country. It will also place a nice hole in a person's head!

How America and Rich Nations Waste Resources

"As we peer into society's future, we- you and I, and our government-
must avoid the impulse to live only for today, plundering for our own
ease and convenience the precious resources of tomorrow. We cannot
mortgage the material assets of our grandchildren without risking the
loss also of their political and spiritual heritage. We want democracy
to survive for all generations to come, not to become the insolvent
phantom of tomorrow."   President Dwight Eisenhower

Our lives are short. We have so many worries about survival, feeding
and sheltering our families. We are befuddled by the constant
bombardment of all the various forms of media and what they are
selling us. Although we get to vote, we feel powerless and sterile against
the tsunami of change, threats and wars. The BIG governments seem to
have total power BUT behind them are the BIG international
corporations that are really running the show. The bottom line is "the
general welfare and happiness of the people" ? …. WRONG! The
bottom line is ALWAYS making a handsome profit at the expense of
the general welfare and happiness of the people! Morality is a word
removed from the voices of absolute power! So what to do in our
meagre and short lifetimes?

Well for a start, education about 'THE SYSTEM' under which we all
live and must survive. Also, the evil rhetoric that pits each of us against
a perceived enemy due to differences: differences in skin colour,
differences in culture, differences in language, differences in religion,
and differences in political beliefs. What we must grasp is that "all
humans are basically the same genetically with similar hopes,
aspirations, dreams and basic needs." But more than half of all people
on the planet are NOT being fulfilled and are NEITHER receiving even

the most basic of life resources for sustainability and survival, let alone the chance of happiness! WHY? ... simple answer: GREED!

We in the rich nations get a most disproportionate slice of the pie. To protect ourselves from the poorer nations, we artificially surround ourselves with massive armies and high technology weapon systems. At the same time, we SELL the crumbs, i.e the antiquated and inferior weapons to the third world for profit. But we get ourselves into a mess as we also SELL more sophisticated weapons and armaments to those countries with resources that we need e.g minerals, gas and oil. Thus we see small Middle East nations with an array of expensive and sophisticated military hardware that inevitably get used in petty and local wars (some of which this author suspiciously feels are 'seeded wars' for further profit!)

HOW STUPID ARE WE, THE COMMON PEOPLE OF THE WORLD FOR PERMITTING OUR GOVERNMENTS TO WASTE OUR RESOURCES AND MONEY ON WEAPONS AND MILITARY GIZMOS!

But we continue to 'vote them in' at each election and despite their 'honey words' they continue on in the same vein with the same evil justifications year after year, decade after decade, century after century!

Let us examine world annual expenditure on military hardware and defence nation by nation for the 'top spending nations'. Without doubt, your country is listed here! Then look at the 'Total Expenditure' per man, woman and child each year. Then look at the 'Grand Total' spent on military and defence across the whole world... it is disgustingly appalling, immoral and completely without justification in a modern world where science, art and medicine have reached such heights. Who is in charge of this evil madness? OK, slowly peruse the table below...

take your time and highlight in your mind the key aspects. Having done this, now think hard on the hundreds of millions of people on the planet in absolute poverty; the millions murdered by bombs and other causes as a result of wars; the 30 000 children dying each day from preventable disease and starvation. I ask you, citizen of the world: "HOW CLEVER ARE WE POOR HUMANS IN THIS, THE 21ST CENTURY?"

The Male Penis and WMDs

A missile or rocket is without doubt a representation of the male penis! The bomb and bullet are also shaped like a phallus. Temples and

Churches invariably have some sort of spire reaching to heaven, erect and majestic. Humans have worshipped the phallus as a religious symbol since the Stone Age, with many primitive and animist religions carving replicas from stone, either roughly hewn or smooth and perfect to mathematical precision. Thus we see the armouries of the superpowers vying for penis superiority and guarding their secret weapons with penile envy! Take fighter jets for example: Each of the superpowers spend anything between $350 million and $1.3 billion **on a single fighter jet** with sophisticated missiles slung underneath. Major Rusnok and Lt Col Kelly are indeed lucky to ride in their most expensive F 35B to obliterate an enemy at speed for the US. Then there are artistically engineered diamonds such as the Lockheed Martin F35 or the F22 Raptor to play in. SAAB has its JAS 290 whilst the Russians and

Chinese have their Sukhoi SU57s and Chengdu J20s respectively, all ready for combat and destruction! Many models have served in the various war scenarios in Afghanistan and the Middle East to evaporate peasant Muslims on the ground! What else are they good for one may

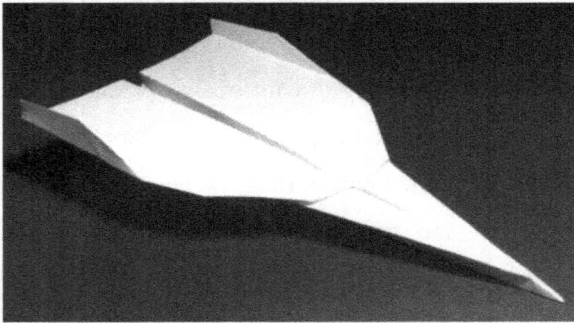

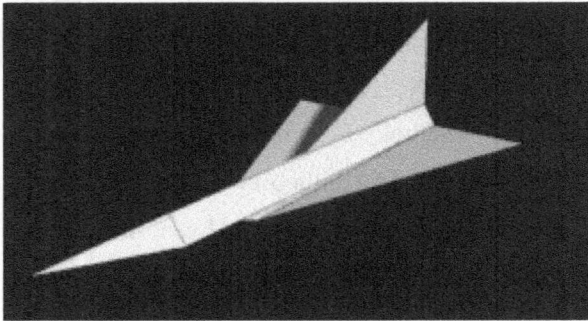

Some of the worlds new top-secret designs estimated at $2.3 billion each!

ask? How many schools and hospitals might be built instead of owning these short term toys?

TABLE OF ANNUAL MILITARY EXPENDITURE FOR TOP SPENDING NATIONS   - 2018

Nation	Annual Military Expenditure $ US billion	Population million	Annual Expenditure per Citizen $ US
Peru	0.85	30.25	$28
Czech Republic	1.25	10.65	$117
Nigeria	1.85	196.00	$9
Ukraine	2.35	44.40	$53
Syria	2.50	18.02	$139
Switzerland	4.50	8.25	$545
Malaysia	4.85	31.02	$156
Norway	5.20	6.50	$800
Egypt	5.20	99.50	$52
Algeria	5.25	40.25	$130
Thailand	5.50	69.20	$79
Argentina	6.00	43.85	$137
Vietnam	6.50	96.00	$68
Iraq	6.50	39.35	$165
Sweden	7.00	10.15	$690
Myanmar	7.25	56.85	$128
Philippines	8.00	93.00	$86
Pakistan	8.20	201.00	$41
Indonesia	8.50	260.00	$33
Afghanistan	8.50	36.40	$234
Mexico	10.25	123.70	$83
Greece	10.50	10.85	$968
Iran	11.00	82.05	$134
Poland	12.50	38.30	$326
Netherlands	14.00	17.25	$812
United Arab Emirates	18.50	9.60	$1,927
Taiwan	20.00	23.80	$840
Israel	20.00	8.50	$2,353
Canada	22.00	36.20	$608
Turkey	26.00	82.00	$317
Spain	26.20	48.85	$536
Australia	28.00	25.01	$1,120
Brazil	28.00	206.40	$136
Italy	40.00	59.40	$673
Saudi Arabia	41.00	28.30	$1,449
South Korea	43.00	51.20	$840
North Korea* estimate	44.00	25.20	$1,746
India	45.00	1300.00	$35
Germany	50.00	82.40	$607
Japan	52.00	127.20	$409
France	64.00	66.40	$964
UK	65.00	66.70	$975
Russia	100.00	144.00	$694
China	175.00	1400.00	$125
USA	750.00	327.00	$2,294
TOTAL	1822	5781	$315
Rest of World	27	1819	$15

	World Annual Expenditure		Annual Expenditure per Citizen $US
GRAND TOTALS	approx:	$US 2.0 trillion	$243

353

Unwarranted Influence

There are a few things that the author would like to comment and highlight:

- Neta Crawford, a co-director of the Cost of Wars Project at Brown University, has estimated that total war spending in Iraq, Afghanistan and Pakistan since 2001 is approaching $5 trillion. Of that, roughly $2 trillion is attributable to Afghanistan.

- The cost of the 2003-2010 Iraq War is often contested, as academics and critics have unearthed many hidden costs not represented in official estimates. The most recent major report on the cost from Brown University totalled just over $1.1 trillion.

- From Ministry of Defence, the total cost of UK military operations in Iraq from 2003 to 2009 was £8.4 billion. ($11.10 billion) Official calculations stated that the Iraq and Afghanistan wars combined cost £20.3 billion ($26.80 billion) up to June 2010.

- Notice that Israel spends a wapping $2300 per capita pa.. the highest in the world but with the USA coming a close second at $2294 per capita per annum.

- North Korea is estimated to spend around $1700 per capita annually with the UAE on $1900 per capita.

- Each of Australia and Saudi Arabia spend more than $1000 per capita annually on military and defence. (not to mention de fence to keep out de dogs an' de rabbits!)

- The USA has a total military budget of $750 billion per annum which is four times that of China and seven and one half times that of Russia. (Mr Trump has edged that figure up closer to a $trillion)

- The world spends approximately $US 2.0 trillion per annum on military hardware which amounts to $US243 for every man, woman and child on the planet. This is a shameful indictment on the leaders of the nations for such immoral waste of resources!

But the saddest thing of all is that these figures are constantly rising. Further, sequestered billions are funnelled away by the 'ugly nuclear giants' towards weapons of mass destruction and their intercontinental delivery systems that will bring such a weapon to your door, no matter where you live on the Earth! How is it that the 'wrong people' always get into government?

The very possession of such hideous destructive weapons is in direct breach of international law regarding the human rights of every one of us that share the planet. The ONLY way forward is for the United Nations to apply the law to bring an end to such madness. And this is where you come in, oh free citizen of the Earth… you MUST raise your voice in protest and DEMAND an end to these weapons. For those countries that disregard the law in question, every type of sanction must be brought to bear upon their society until we have COMPLETE DISARMAMENT!

DEMAND NUCLEAR DISARMAMENT

demandnow.org

Clandestine and Emerging Nuclear Weapons States

It has been no secret that Israel has been a member of 'Le Club Exclusive' for many years now with not a whimper from the UN or the AEIE. How many nuclear weapons it possesses and the precise nature of its delivery systems is not known. One can only surmise that America has taken her under her Eagle wing like a mother protecting its chicks and has been the provider of necessary materials and technology! But this was not always the case. Suspecting that Israel was going to build its own nuclear bomb way back in 1962, the then President John.F. Kennedy wanted to put a stop to it. He was soon to be assassinated (November 1963) and history tells us the rest regarding Israel's secretive Club membership!

As a citizen of the world as well as a citizen of a non-nuclear state, the author feels that his human rights have been swept aside by those powers holding a permanent threat to his safety and well being. He in fact challenges any state owning weapons of mass destruction as now being **'illegal and in contempt of the principles of peace and humanity'** contained in the United Nations Charter. It is clearly the duty of all citizens of the world to protest and similarly the duty of all the non-nuclear nations of the world to protest at the world forum continuously until all have been dismantled.

But one fears that in a progressively more dangerous world, instead of a declining number of these weapons as well as states with their possession, we will experience a new growth industry with new nations scrambling to attain them due to perceived threats from neighbours or just vainglorious national pride. North Korea will not be alone in this regard! If we do not eliminate nuclear weapons

from off the face of the Earth soon, the author predicts a dozen or so additional nuclear weapons states within the next decade. Some will be recklessly open and contemptuous in their decision whilst a few will deny their existence but never the less possess them clandestinely as with Israel currently! Tom Law predicts that all or at least a subset of the following will own or attempt to own nuclear weapons before 2030:

Argentina

Brazil

Egypt

Saudi Arabia

Turkey

Iran

Nigeria

Germany   (clandestine)

Japan   (clandestine)

Indonesia

Taiwan   (clandestine)

Ukraine

Australia   (unlikely)

This then will bring the total number of nuclear weapon states to twenty two! [.. current states include: America, China, Russia, UK, France, India, Pakistan, Israel and North Korea.]

As spelled out in the former book titled 'Nuclear Islam'*, the probability of a nuclear exchange becomes increasingly more likely with the spread of such weapons. Thus it is imperative that the citizens of the planet ensure by legal means and through the United Nations (possibly after reform of that body) that the current situation is wound down until all these weapons are gone forever. Again the author refers to his recent

[* Nuclear Islam, 3rd Edition by Tom Law, Longership Publishing Australia]

357

work titled 'Helter Skelter', also a Longership product, where suggestions are laid down as to possible ways to eliminate nuclear weapons states. With concerted effort it is within the power of ordinary people as well as all the smaller non-nuclear states to pressurize the 'Big Ugly Giants' to come to their senses and realise the dream of a safer world without WMDs.

As stated in the first chapter, it is unlikely that all (or any) of the super powers will give up their weapons unless (1) they have **no veto** on the Security Council and (2) the General Assembly votes in a timetable for total disarmament and a punishment for those that refuse or delay. This might take the form of a hefty fine and/or economic pressure.

In the past we have seen Israel bomb nuclear facilities in Libya, Syria, Iraq and Iran. This was for the purpose of self protection. In this respect, it appears as a failure by the UN. **"It cannot be left to any single sovereign nation to unilaterally destroy property of another nation without reprisal."** Thus we have experienced in recent years devastation across the Middle East partly for the protection of Israel- a country of just 8 million people and a thorn in the side of the world at large! If the Palestinian/Israel war is not resolved in a fair and just way, we may soon see a biblical Armageddon, particularly if WMDs become available to armies or terrorist groups bent on using them.

It is then a logical step not in just preventing new nuclear weapon states, but to denuclearise those that already possess these hideous weapons. It must be achieved through international law and the UN must be constantly vigilant. As well as the IAEA it would be essential to create a sister organisation such as an **'International Nuclear Inspectorate whose job it is to see that no weapons of mass destruction are held by any nation.'** As spelled out in chapter one, only a DEMAND by the world's peoples and ACTION by the UN General Assembly can achieve such a goal.

Let us make the cut-off date **12 midnight, 31st December 2025**.

Hypocrisy of American Nuclear Policy

The author knows what many readers are thinking… if we do not stop new countries such as Iran or North Korea from joining the 'Nuclear Club' then something horrific will eventuate. These countries cannot be trusted with nuclear weapons and delivery systems. But then can any state be trusted? Can we ourselves be trusted? A pissy small nation such as Israel with just under 8 million persons is permitted to have submarines running around the world's oceans with nuclear missiles as well as a nuclear arsenal at home in readiness against an enemy? The Western world aided and abetted this situation, despite the fact that the Middle East is the most volatile part of the globe and if a nuclear war starts, it is most likely to start there! President JFK of the US denied Israel its nuclear program back in 1963. Unfortunately he was snuffed out and nobody got in the way of Israel's nuclear ambitions after that! The gate is open and the horse has bolted you say. Well you would be correct. The world is now faced with only one choice… complete disarmament of all nuclear weapons states. Nothing else is gonna save us! The superpowers are only interested in their own survival and their own interests. For this reason it is fair enough for the smaller nations to gang up on them and pull them down… rhetorically that is!

Added to the previous list are many other countries wishing to 'go nuclear' for electrical energy. This presents the world with further problems of serious pollution for future generations allied with the potential for any nation with a nuclear reactor to graduate to making a nuclear bomb! It is a dilemma. But there is no escaping the fact that in many cases (but not all), **"Nuclear Power states are also Nuclear Weapons States!"**

Israel's Nuclear Arsenal and Weapons of Mass Destruction: A Threat to World Peace

Estimates of the Israeli nuclear arsenal range from a minimum of 200 to a maximum of about 500. Whatever the number, there is little doubt that Israeli nukes are among the world's most sophisticated, largely designed for 'war fighting' in the Middle East. A staple of the Israeli nuclear arsenal are 'neutron bombs', miniaturized thermonuclear bombs designed to maximize deadly gamma radiation while minimizing blast effects and long term radiation- in essence designed to kill people while leaving property intact. The bombs themselves range in size from 'city busters' larger than the Hiroshima Bomb to tactical mini nukes. The Israeli arsenal of weapons of mass destruction clearly dwarfs the actual or potential conventional weapon arsenals of all other Middle Eastern states combined and is vastly greater than any conceivable need for 'deterrence'.

Israel is also thought to possess a comprehensive arsenal of chemical and biological weapons. According to the Sunday Times, Israel has produced both chemical and biological weapons with a sophisticated delivery system, quoting a senior Israeli intelligence official:

"There is hardly a single known or unknown form of chemical or biological weapon.. which is not manufactured at the Nes Tziyona Biological Institute."

Lastly, a nuclear free Israel would make a 'Nuclear Free Middle East' and a comprehensive regional peace agreement much more likely. Until the world community confronts Israel over its nuclear program it is unlikely that there will be any meaningful resolution of the Israeli/Arab conflict.   **From article by John Steinbach,   Global Research, June 30, 2018**

Khilafah Islam

What is the Khilafah?

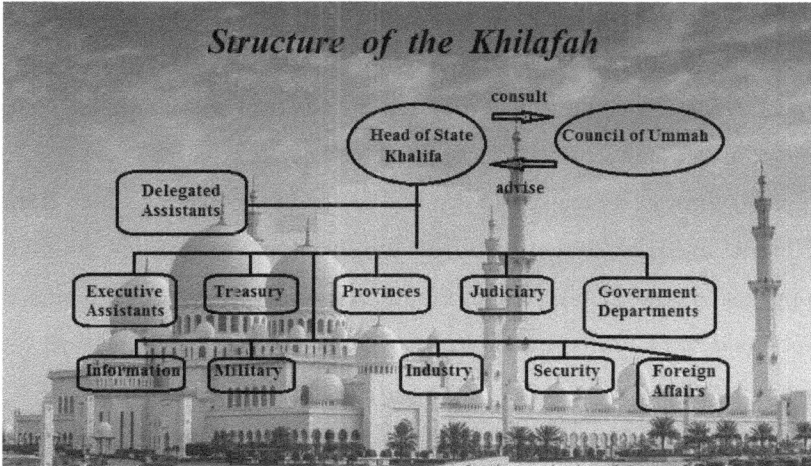

The Khilafah (Caliphate) is a general leadership over all Muslims in the world. Its responsibility is to implement the laws of the Islamic system and convey the Islamic Message to the rest of the world. The Khilafah is also called the Imama as both words have been narrated in many sahih ahadith (complementary writings to the al Koran) with the same meaning.

The Khilafah ruling system bears no resemblance to any of the governments in the Muslim world today. Although many commentators and historians have tried to interpret the Khilafah within existing political frameworks, it is in fact a unique political system.

The Khalifa (Caliph) is the head of state in the Khilafah. He is not a king or dictator but an elected leader whose authority to rule must be given willingly by the Muslims through a special ruling contact called baya. Without this baya he cannot be the head of state. This is completely opposite to a king or dictator who imposes his authority through coercion and force. The tyrant kings and dictators in the Muslim world (past and present) are ample examples of this, imprisoning, torturing Muslims and stealing their wealth and resources.

This contract of baya stipulates that the Khalifa must be just and rule the people by sharia. He is not a sovereign and cannot legislate or enact new laws from his own mind that may suit his personal and family interests. Any legislation he wishes to pass must be derived from the Islamic legal sources through a precise and detailed methodology called ijtihad. If the Khalifa attempts to legislate any law contrary to this or commits oppression against his people, the highest and most powerful court in the State, the Unjust Acts Court (mahkamat mazalim) may impeach the Khalifa and order his removal from office!

The Khalifa has been likened by some to a Pope, who is the Spiritual Head of all Muslims, infallible and appointed by God. But this is not really an apt comparison as the Khalifa is not a priest. His post is an executive post within the Islamic government. He is not infallible and can make mistakes, which is why many checks and balances exist within the Islamic system to ensure he and his government remain accountable.

The Khalifa is not appointed by Allah, rather he is elected by the Muslims and assumes authority through the contract of baya. The Khilafah is not a theocracy. Its legislation is not restricted to religious and moral codes that neglect the problems of society. Shari'ah is a comprehensive system that legislates on political, social, economic, foreign policy and judicial matters. Economic progress, elimination of poverty and enhancing the people's standard of living are all goals the Khilafah will aim to achieve. This is completely opposite to the backward, medieval theocracies founded in Europe during the middle ages where the poor were forced to work and live in squalid conditions in return for the promise of heaven. Historically the Khilafah was an immensely wealthy state with a flourishing economy, high standard of living and a world leader in industry and scientific research for centuries.

The Khilafah is not an empire that favours some lands above others. Nationalism and racism have no place in Islam and are totally prohibited. The Khalifa can be from any race or colour and from any school of thought (mazahib) as long as he is Muslim. The Khilafah is an expansionist state but does not conquer new lands in order to steal their wealth and resources. Rather its foreign policy is to convey the Islamic message alone.

The Khilafah bears no resemblance to the republican system that is widespread in the Muslim world today. The republican system is based on democracy where sovereignty is given to the people. This means they have the right to legislate laws and a constitution. Sovereignty in Islam is to the sharia. No one in the Khilafah, including the Khalifa, can legislate laws from their own minds.

The Khilafah is not a totalitarian state. It cannot spy on its Muslim or non-Muslim citizens. Everyone in the Khilafah has the right to express his or her opposition to policies of the state without fear of arrest or imprisonment. Torture and imprisonment without trial is completely forbidden.

The Khilafah does not oppress its non-Muslim minorities. Non-Muslims (dhimmi) are protected by the state and not forced to leave their religions and adopt Islamic values. Rather, non-Muslim citizens are protected and their homes, properties and lives cannot be violated. Imam Qarafi, a Classical Scholar summed up the responsibility of the Khilafah to the dhimmi when he said: "It is the responsibility of the Muslims to the People of the Dhimma to care for their weak, fulfil the needs of the poor, feed the hungry, provide clothes, address them politely, and even tolerate their harm even if it was from a neighbour, even though the Muslim would have an upper hand (by the fact that it is an Islamic state). The Muslims must also advise them sincerely on their affairs and protect them against anyone who tries to hurt them or their family, steal their wealth, or violate their rights."

Women in the Khilafah are not regarded as inferior or second class citizens. Islam gave women the right to wealth, property rights, rights over marriage and divorce as well as a place in society. Islam established a public dress code for women, the Khimar and Jilbab, in order to establish a productive society free from the type of negative and harmful relationships prevalent in the West.

Establishing the Khilafah and appointing a Khalifa is obligatory on all Muslims in the world, male and female. Performing this duty (fard) is the same as performing any other duty which Allah has ordered us, where no complacency is allowed. Indeed the Khilafah is a vital issue for the Muslims.

The future Khilafah will undoubtedly usher in a new era of peace, stability and prosperity for the Muslim world and beyond, ending years of oppression by some of the worst tyrants this world has ever seen. The days of colonialism and exploitation of the Muslim world will finally come to an end and the Khilafah will utilise all resources at its disposal to further the interests of Islam and Muslims as well as establish an alternative for the people of the world to the Capitalist system.

[Edited from article by Hizb ut Tahrir Wilayah on khilafah.com, March 2018]

3rd March 1924 …   94 years without the Caliphate

"We must put an end to anything which brings about any Islamic unity between the sons of the Muslims. The situation now is that Turkey is dead and will never rise again, because we have destroyed its moral strength, the Caliphate and Islam."

This bold statement, or rather stark warning, was allegedly made by the former British Foreign Secretary, Lord Curzon, at the House of Commons after the Lausanne Treaty of 1923, following the Ottoman defeat in World War One. The reason why Lord Curzon's statement should be taken with so much weight (that is assuming it is true) is because it correlates with the following ḥadith of Prophet Muḥammad:

"The knots of Islam will be undone one by one, each time a knot is undone the next one will be grasped, the first to be undone will be the ruling and the last will be the prayer."

It is now more than 94 years since the destruction of the Ottoman Caliphate, heralding arguably the darkest chapter in Islamic history after the death of Rasul'Allah (Muhammad). The Ummah (Islamic community) continues to suffer from the after effects of this calamitous event, for the very reason which Lord Curzon mentioned: Muslims currently have no collective "moral strength", which is embodied in the form of an inclusive Islamic polity. The Middle East and North Africa were subsequently carved up between Britain and France, as Mark Sykes and Francois Georges Picot planned the future of the former Ottoman territories with a pen and ruler. What followed since was an uninterrupted chain of secular dictatorships and oil rich sheikhdoms. Many of these regimes came to power via military coups (dressed up as liberators), whilst the Gulf monarchies unashamedly enjoyed the fruits of that betrayal post WWI.

History lessons aside, the concept of the Caliphate and the Muslim desire for it continues to be maligned by academics, journalists, Western policy makers and governments. Secular liberals and modernists, both Muslim and non-Muslim from across the political spectrum appear to have adopted the attitude of Lord Curzon but with rehashed rhetoric that a Caliphate is simply incompatible with the modern world, rendering it barbaric and despotic. The irony of this stance is that all seem to conveniently forget that for over a thousand years Islamic civilisation under successive Caliphates, from the Umayyads to the Ottomans, led humanity in science, philosophy, arts and technology. Furthermore, agenda driven critics and muscular ideologues also overlook that not only did every Caliphate have the trappings of a modern state, but they were the beacon and example of modernity for their relevant period in history. One simply cannot do justice in explaining Islam's contribution to the world as we know it today where libraries are filled with books and historical testimonies of non-Muslims who substantiate this undeniable fact.

However, it must be stated from the onset that a Caliphate is not regarded as a utopian state, conceptually or in practice. This was never the case when Prophet Muhammad ruled over Madina or when the Khulafah Rashidun (Rightly Guided Caliphs) expanded the Caliphate or indeed those that came after! In fact, when the Caliphate entered hereditary rule and kingship there were cases of internal corruption, theological deviation and infighting. Rather, this polity is what followed the end of Prophethood and the practical manifestation of Allah's divine law on Earth. This is evident in the following ḥadith of Rasul'Allah:

> *"The Prophets used to manage the political affairs of Bani Israil (i.e the Arabic and Israelite peoples of the Middle East). Whenever a Prophet died another Prophet succeeded him, but there will be no Prophets after me; instead there will be Caliphs and they will number many".*
>
> *The Companions then asked: "what then do you order us?"*
>
> *He replied: "fulfil allegiance to them one after the other. Give them their dues. Verily Allah will ask them about what He entrusted them with".*

The virtues and societal conditions sought from the Caliphate, deduced from the classical scholars after scrutinising the Shari'ah, is to establish social justice, to protect the honour and property of its citizens and the preservation of the Islamic way of life. Now this may be a sour grape for the intolerant 'tolerant' who stubbornly comprehend the Islamic system through the lenses of a secular paradigm, assuming that liberal democracy is the default benchmark against which every governing system should be compared to. [i.e a contemporary self-righteousness defending the current system as the only correct system -ed. TL.] But there is also a political context to this ideological objection of the Caliphate and that is the conflation of Europe's systematic separation of 'Church and State'. This period of secularisation, which is symbolised in the era known as the 'Enlightenment', has never occurred in the Muslim world during the existence of a Caliphate, nor would it be befitting.

Those that attempt and conflate Islam and western Christianity under the arbitrary term "religion" invariably superimpose the pre-reformation Christian history onto Islam; *whereas the two developed quite differently.* The fact of the matter is that Islamic history is not plagued with the same repressive 'church institutions' that stifled human advancement and, further, the classical Islamic governance had already secured the rights that the 'Enlightenment' sought to secure and more. The notion of a Caliph is as an employee that represents and is accountable to the people; Islamic history shows a level of accountability that we still have not yet seen in Western politics! Despite this, there were attempts during the 19th century to minimise the legislative powers of the Caliph and to modernise certain aspects of the declining Ottoman Caliphate to make it more 'palatable' with its thriving European contemporaries; but the idea of a systematic separation of 'religion and state' was unthinkable.

[Without going into depth and detail, it is the moral codes of religion that were seen as inseparable from the state and its laws in the Islamic Caliphate. See the mess that Western countries now endure with morality out of the window and piecemeal attempts to be reintroduced and written, albeit unsuccessfully, into law! -ed. TL.]

Additionally, Islam's worldview that was represented by the Caliphate had always clashed with other empires it encountered; from the Persians, Byzantines, Mongols, Crusaders, right up to the imperial powers of Europe. Hence, after the destruction of the Caliphate on 3rd March 1924, Christian Europe had successfully eradicated the only superpower that it had been in a constant state of conflict with for nearly a millennium (neglecting here the rise of Socialism and appearance of the totalitarian Communist state). Of course, Europe had suffered centuries of bloody internal wars, but the fight against the 'Mohammedans' was a unique one due to cultural and religious dissimilarity.

After the downfall of the Soviet Union in 1989, Francis Fukuyama* had arrogantly stated that humanity had reached the 'end of history', implying that liberal democracy was the only natural form of government to have survived the testing waves of global change. Fukuyama was clearly naive in his assessment of the world because he assumed that in the absence of the Caliphate, the Islamic mind would also be non-existent; he was grossly mistaken. The 9/11 attacks and the subsequent US-led 'war on terror' that followed is a testimony to this. After the invasion of Afghanistan and Iraq and the rise of armed groups in Yemen, Somalia and Pakistan, it became unavoidably clear that the desire for the return of the Caliphate was very much existent. The Arab Spring, or what remains of it, is another example of the Islamic

[*Yoshihiro Francis Fukuyama, born October 27, 1952 is an American political scientist, political economist and author. Known for his book *The End of History and the Last Man* (1992), which argued that the worldwide spread of liberal democracies and free market capitalism of the West and its lifestyle may signal the end point of humanity's socio-cultural evolution and become the final form of human government. However, his subsequent book *Trust: Social Virtues and Creation of Prosperity* (1995) modified his earlier position to acknowledge that culture cannot be cleanly separated from economics. Also associated with the rise of the neoconservative movement from which he has since distanced himself.]

sentiment of the general Muslim masses in wanting Islam to play a greater role in society. Tunisia, Egypt, Libya, Yemen, and more evidently in Syria, are prime examples of this. The revolutions which spread like wildfire in 2011 initially began as grassroot movements in order to attain self-determination in regions which had been ruled by Western-backed dictators for decades. Unfortunately, with the interference of Western powers (which includes Russia) and their regional proxies, the sincere efforts of those who lost their lives during the uprisings had been sidelined and forgotten by political opportunists in search for power. Naturally, cosmetic changes were made to the 'new' post-Arab Spring countries, **but in nearly every case the oppressive regimes and state apparatus remained**.

The emergence of the group known as ISIS, which claimed to have restored the Caliphate on 29 June 2014, was a 'dream come true' for the West. The former chief of the British Armed forces, Sir General Richard Dannatt, justified the occupation of Afghanistan and Britain's involvement in the war on terror by stating that it was to prevent:

"...the historic Islamic caliphate, running through south Asia, the Middle East, North Africa and up through south and south-east Europe."

Lo and behold the West had at last found its medieval Caliphate in the form of ISIS, which in reality was no more than a doctor's sick note allowing it (Britain, America and other capitalist co-conspirators) to continue destructive foreign policy and control in the Middle East. Since, the criminality of ISIS has been used as a stick by Western politicians to beat the Muslims with and a tool to demonise the noble concept of the Caliphate. The media continues to refer to ISIS as an "Islamic State", knowing that the majority of Muslims, including likeminded groups who share the same goal, have unequivocally rejected their claim to the Caliphate.

Most importantly, the abhorrent actions of ISIS cannot be used to pressure Muslims into rejecting the concept of the Caliphate for two very simple reasons:

> Firstly, there is a unanimous consensus amongst classical and contemporary scholars within Sunni Islam that the Caliphate is the ideal form of governance for Muslims and to work for its re-establishment is an obligation. However, Muslims will inevitably differ in the methodology of how the Caliphate should be restored due to theological and political differences; but scriptural evidence and scholarly works emphasising its importance is too overpowering.

> Secondly, the fact that Rasul'Allah's burial was delayed until a Caliph was appointed could not have been a more significant indication of how serious the Companions of Muhammad took the matter of the Caliphate.

"The aforementioned reasons, coupled with the dire situation the Muslim world is currently in as a result of seeking liberation by adopting failed secular ideologies, the only real option remaining for the Ummah is to return to a system which, for all its previous mistakes, protected Islam and safeguarded its citizens from harm."

Those who are adamant that the Caliphate is incompatible with the modern world and thus to anticipate its return is just a romanticised idea, need to appreciate from an Islamic perspective that the Prophet

Muḥammad prophesised its permanent return and Allah has promised the Muslims authority on Earth.

[Original text by Dilly Hussain in Current Affairs, History, Islamic Thought, Latest, News Views, Opinion on www.islam21c.com, March 2018. Tom Law has applied some minor editing.]

A Standard for a true 'Commonwealth of Islamic Nations':

gold, green, white and black

Note there are 56 parallelograms around the edge denoting 56 nations, some of which remain under the yoke of other vainglorious and more powerful nations!

Where to Go from Here?

Where is God? How to address the inequalities in the world today? How to stay human in a world of Artificial Intelligence? Can we turn Climate Change around? How to put an end to senseless wars?

These are all pressing questions for peoples of the world living in the 21st century! We have already discussed the need for reform in the United Nations and a new model for the General Assembly to counter a nation's intent on bellicose actions against a neighbour. But recommendations need momentum and force. This can only be achieved by ordinary people making constant demands until the day is won. The status quo and magnificent imperial international corporations that make huge profits out of the misery of those suffering war possess almost immovable inertia. They will manipulate politicians, the media, the financial sector and go to any lengths to protect their networks and profit machine. THEY WILL RESIST CHANGE!

The Not-so-Intelligent Ape:

Mentioned elsewhere, there are two disabilities that prevent us, or at least greatly impede our attempts at going forward to create a utopian world. Firstly is the limitation of our intelligence. As individuals we cannot absorb all the information thrown at us daily from hard print and digital media. It is overwhelming and we are only able to take in a smidgen of what's on offer; thus most of it passes over our heads and is neither stored nor analysed by our brain. Collectively, humanity has acquired vast scientific and technological knowledge and expertise. Individually, we understand but a very narrow bandwidth of the total spectrum. Even our best and brightest will admit to this. Genetically, we are not much different from our ancestors of one hundred thousand years ago struggling in the hunter-gatherer era! Our brains are marginally bigger due to better and consistent food supplies.

Secondly, our life span is still just above the biblical three score and ten i.e 70 years plus. But this is only true in the wealthier nations. In many poorer nations the average life span of humans is well below this! Taken together, these two facts greatly inhibit our collective progress in an ever complex world of which Mr and Mrs Joe Blow have little understanding. If a utopian world society is represented by a firm and shiny stainless steel amulet, the reality of our situation is a wobbly vibrating rubber band. Our various political structures governing all the separate nations sadly repeat mistakes of the past on an ever grandiose scale. Perhaps a giant computer- 'Deep Thought', possessing all the history and accumulated knowledge of human civilisations over the last two millennia might be better relied upon to work out the answers to our problems and reduce conflict than any of us mere mortals!

Returning to our discussion on 'Demand Now':

You will be labelled a communist, a fascist, a terrorist, a trouble maker extraordinaire, a fifth columnist and a whole host of other insulting acronyms to humiliate you and weaken you so that eventually you leave the field of battle. BUT YOU MUST NOT EVER ALLOW THIS TO HAPPEN! The maggots must be called out and identified. The world is dominated by the dark side, the forces of evil, the ten minute doctors and the war profiteers; the media manipulators and the liars in politics. EDUCATION and raising the intelligence and awareness of all peoples on the planet is the way forward. Science, mathematics and the persuasion of sound logic along with irrefutable evidence must, taken together, be your loadstar and guide.

There is nothing wrong with a belief in God, the creator of the universe and all living things. However, beware of those that state that their slant on religious questions is the only true and correct one. They speak with a forked tongue! Beware those that ask you to join a war and commit murder of innocents for they wish for you to carry out the wishes of Satan and evil. Worse still that you commit suicide in order to kill others! Each of the major religions of the world only approximates the truth and form part of humankind's spiritual search. Taken together they form the petals and sepals of a flower. We do not comprehend everything about our lives, our purpose and the deepest meaning as to why we are here. But in a way this mystery makes our life more beautiful. Those that seek too deeply and play at the darker side of spirituality more often than not become mentally disturbed. In such cases, these individuals have lost opportunity to play their role in assisting humankind. Their actions are detrimental to society. Be aware of your limitations in understanding and go forth as a creative person doing the best works according to your abilities. Be not ashamed of your limitations, for that is what it means to be human!

In your country you must challenge the squandering of resources. Money for large armies and armaments at the expense of infrastructure such as roads, housing, transport systems, hospitals and schools is a travesty. Politicians that allow these things need to be replaced. Immoral media, destructive drug availability, poor role models in high places, excessive display of wealth, overpayment of celebrities and sports professional ... write your own list. Laissez fair attitudes to environment, how each person relates to a complete stranger, the value of protecting family, seeking friendship with those of different skin colour and culture, the elimination of personal weapons such as guns... all these attributes define a safe and healthy society. There is no need to list the negatives as we all know what they are!

So the key to a better world is a combination of these three things:

1   Participation of the individual to question and demand change for the betterment of humankind

2   Participation of each country's representative in the UN General Assembly to move forward incrementally with both law and action to change the world

3   To bring equality of opportunity to every human through education and fair distribution of wealth with a mind to avoid the waste or squandering of resources

The most simplistic of cultures that possess happy and fulfilled people without the stresses of high crime and murder are more sustainable and worthy than those of great material possessions but suffer the worst of those debilitating societal diseases discussed above! A modest house, a modest car, a loving family and dependable friends far outweigh a bag of expensive material things along with loneliness and lack of trust in one's fellows. The Prince and the Pauper is a celebratory tale which exposes the sadness of excessive wealth but lacking in the stuff of life! I am not here rejoicing in poverty either! Poverty is inflicted on sections of society by an uncaring ruler or government that indulges in personal accumulation of wealth through immoral or illegal means without a conscience! (It may also be the result of foolish investment or wasting of national resources on things that are not needed or at least are marked as low priority!) Pure socialism in a totalitarian regime is not the answer either. Some competitiveness is essential for new ideas and invention. Capitalism tempered with a social conscience enables all in society to receive a fair and equitable share. But placing large proportions of one's capital in offshore accounts to avoid paying one's true tax burden is no less than cheating your fellows that share your country. Call them out, call them out!

One sometimes wonders if 'Party Politics' in Western democracies has commenced to fail us in recent years? The best of society are possibly shunned or simply overlooked in favour of those adhering to 'policy' or belonging to an 'old boys and girls network'! There seems to be merit in the 'independent candidate' in contemporary politics. But humans still suffer the 'herd instinct' and tend to gravitate towards a particular party that demonstrates a sub-spectrum of one's personal beliefs and values. I say 'sub-spectrum' as one is never completely satisfied, as an individual, with ALL the policies of one's favoured party. We see this in parliamentary debate where it is not unusual, where a moral issue is under discussion, for a member to 'cross the floor' and vote against her/his own party stance as a matter of conscience! The concentration of media ownership in the modern world is also a concern. When involved in a war, propaganda to lie to and deceive the general public is often the case. "In war, the first casualty is truth!" It has been experienced time and time again. The enemy must always be painted in the most grotesque way. We have inherited this from the Second World War. Unfortunately we also inherited the action of 'bombing the shit out of the bastards' from former wars which now cannot be justified and, in the majority of cases, has been no less than a war crime. These have been cited in earlier chapters but there seems to be no let up in such behaviour by many nations and particularly the super powers. They must all be held to account! Unilateral engagement by any nation to 'right the wrongs' of a rogue nation can no longer be tolerated. "Might is not Right" and the UN General Assembly must take dramatic and swift steps to prevent this in future. The author is not naming culprit nations here, but suspects the reader can quickly list them for their actions over the last couple of decades. There will always be attempts by the richer and more powerful nations to try to create economic and material empires in the world. Innovation and technological advancement will give one nation the edge over others. But this must not be abused. Slowly, such innovations need filter down for all to benefit. With empire comes arrogance and eventually violence in order to maintain a new status quo. History has demonstrated that, even with the best of intentions at the outset, imperialism eventually leads to despotism and cruelty. The General Assembly is the brotherhood/sisterhood of all the nations and must be the vigilant watchdog on this matter. Accumulation of excessive wealth and power always leads to corruption. It is a human weakness that must be tempered!

They're Not Gonna Like It!

The world is at a crossroads where it has the technical knowhow to completely destroy the planet by weapons of mass destruction which include nuclear bombs, chemical agents and biological entities. The recklessness and individual will of the powerful nations cannot be exercised over the rest of the nations any more. UN agencies such as the IEAE and new emerging agencies must be provided with razor teeth to finally eliminate these weapons. There is to be no further compromise or slippery rhetoric for any nation to avoid what is essential for the planet's survival. **There is to be consistency in the application of civil and human rights international law.** There can be no hypocrisy, no conspiratorial secrecy, no sequestering away... only openness, transparency and firm application of the law. No nation can object. All must be equal under and be subject to international law. There is no other way!

Appendices

A   Human Rights Council- Complaints Procedure Form:

available at:
https://www.ohchr.org/en/hrbodies/hrc/complaintprocedure/pages/hrccomplaintprocedureindex.aspx

---

Human Rights Council

Complaint Procedure Form

- **You are kindly requested to submit your complaint in writing in one of the six official UN languages (Arabic, Chinese, English, French, Russian and Spanish) and to use these languages in any future correspondence;**
- **Anonymous complaints are not admissible;**
- **It is recommended that your complaint does not exceed eight pages, excluding enclosures.**
- **You are kindly requested not to use abusive or insulting language.**

I. Information concerning the author (s) of the communication or the alleged victim (s) if other than the author

---

Individual ☐   Group of individuals ☐   NGO ☐
Other   ☐

Last name: ....
First name(s): ....
Nationality: ....
Address for correspondence on this complaint: ....
Tel and fax: (please indicate country and area code) ....
E-mail: ....
Website: ....

Submitting the complaint:

On the author's own behalf: ☐
On behalf of other persons: ☐ (Please specify: ....)

II. Information on the State concerned

Name of the State concerned and, as applicable, name of public
authorities responsible for the alleged violation(s): ....

III. Facts of the complaint and nature of the alleged violation(s)

**The complaint procedure addresses consistent patterns of gross and
reliably attested violations of all human rights and all fundamental
freedoms occurring in any part of the world and under any
circumstances.**

Please detail, in chronological order, the facts and circumstances of the
alleged violations including dates, places and alleged perpetrators and
how you consider that the facts and circumstances described violate
your rights or that of the concerned person(s).

....

....

IV. Exhaustion of domestic remedies

1- Steps taken by or on behalf of the alleged victim(s) to exhaust
domestic remedies– please provide details on the procedures which have
been pursued, including recourse to the courts and other public

authorities as well as national human rights institutions[2], the claims made, at which times, and what the outcome was:

…………………..

2- If domestic remedies have not been exhausted on grounds that their application would be ineffective or unreasonably prolonged, please explain the reasons in detail:

……………………….

V. Submission of communication to other human rights bodies

1- Have you already submitted the same matter to a special procedure, a treaty body or other United Nations or similar regional complaint procedures in the field of human rights?

……………

2- If so, detail which procedure has been, or is being pursued, which claims have been made, at which times, and the current status of the complaint before this body:

……………………….

VI. Request for confidentiality

In case the communication complies with the admissibility criteria set forth in Council resolution 5/1, kindly note that it will be transmitted to the State concerned so as to obtain the views of the latter on the allegations of violations.

Please state whether you would like your identity or any specific information contained in the complaint to be kept confidential.

Unwarranted Influence

Request for confidentiality (*Please tick as appropriate*): Yes ☐
No ☐

Please indicate which information you would like to be kept confidential

Date: .... Signature: ....

N.B. The blanks under the various sections of this form indicate where your responses are required. You should take as much space as you need to set out your responses. Your complaint should not exceed eights pages.

VII. Checklist of supporting documents

Please provide copies (not original) of supporting documents (kindly note that these documents will not be returned) in one of the six UN official languages.

- Decisions of domestic courts and authorities on the claim made (a copy of the relevant national legislation is also helpful): ☐

- Complaints sent to any other procedure mentioned in section **V** (and any decisions taken under that procedure): ☐

- Any other evidence or supporting documents deemed necessary: ☐

VIII. Where to send your communications?

Office of the United Nations High Commissioner for Human Rights

Human Rights Council Branch-Complaint Procedure Unit
OHCHR- Palais Wilson

United Nations Office at Geneva
CH-1211 Geneva 10, Switzerland
Fax: (+41 22) 917 90 11
email: CP@ohchr.org

Website: www.ohchr.org/EN/HRBodies/HRC/Pages/HRCIndex.aspx

B   **List of Antinuclear Organisations:**

- Alliance for Nuclear Accountability
- Alliance for Nuclear Responsibility
- Arms Control Association
- Australian Conservation Foundation
- Bellona Foundation
- Beyond Nuclear
- Campaign Against Nuclear Energy
- Campaign for Nuclear Disarmament   CND
- Campaign for Nuclear Disarmament (NZ)
- Canadian Coalition for Nuclear Responsibility
- Canadian Voice of Women for Peace
- Christian CND
- Citizens' Nuclear Information Center
- Clamshell Alliance
- Coalition for Nuclear Power Postponement
- Committee for Non-Violent Action
- Committee for a Nuclear Free Island
- Committee for Nuclear Responsibility
- Council for a Livable World
- Critical Mass
- Cumbrians Opposed to a Radioactive Environment
- **Demand Nuclear Disarmament   DND**
- Don't Make a Wave Committee
- Earthlife Africa
- East Coast Solidarity for Anti-Nuke Group
- Economists for Peace and Security
- Energy Fair
- Energy Probe
- European Nuclear Disarmament
- Friends of the Earth (EWNI)
- Friends of the Earth Scotland
- Global Security Institute
- Greenpeace Aotearoa New Zealand
- Greenpeace Australia Pacific
- INFORSE-Europe
- Institute for Energy and Environmental Research
- International Campaign to Abolish Nuclear Weapons
- International Physicians for the Prevention of Nuclear War
- Koeberg Alert
- Labour CND
- Legambiente

- Low Level Radiation Campaign
- MEDACT
- Musicians United for Safe Energy
- Natural Resources Defense Council
- Nevada Desert Experience
- Nevada Semipalatinsk
- New England Coalition
- No Nukes group
- No New Nukes Y'all
- No to Nuclear Weapons
- One Less Nuclear Power Plant
- Nuclear Age Peace Foundation
- Nuclear Control Institute
- Nuclear Disarmament Party
- Nuclear Free World Policy
- Nuclear Information and Research Service
- Nuclear Threat Initiative
- NukeWatch
- Oak Ridge Peace and Environmental Alliance
- Operation Gandhi
- Peace Action
- Peace Boat
- Peace Organisation of Australia
- Pembina Institute
- People's Movement Against Nuclear Energy
- Performers and Artists for Nuclear Disarmament
- Physicians for Social Responsibility
- Plowshares Movement
- Public Citizen Energy Program
- Rocky Flats Truth Force
- Sayonara Nuclear Power Plants
- Scientists against Nuclear Arms
- Scottish Campaign for Nuclear Disarmament
- Seeds of hope
- Shad Alliance
- Sierra Club
- Sortir du nucléaire (Canada)
- Sortir du nucléaire (France)
- Stop Rokkasho
- The Seneca Women's Encampment for a Future of Peace and Justice
- The Wilderness Society (Australia)
- Top Level Group
- Trident Ploughshares

- Two Futures Project
- White House Peace Vigil
- Women from Fukushima Against Nukes
- Women Strike for Peace
- Women's Action for New Directions (WAND) previously called Women's Action for Nuclear Disarmament, forerunner organization: Women's Party for Survival
- Women's International League for Peace and Freedom

It should be noted that many of these organisations are also against Nuclear Power Stations for electricity production and include other things such as Uranium mining. Unfortunately this mix of values has not always served the main objective of Nuclear Disarmament. DND has just this one focus, to rid the world of nuclear arms!

International Campaign to Abolish Nuclear Weapons ICAN

The International Campaign to Abolish Nuclear Weapons is a global civil society coalition working to promote adherence to and full implementation of the Treaty on the Prohibition of Nuclear Weapons.
https://icanw.org/au

Other Useful Sites:
https://globalzero.org/
https://cnduk.org/
https://nuclearweaponsfree.org/
https://un.org/disarmament/wmd/nuclear/
https://psr.org/
https://greenpeace.org/Home/What we do
https://concentric.org/films/wpiali-info-resources-anti-nuclear-groups.html
https://demandnow.org/

Other International Organizations to Eliminate Nuclear Weapons:

- The ATOM Project, an International non-profit organisation seeking entry into force of the Nuclear Non-proliferation Treaty and the limitation of all nuclear arsenals
- European Nuclear Disarmament, which held annual conventions in the 1980s involving thousands of anti-nuclear weapons activists mostly from Western Europe but also from Eastern Europe, the United States, and Australia.

- Friends of the Earth International, a network of environmental organizations in 77 countries.
- Global Zero, an international non-partisan group of 300 world leaders dedicated to achieving the elimination of nuclear weapons.
- Global Initiative to Combat Nuclear Terrorism, an international partnership of 83 nations.
- Greenpeace International, a non-governmental environmental organisation with offices in over 41 countries and headquarters in Amsterdam, Netherlands.
- International Campaign to Abolish Nuclear Weapons
- International Network of Engineers and Scientists for Global Responsibility
- International Physicians for the Prevention of Nuclear War, which had affiliates in 41 nations in 1985, representing 135,000 physicians; IPPNW was awarded the UNESCO Peace Education Prize in 1984 and the Nobel Peace Prize in 1985.
- Nuclear Free World Policy
- Nuclear Information and Resource Service
- OPANAL
- Parliamentarians for Nuclear Non-Proliferation and Disarmament, a global network of over 700 parliamentarians from more than 75 countries working to prevent nuclear proliferation.
- Pax Christi International, a Catholic group which takes a sharply anti-nuclear stand.
- Ploughshares Fund
- Pugwash Conferences on Science and World Affairs
- Socialist International, the world body of social democratic parties.
- Sōka Gakkai, a peace-orientated Buddhist organisation, which held anti-nuclear exhibitions in Japanese cities during the late 1970s, and gathered 10 million signatures on petitions calling for the abolition of nuclear weapons.
- The Ribbon International, a United Nations Non-Governmental Organisation promoting nuclear disarmament.
- United Nations Office for Disarmament Affairs
- World Disarmament Campaign
- World Information Service on Energy, based in Amsterdam, The Netherlands
- World Union for Protection of Life

C   Coalition Military Hardware in 2003 Invasion of Iraq

United States of America
Infantry weapons:

- M16A1
- M16A2
- CAR-15
- M60
- MP5
- M249
- M240
- M9 pistol
- M1911 pistol
- Barrett M82
- M24 Sniper Weapon System
- M21 Sniper Weapon System
- M40 Sniper Rifle
- M2HB
- M72 LAW
- AT4
- M47 Dragon

Land-based:
Tanks

- M1 Abrams MBT (Main Battle Tank) 105mm cannon type
- M1A1 Abrams MBT (Main Battle Tank)
- M1A1 HA Abrams MBT (Main Battle Tank) *Heavy Armor*
- M60A1/A3 Patton MBT (Main Battle Tank) (USMC)
- M551A1 Sheridan TTS (Tank Thermal Sight) Armored Reconnaissance Airborne Assault Vehicle

Armoured vehicles

- M2A2 Bradley IFV (Infantry Fighting Vehicle)
- M3A2 Bradley CFV (Cavalry Fighting Vehicle)
- AAVP7A1 Assault Amphibian Vehicle Personnel (USMC)
- LAV-25 Light Armored Vehicle (USMC)
- LAV-AT Light Armored Vehicle (Anti-Tank) (USMC)
- M113A2/A3 APC (Armored Personnel Carrier)
- M113 Armored Personnel Carrier ACAV APC (Armored Personnel Carrier)
- V- 150 APC (Armored Personnel Carrier)
- V -100 APC (Armored Personnel Carrier)
- M901A1 ITV (Improved TOW Vehicle)

Self-propelled artillery/mortars/rockets

- LAV-M Light Armored Vehicle (Mortar) (USMC)
- M106A2 Self-Propelled Mortar Carrier

- M109A2/A3/A4 155 mm SPH (Self-Propelled Howitzer)
- M110A2 8 inch SPH (Self-Propelled Howitzer)
- M270 MLRS Multiple Launch Rocket System
- M91 Multiple Launch Rocket System

Anti-aircraft

- M163 VADS Vulcan Air Defence System
- M48 Chaparral Self-Propelled SAM (Surface-To-Air Missile) Launcher
- M1097 Avenger Humvee
- M167 VADS Vulcan Air Defence System
- MIM-23 Improved Hawk SAM (Surface-To-Air Missile) Launcher
- MIM-104 Patriot SAM (Surface-To-Air Missile) Launcher
- LAV-AD Light Armored Vehicle (Air Defense) (USMC)

Artillery and mortars

- M102 105 mm Towed Howitzer
- M198 155 mm Towed Howitzer
- M58 MICLIC (Mine Clearing Line Charge) Towed
- M224 60 mm Light Weight Mortar
- M252 81 mm Medium Weight Mortar
- M30 107 mm Heavy Weight Mortar

Engineering and recovery vehicles

- M728 CEV (Combat Engineer Vehicle)
- M9 ACE (Armored Combat Earthmover)
- M60 AVLM (Armored Vehicle Launched MICLIC (Mine-Clearing Line Charge))
- M88A1 ARV (Armoured Recovery Vehicle)
- M60A1 AVLB (Armored Vehicle Launched Bridge)
- M139 Volcano Mine System

Command vehicles

- M577A2 ACP (Armored Command Post) Carrier
- AACV7A1 (Assault Amphibian Vehicle Command) (USMC)
- LAV-25C2 Light Armored Vehicle (Command & Control) (USMC)
- M981 FISTV (Fire Support Team Vehicle)

Other vehicles

- M998 HMMWV Humvee
- M151A2 FAV (Fast Attack Vehicle) (USMC)
- M1008 CUCV (Commercial Utility, Cargo Vehicle)
- FAV (Fast Attack Vehicle) / DPV (Desert Patrol Vehicle)
- Kawasaki KLR-250-D8
- M35A2 6×6 2.5-Ton Truck "Deuce And A Half"
- M915 6×4 Army truck medium transportation.
- M915A1 6×4 Army truck medium transportation.
- M925A1 6×6 5-Ton Truck
- M548 Tracked Cargo Carrier
- M992 FAASV (Field Artillery Ammunition Supply Vehicle)

Aircraft;

Helicopters
- Bell AH-1F Cobra (Army)
- Bell AH-1J SeaCobra (USMC)
- Bell AH-1T Improved SeaCobra (USMC)
- Bell AH-1W SuperCobra (USMC)
- Boeing AH-64A Apache (Army)
- Boeing CH-46D Sea Knight (USN)
- Boeing CH-46E Sea Knight (USMC)
- Boeing CH-47D Chinook (Army)
- Sikorsky CH-53D Sea Stallion (USN, USMC)
- Sikorsky CH-53E Super Stallion (USMC)
- Bell EH-1H Iroquois (Huey) (Army)
- Sikorsky EH-60A Quick Fix (Army)
- Boeing HH-46D Sea Knight (USN)
- Sikorsky HH-60H Seahawk (USN)
- Boeing MH-47 (SOA) Special Operations Aircraft (Army)
- Sikorsky MH-53E Sea Dragon (USN)
- Sikorsky MH-60G Pave Hawk (USAF)
- Bell OH-58A Kiowa (Army)
- Bell OH-58C Kiowa (Army)
- Bell OH-58D Kiowa (Army)
- Sikorsky RH-53D Sea Stallion (USMC)
- Kaman SH-2F Seasprite (USN)
- Sikorsky SH-3G Sea King (USN)
- Sikorsky SH-3H Sea King (USN)
- Sikorsky SH-60B Seahawk (USN)
- Bell UH-1H Iroquois (Huey) (Army)
- Bell UH-1N (Huey) (USMC)
- Bell UH-1V Iroquois (Huey) Aeromedical Evacuation (Army)
- Boeing UH-46D Sea Knight (USN)
- Sikorsky UH-60A Black Hawk (Army)

Airplanes
- Grumman A-6E Intruder (USN, USMC)
- Grumman OV1D Mohawk (Army)
- Vought A-7E Corsair II (USN)
- BAe/McDonnell Douglas AV-8B Harrier II (USMC)
- A-10A Thunderbolt II (Warthog) (USAF)
- Lockheed AC-130A (Spectre) Gunship (USAF)
- Lockheed AC-130H (Spectre) Gunship (USAF)
- Boeing B-52G Stratofortress (USAF)
- Boeing B-52H Stratofortress (USAF)
- Grumman C-2A Greyhound (USN)

- Lockheed C-141 Starlifter (USAF)
- Lockheed C-5 Galaxy (USAF)
- McDonnell Douglas C-9B Skytrain II (USN)
- Raytheon C-12 Huron (USAF)
- Lockheed C-130 Hercules (USAF)
- Lockheed C-130F Hercules (USN)
- North American Rockwell CT-39G (USN)
- McDonnell Douglas DC-9 (USN)
- Grumman E-2C Hawkeye (USN)
- Boeing E-3B Sentry AWACS Airborne Warning And Control System (USAF)
- Douglas EA-3B Skywarrior (USN)
- Lockheed EP-3E Aries II (USN)
- Grumman EA-6B Prowler (USN)
- Boeing E-8 Joint STARS Joint Surveillance Target Attack Radar System (USAF)
- General Dynamics EF-111A Raven (USAF)
- Lockheed EC-130E/J Commando Solo (USAF)
- Lockheed EC-130H Compass Call (USAF)
- Boeing EC-135L Looking Glass (USAF)
- McDonnell Douglas F-4E Phantom II (USAF)
- McDonnell Douglas F-4G Phantom II (Wild Weasel) (USAF)
- Grumman F-14A Tomcat (USN)
- Grumman F-14A+(B) Tomcat (USN)
- McDonnell Douglas F-15C Eagle (USAF)
- McDonnell Douglas F-15E Strike Eagle (USAF)
- General Dynamics F-16A Fighting Falcon (USAF)
- General Dynamics F-16C Fighting Falcon (USAF)
- McDonnell Douglas F/A-18A Hornet (USN, USMC)
- McDonnell Douglas F/A-18C Hornet (USN, USMC)
- McDonnell Douglas F/A-18D Hornet (USMC)
- General Dynamics F-111E Aardvark (USAF)
- General Dynamics F-111F Aardvark (USAF)
- Lockheed F-117A Nighthawk (USAF)
- Lockheed HC-130 King (USAF)
- McDonnell Douglas KC-10A Extender (USAF)
- Lockheed KC-130F Hercules (USN, USMC)
- Lockheed KC-130R Hercules (USMC)
- Lockheed KC-130T Hercules (USMC)
- Boeing KC-135E Stratotanker (USAF)
- Boeing KC-135R Stratotanker (USAF)
- Lockheed MC-130E Hercules Combat Talon (USAF)
- North American Rockwell OV-10A Bronco (USMC)
- North American Rockwell OV-10D Bronco (USMC)

- North American Rockwell OV-10D+ Bronco (USMC)
- Lockheed P-3B Orion (USN)
- Lockheed P-3C Orion (USN)
- Boeing RC-135V/W Rivet Joint (USAF)
- McDonnell Douglas RF-4C Phantom II (USAF)
- Lockheed S-3A Viking (USN)
- Lockheed S-3B Viking (USN)
- Lockheed U-2/TR-1 Dragon Lady (USAF)
- Lockheed UP-3A Orion (USN)

Ships:

Command Ships

- *Blue Ridge* class (USS *Blue Ridge*)

Aircraft carriers

- *Midway* class (USS *Midway*)
- *Forrestal* class (USS *Saratoga*, USS *Ranger*)
- *Kitty Hawk* class (USS *America*, USS *John F. Kennedy*)
- *Nimitz* class (USS *Theodore Roosevelt*)

Battleships

- *Iowa* class (USS *Missouri*, USS *Wisconsin*)

Submarines

- *Los Angeles* class (USS *Chicago*, USS *Louisville*)

Amphibious assault ships

- *Tarawa* class (USS *Tarawa*, USS *Nassau*)
- *Iwo Jima* class (USS *Iwo Jima*, USS *Guam*, USS *Tripoli*, USS *New Orleans*)

Guided missile cruisers

- *Leahy* class (USS *Worden*, USS *England*, USS *Richmond K. Turner*)
- *Belknap* class (USS *Horne*, USS *Biddle*)
- *Ticonderoga* class (USS *Valley Forge*, USS *Thomas S. Gates*, USS *Bunker Hill*, USS *Mobile Bay*, USS *Leyte Gulf*, USS *San Jacinto*, USS *Philippine Sea*, USS *Princeton*, USS *Normandy*)
- *California* class (USS *South Carolina*)
- *Virginia* class (USS *Virginia*, USS *Mississippi*)

Destroyer tenders

- *Samuel Gompers* class (USS *Samuel Gompers*)
- *Yellowstone* class (USS *Yellowstone*, USS *Acadia*, USS *Cape Cod*)

Destroyers

- *Spruance* class (USS *Spruance*, USS *Paul F. Foster*, USS *Caron*, USS *Oldendorf*, USS *Moosbrugger*, USS *Leftwich*, USS *Harry W. Hill*, USS *Fife*)

Guided missile destroyers

- *Farragut* class (USS *Macdonough*, USS *Coontz*, USS *Preble*)
- *Kidd* class (USS *Kidd*)

Frigates

- *Knox* class (USS *Marvin Shields*, USS *Francis Hammond*, USS *Vreeland*, USS *Thomas C. Hart*)

- *Oliver Hazard Perry* class (USS *McInerney*, USS *Jarrett*, USS *Curts*, USS *Halyburton*, USS *Nicholas*, USS *Hawes*, USS *Ford*, USS *Samuel B. Roberts*)

Amphibious transport docks

- *Raleigh* class (USS *Raleigh*, USS *Vancouver*)
- *Austin* class (USS *Ogden*)
- *Cleveland* class (USS *Denver*, USS *Juneau*, USS *Shreveport*)
- *Trenton* class (USS *Trenton*)

Ammunition ships

- *Nitro* class (USS *Nitro*, USS *Haleakala*)
- *Kilauea* class (USS *Kilauea*, USS *Santa Barbara*, USS *Mount Hood*, USS *Shasta*, USS *Kiska*)

Dock landing ships

- *Anchorage* class (USS *Anchorage*, USS *Portland*, USS *Pensacola*, USS *Mount Vernon*)
- *Whidbey Island* class (USS *Germantown*, USS *Fort McHenry*, USS *Gunston Hall*)

Tank landing ships

- *Newport* class (USS *Manitowoc*, USS *Peoria*, USS *Frederick*, USS *Cayuga*, USS *Saginaw*, USS *Spartanburg County*, USS *La Moure County*, USS *Barbour County*)

Fast sealift ships

- *Algol* class (USNS *Algol*, USNS *Bellatrix*, USNS *Denebola*, USNS *Pollux*, USNS *Altair*, USNS *Regulus*, USNS *Capella*)

Fleet oilers

- *Neosho* class (USNS *Neosho*, USNS *Hassayampa*, USNS *Ponchatoula*)
- *Cimarron* class (USS *Platte*)
- *Henry J. Kaiser* class (USNS *Joshua Humphreys*, USNS *Andrew J. Higgins*, USNS *Walter S. Diehl*)

Combat stores ships

- *Mars* class (USS *Mars*, USS *Sylvania*, USS *Niagara Falls*, USS *San Diego*, USS *San Jose*)
- *Sirius* class (USNS *Sirius*, USNS *Spica*)

Fast combat support ships

- *Sacramento* class (USS *Sacramento*, USS *Seattle*, USS *Detroit*)

Replenishment oiler ships

- *Wichita* class (USS *Kansas City*, USS *Kalamazoo*)

Minesweepers

- *Aggressive* class (USS *Impervious*)

Repair ships

- *Vulcan* class (USS *Vulcan*, USS *Jason*)

Rescue and salvage ships

- *Edenton* class (USS *Beaufort*)

Sealift ships

- *Wright* class (SS *Wright*, SS *Curtiss*)

Hospital ships

- *Mercy* class (USNS *Mercy*, USNS *Comfort*)

Amphibious cargo ships
- *Charleston* class (USS *Charleston*, USS *Durham*, USS *Mobile*)

Mine countermeasure ships
- *Avenger* class (USS *Avenger*)

Survey ships
- *Chauvenet* class (USS *Chauvenet*)

Light water craft
- LCU-1610 (Landing Craft Utility)
- LCAC (Landing Craft Air Cushion)

United Kingdom

Land-based:
Infantry weapons
- SA80 L85A1
- L1A1 Self-Loading Rifle
- Diemaco C7
- SMG L2A3
- PISTOL L9A1
- L96A1
- L7A1
- L1A2 LAW 80

Tanks
- FV4030/4 Challenger MBT (Main Battle Tank)
- FV4003 Centurion Mk.5 AVRE 165 (Armoured Vehicle Royal Engineers)

Armoured vehicles
- FV101 Scorpion CVR(T) (Combat Vehicle Reconnaissance (Tracked))
- FV102 Striker CVR(T) (Combat Vehicle Reconnaissance (Tracked))
- FV103 Spartan CVR(T) (Combat Vehicle Reconnaissance (Tracked))
- FV104 Samaritan CVR(T) (Combat Vehicle Reconnaissance (Tracked)) *Ambulance*
- FV107 Scimitar CVR(T) (Combat Vehicle Reconnaissance (Tracked))
- FV432 Trojan APC (Armoured Personnel Carrier)
- FV432 Trojan APC (Armoured Personnel Carrier) *Ambulance*
- FV510 Warrior Tracked Armoured Vehicle MCV-80 (Mechanised Combat Vehicle)
- Ferret Armoured Car

Self-propelled artillery/mortars/rockets
- FV432(M) Trojan SPMC (Self-Propelled Mortar Carrier)
- M109 155 mm SPH (Self-Propelled Howitzer) *M109A2*
- M110 8 inch SPH (Self-Propelled Howitzer) *M110A2*
- MLRS (Multiple Launch Rocket System)

Anti-aircraft
- Rapier Field Standard 31(M) Stationary SAM (Surface-To-Air Missile) Launcher

- Rapier Field Standard B2 Stationary SAM (Surface-To-Air Missile) Launcher
- Tracked Rapier TR1 Mobile SAM (Surface-To-Air Missile) Launcher
- Javelin LML (Lightweight Multiple Launcher) SAM (Surface-To-Air Missile) Launcher

Artillery and Mortars

- L118 105 mm Light Gun
- 51 mm Light Mortar
- L16A1 81 mm Mortar

Engineering and recovery vehicles

- FV4205 Chieftain AVLB (Armoured Vehicle Launched Bridge)
- FV180 CET (Combat Engineer Tractor)
- FV106 CVR(T) Samson ARV (Armoured Recovery Vehicle)
- FV434 ARV (Armoured Recovery Vehicle)
- FV512 Warrior MCRV (Mechanised Combat Repair Vehicle)
- FV513 Warrior MRV(R) (Mechanised Recovery Vehicle (Repair))
- CHARRV (Challenger Armoured Repair and Recovery Vehicle)

Command vehicles

- FV105 Sultan CVR(T) (Combat Vehicle Reconnaissance (Tracked))

Other vehicles

- Land Rover Defender
- Leyland 4×4 4-Tonne Lorry
- Bedford 4×4 8-Tonne Lorry
- Mercedes Unimog Support Vehicle
- FV620 Stalwart Amphibious Truck
- Harley Davidson MT530E
- Scammell Commander (TK/TPTR) Tank Transporter
- Scammell Crusader (AVLB) Bridge Transporter
- Scammell S26 Self Loading Dump Truck
- Armstrong 500
- Leyland DROPs (Demountable Rack Off Pickup System)

Aircraft

Rotary-wing

- Aérospatiale-Westland Gazelle AH.1 (AAC)
- Westland Lynx AH.1 (AAC)
- Westland Lynx AH.7 (AAC)
- Westland Lynx HAS.3 (RN)[1]
- Boeing Chinook HC.1B (RAF)
- Westland Sea King HC.4/HAS.5 (RN)[2]
- Westland Puma HC.1 (RAF)

Fixed-wing

- Panavia Tornado GR.1 (RAF) *IDS (Interdictor/Strike)*
- SEPECAT Jaguar GR.1A (RAF)
- Panavia Tornado F.3 (RAF) *ADV (Air Defence Variant)*
- Blackburn Buccaneer S.2B (RAF)

- BAe Nimrod MR.2P (RAF)
- BAe Nimrod R.1 (RAF)
- Britten-Norman Islander AL.1 (RAF)
- Handley Page Victor K.2 (RAF)
- Lockheed Tristar (RAF)
- Lockheed Hercules C.1 (RAF)
- Lockheed Hercules C.3 (RAF)
- Vickers VC10 C.1 (RAF)
- Vickers VC10 K.2 (RAF)
- Vickers VC10 K.3 (RAF)

Ships
Frigates

- Leander Class (HMS Jupiter)
- Broadsword Class (HMS Battleaxe, HMS Brazen, HMS London)

Destroyers

- Type 42 destroyer (HMS Cardiff, HMS Exeter, HMS Manchester, HMS Gloucester, HMS York)

Submarines

- *Oberon* class submarines (HMS Opossum)

Fleet support tankers

- RFA Orangeleaf

Fast fleet tankers

- RFA Olna

Stores ships

- RFA Regent
- RFA Fort Grange

Mine countermeasure vessels

- Hunt Class (HMS Ledbury, HMS Cattistock, HMS Dulverton, HMS Bicester, HMS Atherstone, HMS Hurworth)

Primary casualty reception vessels

- RFA Argus

Fleet repair ships

- RFA Diligence

Kuwait/Free Kuwait

Land-based:
Infantry weapons

- M16A2
- FN FAL
- MP5K

Tanks

- Chieftain tank (Main Battle tank)
- M-84AB MBT (Main Battle Tank)

Armoured vehicles

- BMP-2 IFV (Infantry Fighting Vehicle)
- M113A1 APC (Armored Personnel Carrier)
- FV601 Saladin (Armoured Car)

Aircraft
Helicopters

- Aérospatiale SA.342 Gazelle

Airplanes

- Dassault Mirage F1CK (KAF)
- McDonnell Douglas A-4KU Skyhawk (KAF)

France

Land-based:
Infantry weapons

- FAMAS
- AA-52
- FR F1

Tanks

- AMX-30B2 MBT (Main Battle Tank)

Armoured vehicles

- GIAT AMX-10RC Armoured Car
- Panhard AML-90 Armoured Car
- Panhard ERC-90F4 Sagaie Armoured Car

Artillery and mortars

- TRF1 155 mm Towed Howitzer
- MO-81-61C 81 mm Mortar
- MO-120-RT-61 120 mm Mortar

Anti-aircraft

- GIAT 20 mm 53T2 Towed AAA (Anti-Aircraft Artillery)
- Mistral SAM (Surface-To-Air Missile) Launcher

Other vehicles

- Peugeot P4 4WD
- VLRA (Véhicule de Liaison et Reconnaissance de L'Armée) Truck
- GIAT VAB (Véhicule de l'Avant Blindé)
- GIAT VAB-PC (Véhicule de l'Avant Blindé) (Command)
- GIAT VAB-VCAC/HOT (Véhicule de l'Avant Blindé) ATGM (Anti-Tank Guided Missile) Launching Vehicle
- GIAT VAB-VTM (Véhicule de l'Avant Blindé) Mortar Tractor

Aircraft
Helicopters

- Aérospatiale SA-342 Gazelle
- Aérospatiale SA-330 Puma
- Aérospatiale Super Frelon

Airplanes

- Dassault Mirage F1C-200 (AdA)
- Dassault-Breguet Mirage 2000 (AdA)
- SEPECAT Jaguar A (AdA)
- Dassault Super Étendard

Ships
Aircraft carriers

- *Clemenceau* (R 98)

Qatar
Land-based[edit]
Tanks

- AMX-30S MBT (Main Battle Tank)

Saudi Arabia
Land-based:
Infantry weapons

- H&K G3

Tank

- Auf 100

Armoured vehicles

- V-150

Other vehicles

- M151 Truck, Utility, 1/4-Ton, 4×4

Self-propelled artillery/mortars/rockets

- Astros II MLRS

Artillery and mortars

- M252 81 mm Medium Weight Mortar

Aircraft
Helicopters

- UH-60

Airplanes

- Tornado F3
- McDonnell Douglas F-15 Eagle

Ships

- Badr-class corvette

Italy
Airplanes

- 8 Panavia Tornado IDS *Interdictor/Strike*

Ships

- 1 Audace class Destroyer (Audace)
- 3 Lupo class frigate (Orsa, Lupo, Sagittario)
- 2 Maestrale class frigate (Zeffiro, Libeccio)
- 1 San Giorgio class amphibious transport dock (San Marco)

- 2 Stromboli class replenishment oiler (Vesuvio, Stromboli)

Australia
- Navy
  The frigates HMAS *Anzac* and HMAS *Darwin*
  Each ship carried a single Seahawk helicopter from 816 Squadron RAN
  HMAS *Kanimbla*
  LCM-8 landing craft
  Sea King helicopter Royal Australian Air Force
- Air
  14 F/A-18 Hornet fighter jets
  Three C-130H Hercules transport aircraft
  Two AP-3C Orion maritime patrol aircraft

It is to be noted that around sixty other nations supported the invasion. One has not mentioned the sophisticated communications instruments and networks to coordinate the invasion which included the use of satellites.

E War Against ISIS in Northern Iraq and East Syria 2014-2018

Military Hardware of Western Alliance: Virtually the same as above

Military Hardware of ISIS:

Not much at all really… few crumbs from China, USA, Russia and Czech Republic stolen or purchased from oil sales. Force of 4500 at height of war. Evidence of missiles originating from America.

- Kalashnikovs
- Machine guns
- Various Four Wheel drive vehicles
- Home-made landmines
- Grenades
- Mortars
- Home-made explosive devices
- C4 and other chemicals for explosives
- Al Koran

But who really cares in the US and the West? … just another excuse to destroy many Iraqi cities by bombing the shit out of them and murdering many civilians! But, if it makes us feel good … why not? All this high moral posturing by the Western media was really sickening trying to justify such an immoral war based upon the legacy and false premises of the first Gulf War .. Sadam was creating Weapons of Mass Destruction! This was, in the view of the author, just another 'seeded war' to keep the shareholders happy with their investments in the big military conglomerates! Will we suffer retribution at some future date? One means here 'real retribution' on a grand scale!

And what of reparations? Is the West going to foot the bill to rebuild all those destroyed cities of Syria and northern Iraq?

Unwarranted Influence

F   Syria: Last Days of the Uprising Against Bashir al Assad

Published on 14th March 2018 on khilafah.com

"GHOUTA: Rising from the Ashes"   written by Dr. Nazreen Nawaz

A Talk Delivered in London, Britain, on Saturday 10th March 2018

by Dr. Nazreen Nawaz

Director of the Women's Section in the Central Media Office of Hizb ut Tahrir

Introduction:

"We are standing before the massacre of the 21st century. If the massacre of the 1990's was Srebrenica, and the massacres of the 1980's were Halabja and Sabra and Shatila, then Eastern Ghouta is the massacre of this century right NOW."

- These were the words of a doctor in Eastern Ghouta, one of the suburbs of Damascus, Syria.

- Sisters, when the massacre of Srebrenica in Bosnia happened in 1995, where 8000 Muslim men and boys were executed in cold blood by Serbian forces in what was supposed to be a UN Safe-Haven, the world said….NEVER AGAIN!….But here we are again witnessing a GENOCIDE, and absolute bloodbath, right now against our brothers and sisters in Eastern Ghouta. The horrors that we are seeing and the suffering that our Ummah is enduring is beyond imagination – in a place that was designated as a safe-zone.

- In a matter of just one week in February, more than 500 civilians, including 150 children were killed, as well as around 2000 injured, by the ferocious unrelenting bombardment of the savage Syrian and Russian regimes…and the death toll

400

continues to rise day after day after day – despite the farce of the 30 day UN ceasefire resolution on February the 24th. At one point, airstrikes were coming at 1 every minute.

- They are indiscriminately targeting civilians - men, women, children, babies - in homes, shops, schools, hospitals, ambulances and markets, leaving children buried in the rubble of buildings. Even after the so-called UN truce - Assad's forces dropped chlorine bombs on the Muslims of Ghouta - a chemical which produces a highly corrosive acid in the lungs and severe breathing problems…hence the heartbreaking unbearable images of children and babies gasping for air.

- As a result of the bombardment, families have been forced to take refuge in caves, dugouts or the cold, dark and cramped basement of buildings as they 'wait their turn to die'. Infact, in the town of Harasta, it is said that 80% of the population are living underground. More than 20 medical centres have been destroyed. And so doctors have now resorted to caring for patients, including premature and newborn babies in incubators, in cellars where they face dying from the severe winter cold. The UN Secretary General described the situation as 'Hell on Earth".

- But sisters, this is only the latest chapter of the genocide against the Muslims of Ghouta….because over the last 7 years, since the beginning of the uprising in Syria, 13 000 civilians have been killed in Eastern Ghouta by Assad and Russian forces, including around 1500 children, 1200 people have died due to torture, and there have been 46 chemical attacks (Syrian Network for Human Rights)….including the horrific one in August 2013 which left more than 1400 dead, including 400 children.

- Alongside all this, Eastern Ghouta has been under a brutal siege by the Syrian regime for the last 5 years, described as the longest siege in modern history, leading to severe shortages in food, medicines and fuel. 400 000 people are trapped in this death hole. Doctors are using expired medicines to treat the ill and injured and there is mass starvation that has impacted children the most. According to the UN, around 12% of children under 5 are said to be acutely malnourished and hundreds face dying from starvation.

- In one video that's been circulated widely, there is a mother standing next to her son who has just died from an attack, crying the words - "He died hungry! He didn't eat! He didn't eat. At least he will have food in Jannah." Subhaanallah sisters, the dying wish of mothers - is just that their children have the comfort of food in their stomach before they die! While other mothers are praying that Allah takes the soul of their children - WHY?...to end their pain, to end their suffering....because at least they will not have to endure the unbearable pangs of hunger and the excruciating agony from their injuries - in Jannah. Ya Allah! Can you imagine the scale of suffering sisters, when a mother prefers her own child, the one she loves with all her heart, to die rather than live, because death will stop their agony!

OR can you imagine the level of despair, when the doctors of Eastern Ghouta are so broken having treated child after child, injured from the relentless bombing, with limbs missing, blinded, their tiny bodies ripped apart....that they no longer have the heart to deliver babies from the wombs of dying mothers because they cannot bear the thought of the horrors of the world they will be born into.

Muslims of Ghouta have been Abandoned by the World:

- Sisters, we see the bombs raining down on the heads of the starving children of Eastern Ghouta as they face annihilation. We see row after row of slain children wrapped in their bloodied kaffan (death shroud). We see the tears of the mothers of Ghouta crying out for a morsel of food to feed their young who are dying from hunger. And we see the utter destruction of this blessed land, and our brothers and sisters being slaughtered into submission, bracing themselves for the ground invasion by Assad's butchers and a massacre, perhaps worse than that which we saw in Aleppo.

- And all this is of course alongside the hundreds of thousands of our brothers and sisters who have been massacred across Syria over the last 7 years by Assad's killing machine, aided by his allies. And the tens of thousands who have died in Assad's prisons - 65 000 since 2011 according to some reports - many of them tortured to death (and many more raped).

- And yet despite all these horrors, this unimaginable scale of suffering and bloodshed, the international community, the UN, Western governments, and the regimes of the Muslim world watch on, turning the other way, ignoring the genocide, and giving the butcher Assad and his criminal allies - a free-hand to continue the slaughter with impunity. They have torn up all their conventions on the protection of human life, human rights, and the rights of the child! Clearly, even this 'Living Hell' is not enough to shake their conscience!

- So WHY? Why has the attack on Ghouta intensified over the past few months? And WHY have the Western powers, the UN, and the regimes of the Muslim world ignored this bloodbath of our brothers and sisters?

- To answer this question, sisters, we have to understand the nature of the revolution in Syria. We have to understand that this revolution is no ordinary revolution. NO! It is a BLESSED revolution. Indeed, this whole land of Bilad Al-Sham that Syria is part of is a blessed land and its people are a blessed people.

> **Zaid bin Thabit (ra) said, "We were with the Messenger of Allah collecting the Qur'an on pieces of cloth, so the Messenger of Allah said**: 'Tuba is for Ash-Sham.' **So we said: 'Why is that O Messenger of Allah?'** He said: "Because the angels of Ar-Rahman spread their wings over it."**

- The land of Ghouta also has great significance to us as Muslims.

Abu al-Darda narrated that the Prophet said:

> **"The place of assembly of the Muslims at the time of war will be in al-Ghutah near a city named Damascus, one of the best cities in Syria" (reported by Abu Dawood)**

- In accordance to these words of the Prophet, the uprising in Syria was different to the uprising in the other countries of the Arab Spring like Tunisia, Egypt and Libya. For in Syria, the Muslims were not only calling for the removal of Assad and his regime but they had a distinct call.....and that call was to replace this corrupt oppressive regime with ISLAMIC rule in their land....this was their goal....and you saw it in their chants, in their slogans, in their huge demonstrations from Homs to Aleppo, Damascus to Idlib, Dar'aa to Douma -

> **"Our leader forever is Muhammad, It is for you Allah, it is for you. We are your service Allah, the youth, the people, want the Khilafah."**

- So over the last 7 years, regardless of the political games and posturing that they play on screen....the Western powers, aided by their tools - the UN and their puppet regimes in the Muslim world - Turkey, Saudi, Qatar and others have been united with Assad and his allies - Russia and Iran - in one aim - to crush and contain this Islamic revolution at all costs, no matter how much destruction it takes, no matter how many lives are lost.

- AND it's the carrot and stick approach that's been used - bombing them into submission - in places like Homs, Idlib, Aleppo and Ghouta to try and force them to come to the negotiating table to accept their secular political future for Syria and abandon their Islamic call - and ALL their so-called peace initiatives and proposals - from Geneva to Vienna, Riyadh to Astana - has been for this objective solely - to crush the Islamic revolution for real change and to keep the oppressive secular

Unwarranted Influence

Syrian regime in power - regardless of whether Assad is at the head of it or not - ALL to maintain Western influence over that region of the Muslim world and its resources. (one assumes here that Russia is included in the definition of the West! - ed. TL)

- Sisters, this is why this genocide has been ignored and continues to be ignored by the Western and Muslim governments, because for them...the rivers of blood, formed from the children of Ghouta and across Syria is a price worth paying for their bloodstained political interests in this region! Indeed, it seems there is no limit to the barbarity they are willing to witness to secure their aims.

- Even the funds and weapons given by certain Muslim regimes like Turkey and Saudi to some of the rebel fighters and brigades were never aimed at toppling the Syrian regime - they were never sufficient for that - they were simply a means to divide the brigades, weaken and manipulate them into accepting the plans of the western masters of these regimes...and when they did not achieve their objectives, they simply abandoned them to their killers as we saw in Aleppo and as we see in Ghouta.

- But Alhamdulillah, the Muslims of Syria, as the blessed people described by the Messenger, have kept steadfast to their Deen, rejecting all attempts to terrorise them into abandoning their Islamic call and vision, and fighting on to remove this tyrant regime....and so the bombardment became more and more vicious and bloodthirsty in the hope that it would break their will and force them to surrender.

- So what we see in Ghouta now, which was always a stronghold of the Islamic resistance, is the Syrian regime's attempts to crush and drive out what they see as one of the most significant and remaining pockets of resistance, especially since Ghouta is in a crucially strategic location being near the country's largest military base and international airport, and only a 30 min drive from Central Damascus, the seat of the regime.

We as an Ummah, Cannot Abandon the Muslims of Ghouta:

- Dear sisters, the UN and the governments of the world have abandoned the Muslims of Ghouta and Syria, but we as their Ummah CANNOT!

- We cannot abandon them, because the Prophet said,

"The parable of the believers in relation to the kindness, mercy and compassion they have for each other, is that of the body: when an organ of it falls ill, the rest of the body responds with fever and sleeplessness."

404

- This Ummah is one BODY and as such it is impossible for us to ignore their pain.
- We cannot abandon them because the Prophet said,

> **"Killing a believer is more grievous before Allah than the extinction of the whole world."**

- Telling us about how sacred the blood of a Muslim is and how responding to its spilling is one of the highest actions in Islam.
- We cannot abandon them because Allah(swt) said,

> **"And if they seek help of you for the religion, then you must help"**
> **[Surah al-Anfaal 8:72]**

- And we cannot abandon them because the Prophet said,

Abdullah ibn Umar (ra) narrates that the Prophet said,

> **"A Muslim is a brother of another Muslim, so he should not oppress him, nor should he hand him over to an oppressor. Whoever fulfilled the needs of his brother, Allah will fulfil his needs; whoever brought his (Muslim) brother out of a discomfort, Allah will bring him out of the discomforts of the Day of Resurrection, and whoever screened a Muslim, Allah will screen him on the Day of Resurrection."**
> **[Sahih Bukhari]**

- So as Muslims, we have a heavy, heavy responsibility to end this bloodshed urgently and to NOT ABANDON our brothers and sisters to their oppressors.

Reject Hopelessness:

- But to not abandon them sisters, means first to never lose hope in this situation. We cannot lose hope or feel that there is nothing that can be done or no solution to this problem - because when we do this, we abandon them to their slaughter! And we cannot do that!

- And we should not lose hope sisters - because this Ummah is not helpless - it is 1 billion strong and has some of the strongest armies in the world who could defend our Ummah if mobilised - Turkey (8th most powerful in the world and 2nd largest in NATO); Pakistan (13th largest, 1 1 million personnel - more than France, UK, and Germany combined); Egypt (has over 1000 warplanes) Saudi Arabia (spends $56 billion on its defence budget - more than Russia). So we are NOT helpless as an Ummah, sisters....BUT we have been made to feel helpless by these criminal and cowardly regimes of the Muslim world who use the Muslim armies to maintain their thrones OR to fight wars for selfish national interests OR the interests of western powers rather than for the Ummah.

- Regimes such as in Egypt, Saudi Arabia, and Jordan who instead of sending their armies to defend the children of Ghouta....send them to slaughter and starve the children of Yemen!

- Regimes such as in Turkey, who instead of using its fighter planes and immense arsenal to save the Muslims of Syria.....uses its military to fight on behalf of the interests of western powers.

- Regimes such as in Pakistan, who instead of sending its soldiers to fight the oppressors and killers of this Ummah....send them to fight their Muslim brothers on behalf of the US!

- But most importantly Sisters, we should never lose hope in the help and victory from Allah so that we just accept any proposal for Syria because our DEEN FORBIDS this! Doesn't Allah (swt) say in Surah al Baqara (verse 214) about the believers who came before us who were tested so severely because they held on to their Deen...

> **"They were touched by poverty and hardship and were shaken until [even their] messenger and those who believed with him said, "When is the help of Allah?" Unquestionably (there is NO doubt), the help of Allah is near."**
>
> **[Al-Baqara: 214]**

- And sisters, isn't the Seerah of the Prophet and the history of Islam full of examples of situations where it seemed dire for the believers and the odds seemed stacked against them, but Allah (swt) granted them victory - because of their resilience, and devotion to Him (swt)? In fact, it was at the times when the Prophet and Believers of the past faced their darkest hours and their severest hardships because they held on to their Deen that Allah (swt) sent them His Promises of victory and granted them His Nasr in their struggle for Islam.

- Like the Battle of Ahzab when the enemies of Islam - formed a coalition, 10 000 strong, a well-armed alliance with the shared goal of destroying the Islamic state in Madinah and wiping out Islam. The Muslims were only 3000 in number and the situation in Madinah was dire, they were facing famine and starvation, and it was bitterly cold and there was a drought. They only had a few days to dig a trench all around the borders of the city to try and protect it from the enemy. The ground was hard and they only had spades and pick axes to dig this huge trench.

But it was at this time, that Allah (swt) sent the Prophet a vision and the Believers His Promise of Victory - a vision that made them look beyond the here and now to something greater- The Prophet took a spade and struck a rock while digging - He said,

> "Bismillah, Allahu Akbar, the keys of Ash-Sham are mine, I swear by Allah, I can see its palaces at the moment." Second strike, "Allahu Akbar, Persia is mine, I swear by Allah, I can now see the white palace of Madain." Third strike and the rock shattered into small pieces, "Allahu Akbar, I have been given the keys of Yemen, I swear by Allah, I can see the gates of San'a while I am in my place."

- Sisters, did these Promises of Allah not come true? YES. And Allah also gave victory in the Battle of Ahzab by sending a furious hurricane to destroy the camp of the coalition, forcing them to flee.

- Sisters, it is this strong conviction in the Nasr of Allah that has prevented the Muslims of Ghouta and across Syria from giving up in their revolution for Islam despite 7 years of barrel bombs, airstrikes, chemical attacks, butchery, rape, imprisonment and torture by the Assad regime. As the brutality increased, their resilience and determination to overthrow this tyrant and establish the Rule of Allah increased....For them it was victory or shahada....They are like those described in the verse in Surah Al-i-Imran (verse 173) - When the hypocrites said to them -

> "Indeed, the people have gathered against you, so fear them." But it [merely] increased them in faith, and they said "Sufficient for us is Allah, and [He is] the best Disposer of affairs."

- Sisters, if our brothers and sisters in Syria can keep steadfast through all of this, then surely it is a powerful lesson to us that we should never give up hope in the victory from Allah, and Bi'ithnillah it will be soon!

Work for the Correct Solution to End the Bloodshed:

- So sisters what is it that we can do to bring this victory and end this genocide against our Ummah in Ghouta and Syria? Sisters, if we really want to stop this bloodbath then we must, must work for a solution that will truly end the slaughter of our brothers and sisters for good.

- This means FIRSTLY, not just shedding tears, giving some sadaqa and then returning to our everyday lives. This is not to belittle Sadaqa - Of course the action of giving sadaqa is important but we know that it will NOT end the bloodshed. In fact we don't even know if any of it will reach those who are in desperate need in Ghouta and in other besieged areas! We've seen this week how even the UN aid convey had to turn back from Ghouta due to the shelling and threats of chemical attacks.

- SECONDLY sisters, ending the bloodshed, means NOT making the same mistake again and again and again by placing our hopes on the impotent UN and self-serving Western governments to solve our problems as an Ummah and protect our blood - whether that's through lobbying local MP's, petitioning these governments, demonstrating outside parliament, or any other similar action. These governments and the UN have witnessed the slaughter of 500 000 people in Syria over the past 7 years, they have seen babies burning and suffocating from chemical attacks, they have seen countless hospitals and schools destroyed, every red line crossed, every convention on human rights broken and yet they have stood idly by doing nothing, abandoning the Muslims of Syria to their death!

- ALL their so-called peace-initiatives, interventions and proposed solutions have done, is BUY the butcher Assad more time to torture, rape and kill the Muslims. In fact such is the utter farce of the most recent UN resolution, that just hours after they called for this 30 day ceasefire, the Syrian regime began a new ground offensive in Ghouta followed by a chemical attack. Indeed Allah (swt) says,

> **"The example of those who take protectors other than Allah is that of the spider, who builds for itself a house; but truly the flimsiest of houses is the spider's house; if they but knew."**
>
> **[Al-Ankabut: 41]**

- And history has shown us this again and again and again - whether its Gaza, Myanmar, Kashmir, India, Central Africa or any other land where Muslims have been massacred - that these governments and the UN which is nothing but a tool of these states - will ONLY ever act for the sake of their political and economic interests.....and their interests will never be to aid any revolution based upon Islam that achieves real change for the Muslim world!

- So sisters, we need to stop seeing western intervention in our lands as a solution to our problems....in fact it's been the cause in most instances - we see the mess they made in Iraq, Afghanistan and Libya! The Prophet said

"The believer should not be stung from the same hole twice."

How the Khilafah can Protect the Ummah in Ghouta and Across the World:

- So an Ummah, what can we do to protect the blood of our brothers and sisters of Ghouta and Syria?

- Of course, the first thing is to make sincere Dua to Allah (swt) that He protects our Ummah, destroys the Assad regime and all its allies and grants the Muslims victory in Al-Sham...for ALL-POWER belongs to Allah alone ....and He is truly capable of all things.....But what did our beloved Prophet tell us? He said in one hadith,

"By Him in Whose Hand my life is, you either enjoin good and forbid
evil, or Allah will certainly soon send His punishment to you. Then
you will make supplication and it will not be accepted"

- So what is the Marouf that we must command, and the Munkar that we must Forbid to an END this bloodbath Insha Allah?

- Sisters, is it not blatantly clear, that when the Muslims of Syria are being killed by an ARMY, aided by other armies....then what they need is an ARMY to defend their blood. I ask you sisters, which state is there today, which you sincerely think will send their army to protect the Ummah in Syria?....There is NONE.

- So what we desperately need is a state, ruled by an Islamic leadership and a ruler of taqwa, who truly sees himself as the GUARDIAN of the Ummah, and defender of this Deen, who will mobilise his army urgently to protect the Muslims.

- This state is the righteous Khilafah state, based upon the method of the Prophethood, the System of Allah, which is the shield of the Believers....as the Prophet said,

"Verily the Imam (Khalifa) is a shield from behind whom you fight
and by whom you are protected."

- This is what we need to command sisters - an end to the munkar of the rule of these despicable regimes in the Muslim world....each and every one of them...who have kept silent to or conspired in the crimes against this Ummah, and the urgent establishment of the Islamic leadership of the Khilafah. This is the solution from our Deen, the Qur'an and Sunnah, to protect the blood of the believers! Imam Ghazali (RM) said regarding the Khilafah,

"The security of the world, its inhabitants and properties cannot be achieved except with an obeyed ruler (Sultan Muta`).....This is why it is said that...The deen is the foundation and the Sultan is the guardian..."

- Sisters, it is the Islamic leadership of the Khilafah which will unify the Muslim lands, their resources, their wealth, man-power, strategic assets - such as its waterways, ports, airspace, military bases, and importantly UNIFY the armies of the Muslim world - to create a political, economic and military superpower - a Superpower that will mobilise its soldiers and military arsenal with urgency to defend the believers, remove the oppressors, liberate occupied Muslim land and strike fear into the hearts of those who dare to terrorize or harm the Muslim Ummah - no matter where they live - for this is an Islamic obligation upon the state and the Khalifah, the ruler of the Muslims, from Allah (swt)!

- And this is exactly what happened under the Khilafah of the past:

- In the 12th Century sisters, as we know, the Christian Crusaders occupied Jerusalem and many parts of the blessed land of Palestine. They massacred the Muslims of Jerusalem, thousands were killed, in fact historians describe how the streets ran ankle deep with Muslim blood. However, under the Abbasid Khilafah - the great military commander and Wali (governor) of Egypt - Salahuddin Ayubi - unified the provinces of the Khilafah which had become semi-independent to the state at that time, and then led the unified army of the Khilafah to liberate Al-Quds which once again became a glorious city of security and prosperity under the shade of Islam. The Battle of Hattin in which Salahuddin defeated the Crusaders took part in Ramadan and in the peak of the summer heat. Prior to the battle, some of his advisors advised him to delay the fighting till after Ramadan. However, Salahuddin responded,

"Man's life-span is short, death gives no appointment and leaving the occupiers in the Muslim lands for more than a single day, despite the ability of driving them out is an abominable act that I could not bear."

- So sisters, you have a state, whose capital was in Iraq, a Commander Salahuddin who was Kurdish in origin but governed over the province of Egypt, mobilising an army to liberate Palestine. - This is the nature and capability of the Khilafah which

410

rejects national borders - and views the Ummah as ONE, its land as ONE, its blood as ONE, and its army as ONE.

Conclusion:

- So sisters, will Ghouta and Al-Sham rise from its ashes? Well that depends upon us....it depends upon whether as an Ummah take a stand for our Deen, and whether we focus our attention, time and efforts firmly on the only true solution that will put an end to this nightmare for good - the urgent establishment of this righteous state - the Khilafah.

- If we do, then Insha Allah Ghouta and the whole of Bilad Al-Sham, in fact the whole of the Muslim world can and will rise from its ashes, just like the blessed land of Al-Sham, rose in the past under the shade of the Islamic rule of the Khilafah following its liberation by Salahuddin Ayubi from its Christian crusaders, to become a shining gem of this world, a centre of learning and prosperity.....until its occupation by the Zionists when the Khilafah was destroyed and there was no longer a shield to protect it or its blessed Ummah.

But if we don't focus our attention, time and efforts firmly on this true solution - the establishment of the Khilafah - then unfortunately we will continue to see the slaughter of our brothers and sisters in Syria, AND repeated in land after land after land! Just this week, mobs of extremist Buddhists attacked Muslim homes and shops in Sri Lanka...and we pray that this not the next Myanmar Insha Allah.

- For in the absence of this state today, the Muslims have no champion, no shield, no guardian...and so the tyrants, abusers and killers of Muslims have a free-hand to terrorize and massacre the Believers with no fear.

- Please sisters do not see the Khilafah as a dream....NO! Its establishment is an urgent obligation that our Rabb has placed upon us....described as the Umm al-Furaid (mother of all obligations) by the classical scholars of Islam. And please sisters do not see the Khilafah as a long-term vision, to be established sometime in the distant future...NO! It is an urgent necessity now....because while we distract ourselves with patchwork, plaster strip initiatives to cover what is a huge gaping haemorrhaging wound in this Ummah OR put hope in failed self-serving western and international processes.....we simply prolong the suffering and pain of our Ummah!

- So sisters, match your tears, pain and rage for your Ummah in Ghouta by carrying the dawa for the Khilafah with all your efforts to all you know. Discuss with your friends, family, contacts; arrange circles and talks in your homes, mosques, community; spread the word on social media and all avenues that Allah has given you....about the betrayal and crimes of the Muslim regimes against this Ummah and Deen, expose the plans of the colonialist governments in our lands against the Muslims and Islam, explain to those you know about the utter futility of all western solutions for our problems as an Ummah, and discuss with them the Islamic obligation and urgent need of the Khilafah. And please sisters...do not delay, do it now! For have we not witnessed enough of the bloodshed of our Ummah?!

- Of special importance in your discussions sisters, are those you know in the Muslim armies....make this a special focus....for they have the military power to give the Nussrah (support) for the establishment of the Khilafah. Remind them of the heavy obligation that Allah (swt) has placed upon their shoulders to protect this Ummah! Remind them of the great punishment in the Hereafter of abandoning their brothers and sisters! Ask them why they demean themselves by giving their allegiance to these cowards, traitors and criminals - the Muslim rulers! And call them to embrace the huge honour of becoming the Ansar of today, and the army of the second Khilafah Rashidah so that they will become the heroes of this Ummah and Insha Allah secure the greatest of rewards in the Akhira!

- Dear sisters, do not leave any stone unturned, any opportunity lost in this noble dawa, so that you may witness soon Bi'ithnillah, the tears of pain of your Ummah turn to tears of joy as this glorious state is reborn in our lands and its light and justice spreads to all corners of this world, and may the immense reward of this victory be upon your hands. Ameen.

- O Allah...we ask you to ease the suffering of our Ummah in Ghouta and Syria, protect them and keep them steadfast and patient in their blessed struggle. Lift the oppression from our Ummah across the world and grant us your victory soon. Ameen.

- Allah(swt) has said,

> **"Allah has promised, to those among you who believe and work righteous deeds, that He will, of a surety, grant them in the land, inheritance (of power), as He granted it to those before them; that He will establish in authority their religion, the one which He has chosen for them; and that He will change (their state), after the fear in which they (lived), to one of security and peace: `They will**

**worship Me (alone) and not associate aught with Me.' If any do
reject Faith after this, they are rebellious and wicked."**

[Nur 24:55]

This is the Promise of Allah. And Allah does not fail in His Promise!

Comment by the author:

As seen by Russia's behaviour in the following war scenarios over the past forty years, it is evident that "Russia is no friend to Muslims and Islamic countries!"

Chechnya

Afghanistan

Syria

They have uniquely contributed to the deaths of around three million people and the displacement of around ten million people from their homes.

But let us not be blasé and complacent over Russia's sins as a war mongering nation! The West (led by the United States) has also either sat back making immoral profits or has been directly involved in wars to the detriment and destruction of cities and murder of innocents in the following countries over the past fifty years:

Laos	Libya
Vietnam	Egypt
Afghanistan	Palestine (Gaza)
Iraq	Iran
Syria	Burma
Yemen	Turkey

This omits other conflicts in Central and South America where some interference also took place! A more complete list is provided by William Blum:

INSTANCES OF THE UNITED STATES OVERTHROWING, OR ATTEMPTING TO OVERTHROW, A FOREIGN GOVERNMENT SINCE THE SECOND WORLD WAR.
(* indicates successful ousting of a government)

China 1949 to early 1960s	Ghana 1966 *	Afghanistan 1980s *
Albania 1949-53	Chile 1964-73 *	Somalia 1993
East Germany 1950s	Greece 1967 *	Yugoslavia 1999-2000 *
Iran 1953 *	Costa Rica 1970-71	Ecuador 2000 *
Guatemala 1954 *	Bolivia 1971 *	Afghanistan 2001 *
Costa Rica mid-1950s	Australia 1973-75 *	Venezuela 2002 *
Syria 1956-7	Angola 1975, 1980s	Iraq 2003 *
Egypt 1957	Zaire 1975	Haiti 2004 *
Indonesia 1957-8	Portugal 1974-76 *	Somalia 2007 to present
British Guiana 1953-64 *	Jamaica 1976-80 *	Honduras 2009
Iraq 1963 *	Seychelles 1979-81	Libya 2011 *
North Vietnam 1945-73	Chad 1981-82 *	Syria 2012
Cambodia 1955-70 *	Grenada 1983 *	Ukraine 2014 *
Laos 1958 *, 1959 *,1960 *	South Yemen 1982-84	
Ecuador 1960-63 *	Suriname 1982-84	
Congo 1960 *	Fiji 1987 *	
France 1965	Libya 1980s	
Brazil 1962-64 *	Nicaragua 1981-90 *	
Dominican Republic 1963*	Panama 1989 *	
Cuba 1959 to present	Bulgaria 1990 *	
Bolivia 1964 *	Albania 1991 *	
Indonesia 1965 *	Iraq 1991	

William Blum 2013

https://williamblum.org/essays/read/overthrowing-other-peoples-governments-the-master-list

… which makes the claim of 'Russian Interference' in the 2016 American Presidential elections- even if true- almost laughable !

G   Rohingya

Published on 24th January 2018 on khilafah.com

Only a Righteous Khalifah Will Break the Sick Cycle of Expulsion and Force Repatriation of the Rohingya Muslims

written by Fehmida Binte Wadud

More than 100 Rohingya Muslims have crossed into Bangladesh from Myanmar since Wednesday, with the latest refugees saying army operations are continuing in troubled Rakhine State, raising doubts about plans to send back 655 500 who had already fled. Scores more were waiting to cross the Naf river that forms the border, even as Dhaka prepares to start repatriating next week some of the Rohingya who have escaped from what the Myanmar military calls counter-insurgency operations since late August. In Dhaka, a senior foreign ministry official told Reuters that the deadline of next Tuesday for starting the Rohingya repatriation to Myanmar "may not be possible". "The return has to be voluntary, safe and dignified," said the official, who was part of a 14-member team at talks with Myanmar this week about the repatriation. According to the signed deal 1500 Rohingya would take back by Myanmar government per week and then they would be sheltered in a temporary transit camp in Myanmar before being moved to "houses as per their choices". They would be sheltered in a temporary transit camp in Myanmar before being moved to "houses as per their choices". (Channel News Asia)

Unwarranted Influence

Comment:

The Rohingya issue is not new to the world and it is also not new to Bangladesh. As a neighbouring country of Myanmar, Bangladesh had been witnessing the unspeakable atrocities on the Rohingya Muslims for the last 40 years. Furthermore, the whole world including the human rights organisations and the UN are well aware of the ground reality in the Rakhine state and the position of Myanmar's army backed by the government towards this persecuted Muslim minority. Moreover, the past repatriation result was nothing but a sick cycle of expulsion of the Rohingya Muslims from Rakhine state and then forcefully pushing them back to their land of origin from Bangladesh. Shamefully, to ensure force repatriation, the successive Bangladeshi governments had implemented a series of heinous and inhuman tactics. In 1978, after the exodus of 270 000 Rohingya Muslims, the then government of Bangladesh withheld food ration to ensure their return and 12 000 Rohingya were perished during this repatriation process. Then again from 1992 to 1994, the then Hasina government banned the humanitarian activities of three international NGOs and later used excessive force to ensure the return after protests broke out in the Rohingya camps against force repatriation. And this time again, after the exodus of 650 000 Rohingya Muslims in August, 2017, the current Hasina government hastily signed a repatriation deal full of loopholes with Myanmar to get rid of these unwanted people and hilariously demanding the "safe and dignified" return of the Rohingya population from that very government of Myanmar which is blinded by the extreme form of racism and Buddhist nationalism. Hundreds of Rohingya refugees have already staged protest against this forceful repatriation process in the Kutupalong camp at Cox's Bazar last Sunday and demanded their citizenship, security and guarantee of life before sending them back to their homeland.

But the question is why the world is not trying to stop the ongoing brutal genocide to stop the sick cycle of expulsion and force repatriation? How could Myanmar regime and its killer army be able to continue this horrific persecution on a targeted community for more than three decades? The answer is simple. Dr. Maung Zarni, a UK based Burmese genocide scholar and a human rights activist, answered this question during an interview with a daily newspaper of Bangladesh by saying, it is because "Ending genocide is not profitable. Working with the killer is profitable. Because the killers have monopoly over natural gas, strategic coastlines, deep seaports, visas, etc.(so) it's self interest.... that are in play." This is why the international political players are playing "language games" to undermine the severity of this genocidal crime That is why instead of describing the atrocious activities of Myanmar army as "genocide", the UN named it "ethnic cleansing". This is why NATO or UN Peace Keeping Forces did not invade Myanmar under the pretext of their so called "war on terrorism" or under the banner of protecting humanity although, according to the doctrine "Responsibility to Protect (R2P)" which was endorsed by all the members of UN at the 2005 World Summit, all member state of UN have a responsibility to protect the Rohingya people from genocidal crimes and to punish the perpetrator government of Myanmar. In fact, the cheap slogans of human rights, saving humanity or "Responsibility to Protect"- only come to avail when these slogans are beneficial to the West as it was in Afghanistan, Iraq and Syria. But these slogans will never be used to protect the life, dignity or interest of the Muslim Ummah. Allah (swt) says in the Quran:

"**O you who have believed, do not take as intimates those other than yourselves, for they will not spare you [any] ruin. They wish you would have hardship. Hatred has already appeared from their mouths, and what their breasts conceal is greater.**"

(Surah An-Nisa: 118)

Hence, the Rohingya Muslims of Myanmar do not need any UN resolution, any repatriation deal under UN supervision or crocodile tears of the shameless Muslim rulers to break the cycle of misery. They only need a righteous Khalifah like Umar Ibn al-Khattab under the second Khilafah Rashidah (Caliphate) upon the method of the Prophethood who will send the mighty soldiers of the Khilafah to Rakhine state to punish the criminal government of Myanmar and its killer army and break the shackle of endless misery of Rohingya Muslims. The mighty army of the Khilafah will not only free the Muslims of Arakan, rather, it will free the oppressed Muslims all over the world and restore the Ummah's dignity, security and prosperity by the Will of Allah.

Fehmida Binte Wadud

All very well to sit and wait for something that may never happen... the Rohingya need a solution now in order to save lives! Repatriation with safeguards is probably the best immediate solution overseen by a UN deployment!   Ed. TL

H   Uighur Muslims

Published on 22nd February 2018 by khilafah.com

"It is an Outright Obligation for the Malaysian Government to Protect the Uighur Muslims from Atrocities of the Chinese Regime"   by Abdul Hakim Othman

Deputy Prime Minister, Datuk Seri Dr Ahmad Zahid Hamidi was reported to say that the Royal Malaysian Police (RMP) are conducting a thorough investigation over 11 Uighur Muslims currently detained in this country, and will give due consideration to the request made by the Chinese government to extradite them. Zahid, who is also the Home Minister said that Malaysia would honour the mutual legal assistance between both countries and will cooperate closely with the Chinese police in this matter. All 11 detainees are part of 20 Uighur Muslims who managed to escape from a Thai prison in November last year.

In an open letter to the Malaysian government which was uploaded to a website, Uighur Muslims appealed to the Malaysian government to shelter the detainees and not to deport them back to China. They mentioned in the letter the atrocities and tortures they have faced, to the extent that some of them were murdered by the Chinese regime for no reason other than their religion is Islam and accused of being involved in terrorism. They further stated that they would rather be killed by the Malaysian government than being extradited to China, for at least if they were killed by the Malaysian government, they would be buried in accordance with Islam. These are among their appeals that are apparently ignored by the Malaysian government to date.

Unwarranted Influence

Uighur Muslims are part of the Ummah that were forced to flee for their lives from the cruelty of the Chinese regime. Their only "crime" is because they are Muslims, who have been deprived of their rights for decades, and were restrained from practicing their own religion, apart from being oppressed socio-economically in their very own land. Only those who are politically blind and selfish will fail to see the oppression by the Chinese regime on the Uighur Muslims, whom majority of them live in Xinjiang or East Turkestan.

The Chinese regime justified their atrocities by associating any form of resistance to their authority with the allegation of terrorism. Even if it's true that some of the Uighur Muslims took arms, they will certainly not do that except as a response to the oppression and murders committed by the Chinese regime themselves. They have been oppressed and deprived of their rights for decades, and their cry are never heard by the Muslim rulers. The Prime Minister of Malaysia himself not only failed to aid Muslim Uighurs, but in turn established a close relationship with that anti-Islam communist regime who murdered them.

Hizb ut Tahrir / Malaysia hereby stresses and reminds the Malaysian government that these Uighur Muslims are our brothers and it is an outright obligation for the government to protect them from the atrocities by the Chinese regime. Furthermore, the Malaysian government must provide shelter and fulfil all their needs, including granting citizenship to them along with all the rights that come with it. It is forbidden (haram) for the government to deport them or allow the Chinese regime to take them away which shall endanger their lives. Rasulullah said:

> **"A Muslim is a brother of another Muslim, so he should not oppress him, nor should he hand him over (to an oppressor)"**
>
> **[Narrated by Bukhari and Muslim].**

Moreover, the government should have urged the Communist Chinese regime to end all forms of atrocities on the Muslim in their country, regardless of their location or ethnicities. All diplomatic and trade relations with the Chinese regime must be cut as long as their hostility towards Islam remain.

O Malaysian government! Even though we are very certain that you are not going to do all those, but as an Islamic political party that works for the sake of this Ummah, Hizb ut Tahrir will never stop reminding you of your responsibility. At the very same time, Hizb ut Tahrir will keep working to resume the complete Islamic way of life by re-establishing the Righteous Caliphate on the method of Prophethood, which

419

upon its establishment soon, our Muslim Uighur brothers and all the oppressed Muslims shall be saved Insha Allah. O government who does not rule with what Allah (swt) has bestowed! Take heed that your time of ruling is not long. With only remnants of your time left, do help our Muslim brothers and do implement what Allah (swt) and His Messenger have commanded you to, because at the moment when the Uighur Muslims ask for their unfulfilled rights in the Mahshar, no one can save you from His (swt) severe torment!

Abdul Hakim Othman

Spokesperson of Hizb ut Tahrir in Malaysia

For more on the plight of the Uighur peoples under Chinese communism, see "All on that Day" by Tom Law, Longership Publishing Australia, ISBN 9780980725810 available on Amazon.   Ed. TL

Unwarranted Influence

I   Al-Ghouta

Published on 11th March 2018 by khilafah.com

"O People of Al-Ghouta, You have Allah"   **by Dr. Osman Bakhach**

More than 2000 air strikes were launched by the Russian Air Force (1150 raids) and the Syrian Air Force (900 raids) which destroyed the people and the land; it destroyed hospitals, vegetable markets and bakeries, killing 900 martyrs and injuring 2000 unarmed civilians. The whole world is complicit with the butcher of Damascus and the Moscow criminal, in their relentless brutality to annihilate the people of Ghouta, the heroes who refused to bow down to Pharaoh, or Nero of the century, Bashar. But Bashar is nothing more than a puppet who gave "legitimacy" to the Russian air force's intervention, which reflects Putin's deep-rooted hatred of Islam and Muslims.

The Western countries' silence, the so-called "international community", reveals their participation in this sinful aggression. These countries have already raised the slogan, "Never Again" to prevent the recurrence of the so-called Holocaust. Yet it was not implemented in Srebrenica-Bosnia in 1995, when UN peacekeepers handed over Muslims to the criminal gangs of Serbs and gave them the green light to commit the Holocaust against 11 000 Muslims; neither it was implemented in Rwanda in 1994 nor in Central Africa in 2016. Nor in Myanmar in 2017.

No wonder Col. John Thomas of the US Central Command Public Affairs Office told the *Daily Beast* Newspaper:

> **"Those aren't our issues," "CENTCOM has no part in anything in Syria other than the defeat of ISIS and some counterterrorism authority,"**

Stopping the biggest terrorist, Bashar al Assad, a loyal American agent, is not part of the US military mission in Syria. UN Under-Secretary-General for Political Affairs Jeffrey Feltman, continuing the criminal play, told a UN Security Council session on 28/2/2018, on the humanitarian situation in Syria that the United Nations will continue:

421

"to call forcefully for justice and accountability, those responsible for the catalogue of horrors that mark daily life in Syria...must be held accountable"

This green light explains Lavrov's statement:

"There are groups in both Eastern Ghouta and Idlib, which are presented as moderates by their Western partners and sponsors, including Ahrar Al-Sham and Jaish Al-Islam, they are cooperating with Ahrar Al-Sham movement,"

adding that the Syrian regime and Moscow will continue to target them. Yes. Lavrov accuses Ahrar Al-Sham movement, which is waging a fierce war against Hay'at Tahrir Al-Sham in Idlib that it is cooperating with this branded "terrorist" organization, to justify the destruction campaign based on the scorched earth policy in Ghouta.

That is why neither Russia nor the United Nations accepted Jaish Al-Islam and Failaq Ar-Rahman's offer; to take out the elements of Hay'at Tahrir Al-Sham from Al-Ghouta. Taking them out destroys the pretext of fighting the terrorists. And leaving them inside justifies the bombing of children and women and blowing up of hospitals, vegetable markets, bakeries, pharmacies and ambulances. All this under the watchful eyes and ears of the "international community" which raises the banner of civilization and human rights!!

And is also under the sight and hearing of Muslim rulers who are busy serving the interests of their masters, the colonial West. And it is under the sight and hearing of the leaders of the armies in Muslim countries. These armies, which drain thousands of billions of Muslim wealth, if they do not carry out their duties to protect Muslims and defend their honour and blood, what is the purpose of their existence?

The Prophet said:

"Whoever abandons a Muslim in a place where his sanctity is violated and his honour is reduced, Allah will abandon him in the place where he loves to be supported by Allah. And whoever supports a Muslim in a place where his sanctity is violated and his honour is reduced, Allah will support him in the place that he loves to get His (swt) support."

O Allah we are defeated, make us victorious.

Dr. Osman Bakhach

Director of the Central Media Office of Hizb ut Tahrir

J   **Turkey Enters Syria**

Published on 30th January 2018 by khilafah.com

"What is behind the Turkish Operation 'Olive Branch' in Northern Syria?"
Editorial

Question:

It has been noted that Erdogan's movements in Syria have calmed down relatively after Operation Shield of the Euphrates and Erdogan's abandonment of Aleppo, and allowing the regime to take control over Aleppo, but he resumed the operation in the name of Olive Branch heading towards Afrin since Saturday, 20/01/2018, through artillery and air shelling. According to the statement issued by the Turkish Chief of Staff on Sunday 21/01/2018: The Olive Branch Operation, which started on Saturday according to the plan drawn for it, and the ground operation began on Sunday morning. (Turk Press, 21/01/2018) and it is ongoing, so what is behind this operation 'Olive Branch'? May Allah reward you with the good.

Answer:

1- Before starting to analyze what took place, we must draw attention to a very important matter that forms the basis of the current Turkish policy, that will shed light on the movements of Erdogan and his actions and statements, as Turkey's Erdogan is clearly pro-American, he does so in exchange for America's support to stay in power as it brought him into power. The evidence for this is what the pro-Turkish government As-Sabah Newspaper stated on 18/4/2017: "The US president telephoned the Turkish President Erdogan last night to congratulate him on the outcome of the April 16 referendum on constitutional reforms and the presidential system". Erdogan mentioned to him that "he launched a good campaign for it and that he observed it personally". He said to Erdogan: "I give attention to our friendship and there are very important things that we will do together." Hence Erdogan's policy in Syria was in fact assisting America's plans to install the regime and pressure the factions to withdraw from vital areas of the regime. The example for that is the recent order to surrender Aleppo, and the empowerment of the regime, he made up issues and pulled out factions to fight instead of fighting in their areas to prevent the regime from entering them under the pretext of the battle of the Euphrates Shield. At a time when the regime went to Aleppo and focused its attack there, knowing that the battle of the Euphrates Shield was originally given the American blessing, Turkey has entered Jarabulus region in 2016 with America's encouragement when former US Vice President Joseph Biden came to Ankara and announced from there his open support for the entry of the Turkish army on 24/8/2016 and asked the forces of the units of protection of the Kurdish people to withdraw from the Turkish forces under the name of the Euphrates Shield. We mentioned in the Answer to Question on 25/9/2016 that:

"In order to make the American plans work, that focused on Aleppo, the Turkish troops had to be re-imposed blockade, and here America worked on two axes to restore the siege on Aleppo: First: the introduction of the Turkish army to in northern Syria, starting with the area of Jarabulus meanwhile Turkey announced operation "Euphrates Shield" and calling the pro-Turkish rebels from southern Aleppo to fight ISIS, that is, weakening the real points of clashes in Aleppo! And creating new infighting points and pushing away as many opposition from fighting in Aleppo! etc."

This is how Erdogan withdrew the factions loyal to him to fight in the areas of Al-Bab and leave Aleppo almost empty of resistance, except for a few believers who stood firm. Meanwhile most factions responded to Erdogan's call to the Euphrates Shield and he is repeating this betrayal again.

2- These movements are still in place and the latest is not the last to enable the Syrian regime to control the important areas in Idlib and to remove the loyal fighting factions to the orders of Turkey to focus on Afrin and forget its homeland Idlib; that the criminal regime is advancing towards in coordination with America, but under a guise of tensions between Turkey and America to prevent the preparation of new forces linked to America! Note that America is advancing from Turkey towards Syria and arming its puppet organizations, including the protection units of the Kurdish people, which have a majority within the Syrian Democratic Forces linked to America, where Erdogan opened Incirlik Base ... Thus Erdogan repeats the scenario of the Euphrates Shield to facilitate the entry of the regime in Idlib. Operation Olive Branch was devised to facilitate the entry of the regime in Idlib. The Syrian regime while moving towards Idlib and surrounding Abu al-Duhur Airport, Erdogan pushed the fight towards Afrin!

About 25 thousand of the opposition are participating in this operation as confirmed by the military commander in the Sham Legion, Yasser Abdul Rahim, that about 25 thousand armed men from the Free Syrian Army are participating in the Turkish military operation in Afrin (Russia Today, 23/1/2018), known to America along with its approval. The Turkish Minister of Foreign Affairs Mevlüt Çavuşoğlu stated that he discussed the Syrian crisis and the issue of border security units with US Secretary of Defense James Mattis on Monday evening (15/1/2018) in Canada. He stated that he met with US Secretary of State Tillerson also on Tuesday evening (16/1/2018) on the sidelines of the Foreign Ministers' Meeting on Security and Stability on the Korean Peninsula in Vancouver, Canada.

Çavuşoğlu said that Mattis said:

"We have been asked not to believe the news that is being published about (the formation of a new army in northern Syria)," adding that he was "following up the matter himself and would remain in contact with us." (Anadolu news agency 17/1/2018)

3- This confirms the American statements in the past two days. They confirm that Olive Branch, the issue of Afrin and the movements of the Turkish army and the Free Syrian Army is with the full approval of America and Russia, which entered Syria in coordination with America, here are some of these statements:

- The Turkish military campaign in Afrin began yesterday on Friday, with the first stages of the bombing of certain areas of Afrin at a high rate since Thursday/Friday night, with the start of the withdrawal of the Russian military police from Afrin and its environs. Nurettin Canikli considered it "the beginning of the attack on the ground," according to Al Jazeera Channel ... Al-Araby Al-Jadeed learned from a Turkish source that:

"Another offer was made, to control of the city in exchange for the consensus between Ankara and Moscow on the way of its management. The Turkish government is ensuring by a large proportion the reconstruction similar to the Euphrates Shield, and by pressuring the Syrian opposition to attend the Sochi conference, while the Russians insisted on handing over the city after its control by the Syrian regime and the absence of any opposition forces in it and also allowing the regime to make further progress in the province of Idlib. Meanwhile, Turkish Defense Minister Nurettin Canikli in a television interview yesterday confirmed, "We know that Russia supports the regime greatly" …" As for the Turkish expectations of the operation, the Turkish source said to Al-Araby Al-Jadeed "The operation is expected to continue for a maximum of five to six months .. The source pointed out "the diplomatic channels did not break with Washington." (Al-Araby Al-Jadeed, 20/01/2018)

"On 20 January, Turkey resorted to its armed forces near Afrin in north-west Syria … Moscow is concerned about this information," the Russian Foreign Ministry said in a statement, noting that it was "closely following the development of the situation." "Russia remains committed to its position regarding the search for solutions to the conflict in Syria, based on the preservation of the territorial integrity of this country and respect for its sovereignty," the ministry said). (Rudaw, 20/01/2018)

The United States wants the Turkish military operation to remain limited in time and scope, and it urged "self-restraint" and to ensure that the rest of the military operations are limited in scope and duration, to minimise the damages to "civilian lives." State Department spokeswoman Heather Nauert said:

"We urge Turkey to exercise restraint and ensure that its military operations remain limited in scope and duration and scrupulous to avoid civilian casualties."

US Defense Secretary Jim Mattis said on Sunday that Turkey informed the United States before the move, noting that Washington is communicating with Ankara on developments in the situation. She said that Foreign Minister Sergey Lavrov and his US counterpart, Rex Tillerson, have discussed "measures in order to ensure the preservation of stability north of the country". The Turkish foreign minister discussed the military operation with his US counterpart, but did not yet reveal what took place between the two parties (BBC Arabic, 22/01/2018)

US Secretary of State Rex Tillerson said his country hopes to work with Turkey to establish a safe area in northwestern Syria to meet Ankara's security needs... The head of the US Central Command, General Joseph Votel, confirmed that Turkey briefed his country on its military operation in Afrin, pointing out that the city does not fall within the scope of American military operations. The Department of Defense calls for "not to escalate tension," noting that it understands Turkey's security concerns in the region. (Russia Today, 23/01/2018)

- The Central Command of the US army said Turkey briefed them on the military operation in the Syrian city, Afrin, stressing at the same time that the city does not fall within the scope of US military operations. General Joseph Votil, Commander of the Central Command, in a press statement on Sunday said that his country does not pay particular attention to the Turkish operations area. (Quds Press, 21/01/2018)

- US Secretary of State Rex Tillerson said that his country hopes to work with Turkey to establish a safe area in north-west Syria to meet Turkey's security needs; this was on the third day of Operation Olive Branch launched by the Turkish armed forces and the Free Syrian Army. The region of the Syrian city of Afrin, the US Secretary of State:

> **"let us see if we can work with you to create the kind of security zone you might need... So we're in discussions with the Turks and some of the forces on the ground as well as to how we can stabilize this situation and meet Turkey's legitimate concerns for their security." (Turk Press, 23/01/2018)**

- And the statements of US Secretary of State Rex Tillerson on the announcement of his country's intention to form an army of 30 thousand fighters, whose task is "guarding the border," which angered Ankara and made Tillerson comment to reporters on board a US government plane, "The country does not intend to establish any border force in Syria". Adding that according, to Anatolia, his country is clarifying to Turkey the news agencies' reports of the United States' intention to establish a border security force in Syria, on this, Nauert said, "You take the fight off of ISIS, and that is exactly why we are there, and that's one of the things that the Secretary and others with the State Department have highlighted to Turkish officials." (Orient, 19/01/2018)

Unwarranted Influence

- Last Tuesday, US Defense Department spokesman Eric Bahon said his country understood Turkey's concerns about the border security force it plans to build in Syria, citing the issue with Turkish officials.

Bahon pointed out that his country is in regular and close contact with Turkey; its partner in NATO. Bahon used the phrase "supposed border security force" in his answer ... Today, Thursday, US Secretary of State Rex Tillerson came out to announce that the United States had no plans to establish any border force in Syria, commenting on news reports on this issue. He added in a press statement: "This issue is perceived and defined in the wrong way, and some people spoke in the wrong way, we are not creating any border force". (Yenisafak Arabic, 17/01/2018)

It is clear from previous statements that Olive Branch is a branch carried by Turkey in coordination with America and Russia ... and that America's statements at the beginning of establishing a 30 thousand border force are only to give the justification for the Afrin operation, America then changed the statement to a kind of an open denial after its goal has been achieved!

4- Therefore, the Turkish moves in Syria are to serve American projects by instilling the secular system in Syria. The loud statements from Erdogan are just to deceive the naive of the people with fiery words and statements that do not translate into actions, like the time when he said, we will not allow another Hama; but the regime committed in every city and town more than what took place in Hama ... as well as artificial movements that do not produce honest deeds. He deceives people with misleading statements that fool the naive as he said about Trump's decision to recognize al-Quds (Jerusalem) as the capital of the Jewish entity. Erdogan threatened that he could sever his relationship with the Jewish entity if Jerusalem was recognized as a capital of this entity. But he didn't cut his ties with America that took this decision, but rather it supports the Jewish entity and provides it with all means to maintain its survival. He also called for a two-state American solution, which includes the transfer of 80% of Palestine to the Jews, and he called for East Jerusalem as the capital of Palestine, surrendering the west of Jerusalem to the Jews. This is in addition to what he did and still is carrying out in Syria, and even his betrayals, which have reinforced the presence of the Russian and American enemies and the Syrian regime, whether by handing over Aleppo or opening American bases to intervene in Syria or to open the Turkish airspace for Russian aviation or the meetings of Astana, in which he pressured the leaders of the armed factions to accept their decisions and bring calm to the battle fronts and deescalate and withdraw from areas and surrender them to the regime and then surrounded Idlib and many more areas. Then comes this new chapter the "Olive Branch" to facilitate the entry of the regime to Idlib!

Finally, we address all factions and say do not be fooled by Erdogan's actions, and not to surrender Idlib to the regime ... and not to forget what happened to them in Aleppo, but to remember the Hadith narrated by Bukhari from Abu Hurayrah (may Allah be pleased with him) from the Prophet who said:

"A believer is not bitten from the same whole twice". So how then if he is bitten many times?

"Indeed in that is a reminder for whoever has a heart or who listens while he is present [in mind]."

Comments from the author:

These extracts in the Appendices have been placed here for the reader to absorb other points of view on the war in Syria and the involvement of outside countries such as Russia, the US and allies, Turkey etc. In no way are they to be taken as being the thoughts or viewpoints of this author who, firstly, does not claim to be a Muslim and secondly, cannot claim to have accessed the minutiae of detail of the war. They serve purely to provide the reader with views held by persons with a stake in the outcome of the conflict by virtue of their nationality or former nationality!

K   Islamic Organisations Listed as Terrorist:

- Abu Sayyaf Group (ASG)
- Al-Murabitun
- Al-Qa'ida (AQ)
- Al-Qa'ida in the Arabian Peninsula (AQAP) Yemen etc.
- Al-Qa'ida in the Indian Subcontinent (AQIS)
- Al-Qa'ida in the Lands of the Islamic Maghreb (AQIM)
- Al-Shabaab
- Ansar al-Islam (formerly known as Ansar al-Sunna)
- Boko Haram
- Hamas' Izz al-Din al-Qassam Brigades
- Hizballah's External Security Organisation (ESO)
- Islamic Movement of Uzbekistan
- Islamic State (formerly listed as Al-Qa'ida in Iraq)
- Islamic State East Asia
- Islamic State in Libya (IS-Libya)
- Islamic State Sinai Province (IS-Sinai)
- Jabhat al-Nusra (alias Jabhat Fatah al-Sham)
- Jaish-e-Mohammed
- Jamiat ul-Ansar (JuA) (formerly known as Harakat Ul-Mujahideen)
- Jemaah Islamiyah (JI)
- Kurdistan Workers' Party (PKK)
- Lashkar-e Jhangvi
- Lashkar-e-Tayyiba
- Palestinian Islamic Jihad

L   Websites to Assist Refugees and Those in Need:

https://amnesty.org.au/DonateToday/PleaseDonateNow

https://anglicare.org.au/directory-category/migrant-refugee-support

https://vinnies.org.au/Refugee-Services

https://refugeecounci..org.au

https://refugeecounci..org.au/Charity

https://unrefugees.org.au

https://refugeecounci..org.au/

https://carad.org.au/

https://asrc.org.au/

https://julianburnside.com.au/asylum-seekers/asylum-seeker-organisations/

https://roads-to-refuge.com.au/refugees-australia/supporting-arrival.html

https://refugeeswelcome.org.au/

https://vinnies.org.au/page/Our_Impact/Asylum_Seekers_Migrants_Refuge
es/

https://redcross.org.au/migration-support.aspx

https://redcross.org.uk/What we do/Refugee support

https://sanctuaryaustraliafoundation.org.au/

https://riserefugee.org/

https://ssi.org.au/

https://arcrelief.org/

Canada:

https://ccrweb.ca

https://www.nccpeterborough.ca/?page_id=10560

https://www.com-management.org/home/2017/2/11/refugees-citizen-power

https://auraforrefugees.org

https://novascotiaimmigration.com/support-for-refugees/

https://soscanada2000.com/migration/newact/refugee/refasspro.html

https://redcross.ca/how-we-help/migrant-and-refugee-services

Here are some smaller groups to consider helping:

Syrian American Medical Society provides medical treatment on the ground in southern Syria as well as for refugees in Turkey, Lebanon, and Jordan.

Karam Foundation is a Chicago-based charity that operates out of Turkey to raise funds for rebuilding schools in Syria and securing educational opportunities for Syrian children.

Sunrise USA is a US-based non-profit to provide emergency-relief programs to Syrians, both internally displaced and refugees abroad. They deliver food, support education, establish trauma-care facilities, and facilitate orphan sponsorships.

Islamic Relief USA is a larger non-profit; provides food, clothing, housing necessities and medicine for refugees in neighboring countries. To support these efforts, specify "Syrian Humanitarian Aid" on the donation page.

Project Amal Ou Salaam is a grassroots initiative sponsoring schools in Syria, Jordan and Turkey; it also organizes arts, drama, sports and photography workshops for refugees in and outside of Syria.

National Syrian Project for Prosthetic Limbs is a program, operated by UK-based Syria Relief that builds prosthetics and offers physical therapy to Syrians who've lost their limbs in the conflict.

M   Complete List of Nazi Death Camps and Work Camps of WWII

The camps are classified by countries, based on the 1939-1945 borders. When known, the name of each sub-camp or external kommando is followed by the name of the company which used inmates as slaves. A star means that the inmates of the camp were women.

This list is far from complete. It is estimated that the Nazis established 15 000 camps in the occupied countries. There were several small camps which were created for limited time operations against local populations. Most of these camps were destroyed by the Nazis themselves, sometimes after two or three months of activity. This list does not contain the names of the ghettos created by the Nazis, even if several ghettos e.g Theresienstadt Ghetto had their own external kommandos (work teams).

The list is based on information found in the following two books:

- "Le livre des Camps" by Ludo Van Eck, published in 1979, editions Kritak (Belgium). This book was never re-published or translated into English, but still possible to purchase at the Museum of **Breendonck**, Belgium.

- "Atlas of the Holocaust" by Martin Gilbert 1982.

Thanks also go to Mark Vardasz and Andreas Baumgartner for their valuable assistance in completing the list.

- **Germany:**
    - o   **Bergen-Belsen** (probably 2 sub-camps but location is unknown)
    - o   **Börgermoor** (no sub-camp known)
    - o   **Buchenwald** (174 sub-camps and external kommandos)
    - o   **Dachau** (123 sub-camps and external kommandos)
    - o   **Dieburg** (no sub-camp known)
    - o   **Esterwegen** (1 sub-camp)
    - o   **Flossenburg** (94 sub-camps and external kommandos)
    - o   **Gundelsheim** (no sub-camp known)
    - o   **Neuengamme** (96 sub-camps and external kommandos)
    - o   **Papenburg** (no sub-camp known)
    - o   **Ravensbruck** (31 sub-camps and external kommandos)

- o **Sachsenhausen** (44 sub-camps and external kommandos)
- o **Sachsenburg** (no sub-camp known)
- **Austria**:
  - o **Mauthausen** (49 sub-camps and external kommandos)
- **Belgium:**
  - o **Breendonck** (no sub-camp known)
- **Czechoslovakia**:
  - o **Theresienstadt** (9 sub-camps)
- **Estonia:**
  - o **Vivara**
- **Finland:**
  - o **Kangasjarvi**
  - o **Koveri**
- **France:**
  - o **Argeles**
  - o **Aurigny**
  - o **Brens**
  - o **Drancy**
  - o **Gurs**
  - o **Les Milles**
  - o **Le Vernet**
  - o **Natzweiler-Struthof** (70 sub-camps and external kommandos)
  - o **Noé**
  - o **Récébédou**
  - o **Rieucros**
  - o **Rivesaltes**
  - o **Suresnes**
  - o **Thill**

Work camps created by the Government of Vichy in Morocco and Algeria. Following the Atlas of the Holocaust by Martin Gilbert, thousands of Jews were sent to these camps by the French pro-nazi government of Petain:

- o **Abadla**

- o Ain el Ourak
- o Bechar
- o Berguent
- o Bogari
- o Bouarfa
- o Djelfa
- o Kenadsa
- o Meridja
- o Missour
- o Tendrara

- Holland:
  - o Amersfoort
  - o Ommen
  - o Vught (12 sub-camps and external kommandos)
  - o Westerbork (transit camp)

- Italy:
  - o Bolzano
  - o Fossoli
  - o Risiera di San Sabba (no sub-camp known)

- Latvia
  - o Riga
  - o Riga-Kaiserwald
  - o Dundaga
  - o Eleje-Meitenes
  - o Jungfernhof
  - o Lenta
  - o Spilwe

- Lithuania
  - o Kaunas
  - o Aleksotaskowno
  - o Palemonas
  - o Pravieniskès
  - o Volary

Unwarranted Influence

- **Norway:**
  - **Baerum**
  - **Berg**
  - **Bredtvet**
  - **Falstadt**
  - **Tromsdalen**
  - **Ulven**
- **Poland:**
  - **Auschwitz/Birkenau** - Oswiecim-Brzezinka (extermination camp - 51 sub-camps)
  - **Belzec** (extermination camp - 1 sub-camp)
  - **Bierznow**
  - **Biesiadka**
  - **Dzierzazna & Litzmannstadt** These two camps were "Jugenverwahrlage" i.e children camps. Hundreds of children and teenagers considered as not good enough to be "Germanized" were transferred to these places (read up about **Lebensborn**) and later sent to the extermination centres.
  - **Gross-Rosen** - Rogoznica (77 sub-camps)
  - **Huta-Komarowska**
  - **Janowska**
  - **Krakow**
  - **Kulmhof - Chelmno** (extermination camp - no sub-camp known)
  - **Lublin** (prison - no sub-camp known)
  - **Lwow (Lemberg)**
    - Czwartaki
    - Lemberg
  - **Majdanek** (extermination camp - 3 sub-camps)
  - **Mielec**
  - **Pawiak** (prison - no sub-camp known)
  - **Plaszow** (work camp but became later sub-camp of Majdanek)
  - **Poniatowa**
  - **Pustkow** (work camp - no sub-camp known)

- o **Radogosz** (prison - no sub-camp known)
- o **Radom**
- o **Schmolz**
- o **Schokken**
- o **Sobibor** (extermination camp - no sub-camp known)
- o **Stutthof** - Szutowo (40 sub-camps and external kommandos)
- o **Treblinka** (extermination camp - no sub-camp known)
- o **Wieliczka**
- o **Zabiwoko** (work camp - no sub-camp known)
- o **Zakopane**

- **Russia:**

The true number of concentration and extermination camps established in occupied Soviet Union by the Nazis is unknown. The following list contains the name of the major camps. Some of these camps were under Romanian control e.g. Akmétchetka or Bogdanovka where 54 000 were executed between December 21st and December 31st, 1941.

- o **Akmétchetka**
- o **Balanowka**
- o **Bar**
- o **Bisjumujsje**
- o **Bogdanovka**
- o **'Citadelle'** - The real name of this camp is unknown. The camp was located near Lvov where thousands of Russian POWs were killed.
- o **Czwartaki**
- o **Daugavpils**
- o **Domanievka**
- o **Edineti**
- o **Kielbasin** (or **Kelbassino**)
- o **Khorol**
- o **Klooga**
- o **Lemberg**
- o **Mezjapark**
- o **Ponary**

- o **Rawa-Russkaja**
- o **Salapils**
- o **Strazdumujsje**
- o **Yanowski**
- o **Vertugen**

  - for all these camps, no sub-camp known.

- **Yugoslavia:**
  - o **Banjica**
  - o **Brocice**
  - o **Chabatz**
  - o **Danica**
  - o **Dakovo**
  - o **Gornja reka**
  - o **Gradiska**
  - o **Jadovno**
  - o **Jasenovac**
  - o **Jastrebarsko**
  - o **Kragujevac**
  - o **Krapje**
  - o **Kruscica**
  - o **Lepoglava**
  - o **Loborgrad**
  - o **Sajmite**
  - o **Sisak**
  - o **Slano**
  - o **Slavonska-Pozega**
  - o **Stara-Gradiska**
  - o **Tasmajdan**
  - o **Zemun**

  for all these camps, no sub-camp known

Note: **Revised estimates of murdered Jews place the figure as high as 6 700 000.**

N   The Ten Commandments: Exodus 20 King James Version

And God spake all these words, saying:

I am the LORD thy God, which have brought thee out of the land of Egypt, out of the house of bondage.

Thou shalt have no other gods before me.

Thou shalt not make unto thee any graven image, or any likeness of any thing that is in heaven above, or that is in the earth beneath, or that is in the water under the earth.

Thou shalt not bow down thyself to them, nor serve them: for I the LORD thy God am a jealous God, visiting the iniquity of the fathers upon the children

unto the third and fourth generation of them that hate me;

And shewing mercy unto thousands of them that love me, and keep my commandments.

Thou shalt not take the name of the LORD thy God in vain; for the LORD will not hold him guiltless that taketh his name in vain.

Remember the sabbath day, to keep it holy.

Six days shalt thou labour, and do all thy work:

But the seventh day is the sabbath of the LORD thy God: in it thou shalt not do any work, thou, nor thy son, nor thy daughter, thy manservant, nor thy maidservant, nor thy cattle, nor thy stranger that is within thy gates:

For in six days the LORD made heaven and earth, the sea, and all that in them is, and rested the seventh day: wherefore the LORD blessed the sabbath day, and hallowed it.

Honour thy father and thy mother: that thy days may be long upon the land which the LORD thy God giveth thee.

Thou shalt not kill.

Thou shalt not commit adultery.

Thou shalt not steal.

Thou shalt not bear false witness against thy neighbour.

Thou shalt not covet thy neighbour's house, thou shalt not covet thy neighbour's wife, nor his manservant, nor his maidservant, nor his ox, nor his ass, nor any thing that is thy neighbour's.

... and more succinctly :

The Ten Commandments, also known as the Decalogue, found in the Ark of the Covenant are:

1. You shall have no other gods before Me.
2. You shall not make for yourself an idol in the form of anything.
3. You shall not misuse the name of the Lord your God.
4. Remember the Sabbath day by keeping it holy.
5. Honour your father and your mother.
6. You shall not murder.
7. You shall not commit adultery.
8. You shall not steal.
9. You shall not give false testimony against your neighbour.
10. You shall not covet your neighbour's house, wife, or property.

Moses with Tablets of the Ten Commandments

O   **Table of Acronyms**

ABM   antiballistic missile

AEOI   Atomic Energy Organisation of Iran

AI   Amnesty International

AIPAC   American Israel Public Affairs Committee

Al-Qaeda   Islamic Terror Group founded by Osama bin Laden

ASEAN   Association of Southeast Asian Nations

CIA   Central Intelligence Agency

CM   cruise missile

CTBT   Comprehensive Nuclear Test Ban Treaty

DOE   Department of Energy

DU   depleted uranium

EMP   electromagnetic pulse

EPA   Environmental Protection Agency

EURATOM   European Atomic Energy Community

HEU   highly enriched uranium

IAEA   International Atomic Energy Agency

ICBM   intercontinental ballistic missile

ICC   International Criminal Court

ICCPR   International Covenant on Civil and Political Rights

ICJ   International Court of Justice

IED   Improvised Explosive Device

IHL   International Humanitarian Law (law for armed conflict)

ISI   Inter-Services Intelligence (Pakistan)

ISIS/ISIL   Islamic State (terror organisation)

KGB/FSB   Committee for State Security now Federal Security Service (Russia)

LEU   low enriched Uranium

LIS   laser isotopic separation

MAD   mutually assured destruction

MI6   British Secret Intelligence Service, section 6

MOSSAD   National Intelligence Agency of Israel

MRV   multiple re-entry vehicle

NASA   National Air and Space Administration

NATO	North Atlantic Treaty Organisation
NPP	nuclear power plant
NPR	Nuclear Posture Review
NPT	Non-proliferation of Nuclear Weapons Treaty
NRC	Nuclear Regulatory Commission
NSA	National Security Agency (US)
NSG	Nuclear Suppliers Group
OECD	Organisation for Economic Cooperation and Development
Pu139	plutonium 139
SIPRI	Stockholm International Peace Research Institute
START	Strategic Arms Reduction Treaty
TNT	trinitrotoluene
U235	uranium 235
U238	uranium 238
UI	The Uranium Institute
WHO	The World Health Organisation
WMD	weapon of mass destruction
WWI	World War One 1914-1918
WWII	World War Two 1939-1945

P   Russian Armed Forces in Syria 2016-2018

Naval ships

3 Buyan-M-class corvettes

1 Gepard-class frigate

2 *Admiral Grigorovich*-class frigate

2 Vishnya-class intelligence ship

4 Improved Kilo-class submarines

1 *Slava*-class cruiser

Kuznetsov aircraft carrier battlegroup

1 *Kuznetsov*-class aircraft carrier

1 *Kirov*-class battlecruiser

2 *Udaloy*-class destroyers

support vessels

Strategic bombers

14 Tu-22M3

6 Tu-95MSM

5 Tu-160

Tactical bombers

12 Su-24M2

8 Su-34

Attack bombers

4 Su-25SM

Fighter aircraft

4 Su-27SM

4 Su-30SM

4 Su-35S

4 MiG-29SMT

Interceptor aircraft

MiG-31BM

Reconnaissance aircraft

A-50U

Il-20M1

Tu-214R

Attack helicopters

12 Mi-24P/35M

6 Mi-28N

4 Ka-52

Utility helicopters

4 Mi-8AMTSh

UAV

Orlan-10

Ground arms and equipment

UGV

Uran-6

MRAP

Kamaz Typhoon

IMV

GAZ Tigr

Iveco Rys

SRBM

2 9K720 Iskander (SS-26) missile launchers

SAM

SA-22, other anti-aircraft and anti-missile weapons,

including S-400, S-300VM, and Vityaz (S-350E)   **Wikipedia**

IS, Free Syrian Army and other Rebel Groups:

Same as against US and allies: hardly any at all really!

Not surprising to see so many civilian casualties considering Goliath is fighting puny David! Hail to the Heroic Russians!

Bibliography

Abbas, Hassan; Pakistan's Nuclear Bomb, Penguin 2018
Addison, Paul and Crang, Jeremy A; Firestorm: The Bombing of Dresden, 1945,
Pimlico 2006
Albright, David, Berkhout, Frans & Walker, William; World Inventory of Plutonium and
Highly Enriched Uranium, 1992
Aldrich, Richard J; The Hidden Hand, Britain, America and Cold War Secret
Intelligence, John Murray 2001

Anderson, Duncan; The Falklands War 1982, Osprey Publishing 2002
Arnold, Anthony; Afghanistan: The Soviet Invasion in Perspective, Hoover
International Studies 1985
Australian Department of Defence; The War in Iraq. ADF Operations in the Middle East
in 2003, ADF 2004

Ayaan, Hirsi Ali; Heretic: Why Islam Needs a Reformation Now, Fourth Estate 2015

Ayaan, Hirsi Ali; Infidel, Atria Paperback 2008

Baird & Marzuki; War Crimes in Japan Occupied Indonesia, Potomac Books 2015

Bari, Muhammad Abdu; The Rohingya Crisis: A People Facing Extinction, 2018

Bodden, Valerie; The Bombing of Hiroshima & Nagasaki, The Creative Company 2007
Borshoff, John; Policy and Future Scenarios in the Uranium Industry, Paladin Resources
(taped interview), March 2006

Boyle, Francis A; The Criminality of Nuclear Deterrence, Clarity Press 2015
Bubalo, Anthony; Remaking the Middle East, Lowy Institute, Penguin 2018
Byman,Daniel; al-Qaeda Islamic State and Global Jihadist Movement, OUP 2015
Caldecott, Dr Helen; If You Love This Planet, WW Norton 1992
Calic, Marie-Janine; A History of Yugoslavia (Central European Studies), 2019
Carroll, Ian; Israel and Palestine: The Complete History, Dark River 2018
Carroll, James; House of War: The Pentagon and the Disastrous Rise of American
Power, Houghton Mifflin Harcourt 2007
Cassman, Daniel; Moro National Liberation Front-Mapping Militant Organizations,
Stanford University 2015
Chang, Iris; The Rape of Nanking, Basic Books 2012
Chehab, Zaki; Iraq Ablaze: Inside the Insurgency, IB Tauris 2006
Cheshire, Leonard; The Light of Many Suns: The Meaning of the Bomb, Methuen 1985
Ching Fatt Yong; The Origins of Malayan Communism, South Seas Society 1997
Cixin Liu; The Three-Body Problem, Head of Zeus 2016
Cixin Liu; 刘慈欣, 三体, Chongqing Publishing Group 2008
Clavell, James; Gai-Jin, Hodder & Stoughton 1993
Cobain,Ian; The History Thieves: Secrets, Lies and the Shaping of a Modern Nation,
Portobello Books 2017
Cockburn, Patrick; Age of Jihad, Verso 2016
Coll, Steve; Directorate S: The C.I.A. and America's Secret Wars in Afghanistan and
Pakistan, Penguin Press 2018
Coll, Steve; Ghost Wars, Penguin Press 2004
Cumings, Bruce; The Korean War: A History, Modern Library 2011
DABIQ 1437 Issue 15 pp 40-45, Magazine of Islamic State 2016
Dawood, N. J.; The Koran, Penguin 2015

Unwarranted Influence

Dennis, Peter and Grey, Jeffrey; Emergency and Confrontation: Australian Military Operations in Malaya & Borneo 1950-1966, Official History 1996

Dietl, Wilhelm; Holy War: From Egypt to Iran to Lebanon-A Revealing, Unique Look At the Brotherhood-The Terrorist Underground That is Keeping the Mideast in Turmoil, Macmillan 1984

Edwards, Aaron; Defending the Realm? The Politics of Britain's Small Wars Since 1945, Manchester University Press 2012

Engbrecht, Shawn; America's Covert Warriors: Inside the World of Private Military Contractors, Potomac Books 2011

Farr, US Army Lt. Col. Warner; The Third Temple Holy of Holies Israel's Nuclear Weapons, USAF Counterproliferation Center, Air War College 1999

Fauré, Marie and 50 Minutes; La guerre de Gaza 2006-2014: Les temps forts du conflit israélo-palestinien, Grand Batailles Num 41 2015

Foad, B Salem; Life of the Profet Muhammad, Goodword Books 2003

Gabriel, Richard A and Boose Jr, Donald W; The Great Battles of Antiquity 1994

Gaffney, Mark; Dimona, The Third Temple:The Story Behind the Vanunu Revelation, Amana Books 1989

Gardner, Robert; Islam- Empire of Faith, Gardner Films 2000

Geller, Pamella; Stop the Islamization of America, WND Books 2011

Gibon, Edward; The Decline and Fall of the Roman Empire, two vols., The Modern Library Inc., New York

Gibran, Kahlil; The Profit, Senate 2004

Goeritno, Ir. KGPH, Soeryo, Hitler Mati di Indonesia: Rahasia Yang Terkuak, Indonesia: Titik Media 2010

Gold, Dore; Hatred's Kingdom, Regnevy Publishing 2004

Government of France: Geneva Protocol, Protocol for the Prohibition of the Use in War of Asphyxiating, Poisonous or other Gases, and of Bacteriological Methods of Warfare, Government of France Publication 1931

Grant, R.G ; World War I: The Definitive Visual History, DK 2014

Greenwald, Glenn; No Place to Hide: Edward Snowden, the NSA and the Surveillance State, Hamish Hamilton 2014

Hanson, Victor Davis; The Second World Wars: How the First Global Conflict Was Fought and Won, Hachette Book Group 2017

Harper, Timothy Norman; The End of Empire and the Making of Malaya, Cambridge University Press 2001

Harris, Robert and Paxman, Jeremy; A Higher Form of Killing: The Secret History of Chemical and Biological Warfare, Random House 2002

Hart, Basil Liddell; History of the Second World War. Volume 6, Purnell 1969

Hart, Peter; The Great War: A Combat History of the First World War 1914-1918, Profile Books 2015

Hartung, William D; Prophets of War: Lockheed Martin and the Making of the Military-Industrial Complex, Nation Books 2012

Hassan, Mona; Longing for the Lost Caliphate: A Transregional History, Princeton University Press 2016

Hersh, Seymour; The Samson Option: Israel's Nuclear Arsenal and American Foreign Policy, Random House 1991

Heydarian,Richard Javad; The Rise of Duterte: A Populist Revolt against Elite Democracy, Springer Nature 2018

Hoffman, JS; Greenhouse Effect and Sea Level Rise, Van Nostrand Reinhold 1984

Hoffman,B; Inside Terrorism, Columbia University Press 1999

Holbrook, Donald; The Al-Qaeda Doctrine, Bloomsbury Publishing 2014

Horton, Scott; The Lords of Secrecy, Nation Book 2015

Hunt, Patrick; When Empires Clash: 12 Great Battles of Antiquity 2017

Ibrahim, Azeem and Yunus, Muhammad; The Rohingyas: Inside Myanmar's Genocide, C.Hurst & Co 2018

Ingrao, Charles W and Emmert,Thomas A; Confronting the Yugoslav Controversies: A Scholars' Initiative, Purdue University Press 2012

Iran, Lonely Planet, 2004

Isaacs, Hardy, Brown et al.; Pawns of War, Boston Publishing Company 1987

Isby, David and Volstad, Ronald; Russia's War in Afghanistan, Osprey Publishing 1986

Itali, Talal; The Quran: English Translation, ClearQuran 2017

Johnson, Alison; Gulf War Syndrome : Legacy of a Perfect War, MCS Information Exchange 2001

Jowett, Philip; China's Wars: Rousing the Dragon 1894-1949, Bloomsbury Publishing 2013

Karlsch, Rainer; Hitler's Bombe, Deutsche Verlags-Anstalt 2005

Keyes, Daniel C ; Medical Response to Terrorism : Preparedness and Clinical Practice, Lippincott Williams & Wilkin 2005

Khan, Yasmin; The Great Partition: The Making of India and Pakistan, Yale University Press 2017

King, Gilbert; Dirty Bomb: Weapons of Mass Disruption, Chamberlain Bros 2004

Kroenig, Matthew; The Logic of American Nuclear Strategy, Oxford University Press 2018

Kurlantzick, Joshua; A Great Place to Have a War: America in Laos and the Birth of a Military CIA, Simon & Schuster 2018

Langewiesche, William; The Atomic Bazaar: The Rise of the Nuclear Poor , Farrar Straus and Giroux 2007

Law, Tom; China Collection, Longership Publishing Australia 2014

Law, Tom; Nuclear Islam, Longership Publishing Australia 2016

Law, Tom; Guns Off Cops Guns Off Everyone, Longership Publishing Australia 2016

Law, Tom; Return to Anmalia, Longership Publishing Australia 2015

Leigh,Davidand, Harding, Luke; WikiLeaks: Inside Julian Assange's War on Secrecy, Faber & Faber 2011

Lewis, John W and Litai Xue; China Builds the Bomb, Stanford University Press 1988

Lister, Charles R; The Syrian Jihad, OUP 2016

Lukacs, John; Five Days in London May 1940, Yale Nota Bene 2001

Malkasian, Carter; The Korean War, Osprey 2001

Masters, Chris; No Front Line , Allen and Unwin 2017

McCants, William; Abu Bakr al Baghdadi Leader of ISIL, ebook 2015

McClelland, Royal Commissioner Mr Justice; The Report of the Royal Commission into British Nuclear Tests in Australia, Australian Government Publishing Service, Canberra

McLaren, Colin; JFK The Smoking Gun, Hachette Australia 2013

McSmith, Andy; The Iraq Report, Independent Print 2015

Miller, Jonathan; Rodrigo Duterte: Fire and Fury in the Philippines, 2018

Müller, Rolf-Dieter; Schönherr, Nicole; Widera, Thomas, eds.; Die Zerstörung Dresdens: 13. bis 15. Februar 1945. Gutachten und Ergebnisse der Dresdner Historikerkommission zur Ermittlung der Opferzahlen, V&R Unipress 2010

Neville, Leigh; Special Forces in the War on Terro, Osprey Publishing 2015

Nye Jr, Joseph S; The Paradox of American Power, Oxford University Press 2002

Oberdorfer, Don; The Two Koreas: A Contemporary History, Basic Books 2014

On Walden Pond and Civil Disobedience, Henry David Thoreau, Dover Publications 1995

Palazzo, Albert; Australian Military Operations in Vietnam, ADF Publication 2015

Pearman, G I; Greenhouse- Planning for Climate Change, CSIRO 1988

Perkovich, George; India's Nuclear Bomb: The Impact on Global Proliferation, University of California Press 1999

Pittock, A Barrie; Climate Change, CSIRO 2005/EARTHSCAN 2005

Power, Samanthea; A Problem from Hell- America and the Age of Genocide, Flamingo 2002

Pritchard, R John; Judgement: International Military Tribunal for the Far East, Chapter VIII: Conventional War Crimes (Atrocities) November 1948

Pritchard, R John; The Tokyo Major War Crimes Trial: The Judgement, Separate Opinions, Proceedings in Chambers, Appeals & Reviews of the International Military Tribunal for the Far East , 2002

Qiu Jin; The Culture of Power: Lin Biao and the Cultural Revolution, Stanford University Press 1999

Razoux, Pierre and Elliot, Nicholas; The Iran-Iraq War, Harvard College 2015

Rebiya, Kadeer & Cavelius, Alexandra; Dragon Fighter- One Woman's Epic Struggle for Peace with China, Kales Press 2011

Return to Animalia, Tom Law, Longership Publishing Australia 2015

River, Charles; The Gulf War: The History and Legacy of Operation Desert Shield and Operation Desert Storm, Charles River 2018

Rummel, R.J.;Statistics of Democide, University of Virginia 1997

Sánchez, Juan Reinaldo; La vida oculta de Fidel Castro, Ariel 2014

Sardar, Ziauddin & Davies, Merryl Wyn; American Dream, Global Nightmare, Icon Books 2004

Sardar, Ziauddin & Davies, Merryl Wyn; Why Do People Hate America?, Icon Books 2003

Shami. Salman; The Blasphemy Law , Shami Business 2017

Smalley, Dr David L Smalley; Biowars The Hidden Battles, 2012

Snedden, Christopher; Kashmir The Unwritten History, 2013

Steinberg, Mark; The Russian Revolution 1905-1921, Oxford University Press 2017

Stockholm International Peace Research Institute (SIPRI)

Sunardiman, Dr Imam & Sarana, Dr Indo Prima; Atlas Indonesia & Dunia, 2000

Szulc, Tad; Fidel: A Critical Portrait, Post Road Press 2000

Tang Tsou; The Cultural Revolution and Post-Mao Reforms: A Historical Perspective, University of Chicago Press 1986

Thompson, Dorothy; Over Our Dead Bodies: Women Against the Bomb, Virago, 1983

Timmerman, Kenneth; Countdown to Crisis: The Coming Nuclear Showdown with Iran, Crown Forum 2005

Treisman, Daniel; The New Autocracy: Information, Politics, and Policy in Putin's Russia, The Bookings Institution 2018

US Government and US Military DoD; 2018 American Nuclear Posture Review (NPR) and National Defense Strategy - New Trump Administration Policies on Nuclear Weapons, Threat from Russia, China, North Korea, and Iran, Triad Modernization, 2018

US Government; Russian and Chinese Nuclear Arsenals: Posture, Proliferation and the Future of Arms Control, Committee on Foreign Affairs 2018

US Government; War in the Balkans 1991-2002, US Government Publication 2016

Walker, Frank; Traitors, Hachette Australia 2017

Ward, Geoffrey C. and Burns, Ken; The Vietnam War: An Intimate History, Alfred A Knoff 2017

Warrick, Joby; Black Flags, The Rise of ISIS, Anchor Books 2016

Wasserstein, Bernard; Israel and Palestine: Why They Fight and Can They Stop? , Profile Books 2004

Weiner, Tim; Legacy of Ashes: The History of the CIA, Anchor 2008

Wiles, Robert; The Information Paradox, Information Press 2014

World Nuclear Power Reactors, IAEA Database

Websites and Newspapers:

247wallst.com/
aljazeera.com
armscontrol.org/files/images/Warhead_Inventories_C.png
apnews.com/
bbc.com
clarion-defence.com
edition.cnn.com
demandnow.org
en.wikipedia.org/wiki/American-led_intervention_in_the_Syrian_Civil_War
en.wikipedia.org/wiki/List_of_Islamist_terrorist_attacks
globalresearch.ca
hizb.org.uk
hizb.org.uk/islamic-culture/3rd-march-1924-matter/
*hizb.org.uk/resources/leaflets/3rd-march-1924-the-day-state-founded-by-rasoolallah
-saw-was-abolished/*
ipcc-ddc.cru.uea.ac.uk
islam21c.com
khaama.com/3rd-march-1924-the-forgotten-day-2850/
khilafah.com
metro.co.uk/2017/08/15/when-and-why-was-india-partitioned-6837615/?ito=cbshare
msn.com/en-au
*newsweek.com/down-its-luck-syria-and-iraq-isis-outsources-terror-attacks-pakistani-taliban-
650926*
npt3.htm
nuclearweaponarchive.org/Nwfaq/Nfaq7.html
quora.com
sipri.org
*ummulfaraidh.wordpress.com/2014/03/03/3rd-march-1924-the-destruction-of-the-islamic-
khilafah/*
ushmm.org
washingtoninstitute.org/policy-analysis/view/ascent-of-the-pyd-and-the-sdf
world-nuclear.org

Associated Press
Australian Federal Police
Canberra Times
Dabiq: ISIL propaganda
Daily Mail
Daily Telegraph UK
New York Times
Sydney Morning Herald
Sydney Morning Herald
The Australian
The Guardian (Australia and UK)
The Jakarta Post
The Jerusalem Post
The Melbourne Age
The Straits Times
Washington Post

Other Titles at Longership

Stonehouse One by Chas Rose describes perhaps his greatest work.. the building of a house set in rural Australia for his young family. The story tells of the planning and arduous tasks of rock collecting, cutting out timbers and gradual construction. This labour of love took several years to complete whilst working as a school teacher in a small village of East Gippsland. "It embraces my Scottish heritage… " so he claims in this extraordinary tale of a man's determination to fulfil his life-dream.

ISBN 9780648226871

Tears from a Persian Rose

A short booklet on rules and values by which to guide one's life. A religious text that is general and not specifically belonging wholly to any of the major religions. Values that have been handed down over the millennia and consequently never changing in human civilisation.

ISBN 9780648226857

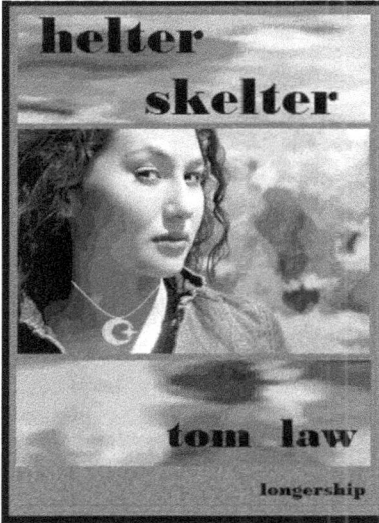

Helter Skelter

ISBN 9780994315724

So where are we headed? Tom Law's recent tome paints an extremely dark picture of how the myriad of world civilizations will experience an horrific end unless the most vile elements of capitalism (i.e the armaments industries) are not curtailed with a heavy hand. An unconventional read with epithets interwoven with futuristic fiction.

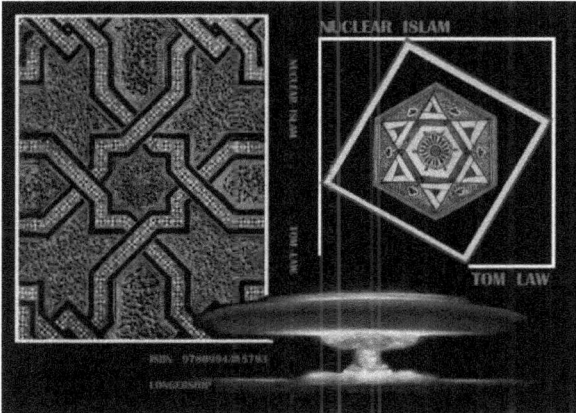

Nuclear Islam 3rd Edition   ISBN   9780994315793

This expose on what our future holds if we continue down the nuclear road looks at the various scenarios from conventional nuclear power plants. Also discusses the causes and outcomes of Islamic terror and how we can heal the divisions between the various religions on the planet. Population expansion is beyond our control- taken together with finite resources, the planet faces some tough times ahead!

451

Return to Animalia

ISBN 9780994315700

Politics of contemporary Australia as seen through the eyes of perhaps a very British Australian. A disquieting diatribe on many issues with solutions given as possible suggestions. Could easily be construed as unapologetic extremism by some, but sensible remedies by others- depending on one's perspective!

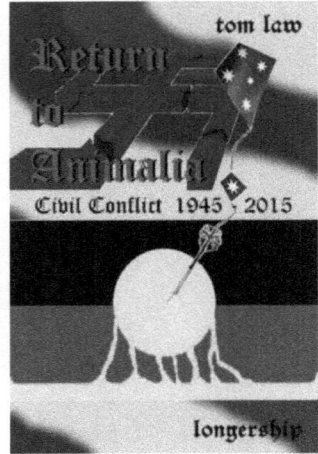

China Collection.

ISBN 9780980725889

This is a collection of four books of poetry by Tom Law on political and environmental observations written over a period of six years whilst working in Jiangsu province, China as a science teacher. It is a commentary on Chinese life, politics with a little romanticism thrown in. There are also references to world events over the period particularly the Middle East conflicts

Guns Off Cops Guns Off Everyone!

ISBN   9780994315779

A hard look at US policy on guns and the continual high rate of killings by guns in that country. Also describes the role of the armaments industries in wars around the world and the development of the new weapons.

LONGERSHIP

All available at:

amazon.au   amazon.com   amazon.ca   amazon.co.uk   amazon.de   amazon.fr

amazon.it   amazon.es   amazon.in   amazon.co.jp   amazon.cn   amazon.id

...   also, for a comprehensive list of titles please go to: longership.com

Unwarranted Influence

A member of the Syrian Civil Defense (White Helmets) carries an injured child rescued from rubble, Damascus March 2018.   Photo by Abdulmonam Eassa

https://www.savethechildren.org.au/Donate/Monthlydonation

Jesus called them *unto him* saying: "Suffer little children to come unto me, and forbid them not: for of such is the kingdom of God"

Detail, Christ Carrying the Cross, Mathis Grünewald 1522

United Nations International Children's Emergency Fund

Almost 30 000 children under the age of five die every day, mainly from preventable causes. No child should live in fear of war, poverty or disease.

More than 70 per cent of almost 11 million child deaths every year are attributable to six causes: diarrhea, malaria, neonatal infection, pneumonia, preterm delivery, or lack of oxygen at birth.

These deaths occur mainly in the developing world. An Ethiopian child is 30 times more likely to die by its fifth birthday than a child in Western Europe. Among deaths in children, South-central Asia has the highest number of neonatal deaths, while sub-Saharan Africa has the highest rates. Two-thirds of deaths occur in just ten countries.

The majority are preventable! Some of these deaths occur from illnesses like measles, malaria or tetanus. Others result indirectly from marginalization, conflict and HIV/AIDS. Malnutrition and the lack of safe water and sanitation contribute to half of all these children's deaths.

But disease isn't inevitable, nor do children with these diseases need to die. Research and experience show that six million of the almost 11 million children who die each year could be saved by low-tech, evidence-based, cost-effective measures such as vaccines, antibiotics, micronutrient supplementation, insecticide-treated bed nets and improved family care and breastfeeding practices.

These measures are the basis for UNICEF's actions to help children survive, carried through with hundreds of allies and via offices in the field - and well-travelled staff - all over the world.

https://www.unicef.org

Unwarranted Influence

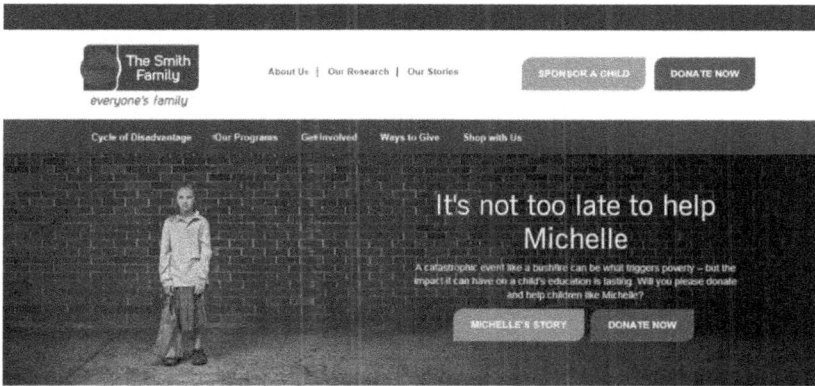

The Smith Family is a children's charity helping disadvantaged

https://www.thesmithfamily.com.au/

https://demandnow.org

DEMAND NUCLEAR DISARMAMENT

Request your nation's representative in the UN General Assembly to:

1. DEMAND an end to all weapons of mass destruction, nuclear weapons in particular. (to include testing, manufacture and storing of these weapons)

2. DEMAND the destruction of delivery systems capable of reaching far beyond a nation's border (e.g ICBMs).

3. DEMAND a strict limitation to the possession of conventional armaments and military hardware by any nation.

4. DEMAND strict limitations on the manufacture of armaments and military hardware solely for the purpose of selling to other nations for profit.

5. DEMAND stringent rules on the selling or trading of armaments and military hardware.

6. DEMAND punitive measures, to be of an economic nature, against nations that disregard the Assembly's rulings on these issues of disarmament.

Send your complaint to the Human Rights Council of the United Nations today!

https://demandnow.org

The International Red Cross and Red Crescent Movement

The International Red Cross and Red Crescent Movement is a global humanitarian network of 80 million people that helps those facing disaster, conflict and health and social problems. It consists of the International Committee of the Red Cross, the International Federation of Red Cross and Red Crescent Societies and the 191 National Red Cross and Red Crescent Societies.

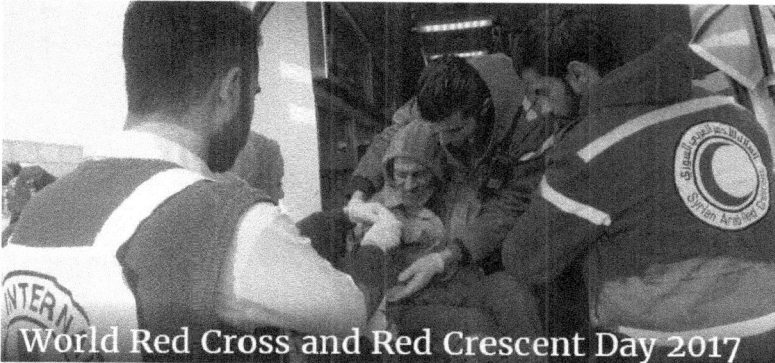

World Red Cross and Red Crescent Day 2017

https://www.icrc.org/en/who-we-are/movement

Unwarranted Influence

About the Author

Tom Law has lived on and off in East Gippsland, Victoria, Australia for a period of nigh on forty years. Originally from England, he was educated at Melbourne High School and later at Monash University. He describes his academic progress as chequered.. "The problem with education is that it can get in the way of living..."   But Tom never lets the dust settle

photo by: Zhang Yumin

under his feet and seriously views learning as his life-blood along with exploration of everything. As a teacher of Chemistry he has worked in many different countries: Indonesia, China and Australia in particular.

Building his life and home "among the gum trees" he has developed a deep affinity and love for the natural environment of this unique part of Australia "Very few places experience the convergence of bird life from such a wide range of habitats.. forest, high plains and coastal dwellers all breeze in and out of this area, depending on the season and prevailing weather. Migratory types such as swallows visit from as far away as China. When I first came here as a young man I could distinguish between a wattle tree and a eucalyptus but that is where it ended. Now I can view a Blackwood and differentiate it from a variety of these trees."

Tom built his first house from natural materials at hand.. stone, timber, slate and whatever could be recycled from earlier building materials left over from the gold era of the mid-nineteenth century. "So many cultures have made an impact on this area in a brief frenetic period of gold mining. They came from China, Europe and North America in search of their fortunes. Some stayed, some died penniless and others returned home after some success. What now takes less than a two hour drive to a large regional town took three days at least by wagon and horse. The local cemetery tells tales of woe and grief from a bygone age of hardship and struggle difficult to comprehend in modern times."

Tom has two adult sons from his first marriage plus a daughter and son from his second marriage to an Indonesian lady.

Unwarranted Influence

www.ingramcontent.com/pod-product-compliance
Lightning Source LLC
Chambersburg PA
CBHW020652270326
41928CB00005B/86